W9-AAL-448

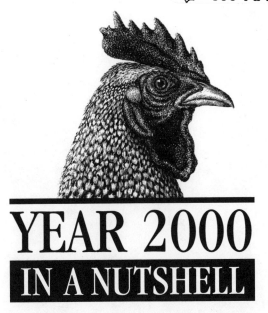

YEAR 2000
IN A NUTSHELL

A Desktop Quick Reference

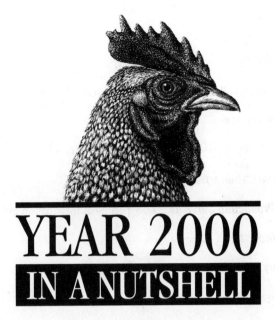

YEAR 2000
IN A NUTSHELL

A Desktop Quick Reference

Norman Shakespeare

O'REILLY™

Cambridge · *Köln* · *Paris* · *Sebastopol* · *Tokyo*

Year 2000 in a Nutshell

by Norman Shakespeare

Copyright © 1998 O'Reilly & Associates, Inc. All rights reserved.
Printed in the United States of America. Cover illustration by Susan Hart, Copyright © 1998 O'Reilly & Associates, Inc.

Published by O'Reilly & Associates, Inc., 101 Morris Street, Sebastopol, CA 95472.

Editors: Tim O'Reilly and Troy Mott

Editorial and Production Services: *TIPS* Technical Information Publishing Solutions

Production Editor: Paula Carroll

Printing History:

> September 1998:   First Edition.

Nutshell Handbook and the Nutshell Handbook logo are registered trademarks of O'Reilly & Associates, Inc. The association between the image of a rooster and the topic of the Year 2000 is a trademark of O'Reilly & Associates, Inc.

Many of the designations used by manufacturers and sellers to distinguish their products are claimed as trademarks. Where those designations appear in this book, and O'Reilly & Associates, Inc. was aware of a trademark claim, the designations have been printed in caps or initial caps.

While every precaution has been taken in the preparation of this book, the publisher assumes no responsibility for errors or omissions, or for damages resulting from the use of the information contained herein.

This book is printed on acid-free paper with 85% recycled content, 15% post-consumer waste. O'Reilly & Associates is committed to using paper with the highest recycled content available consistent with high quality.

ISBN: 1-56592-421-5

Table of Contents

Part IV: Date Function Reference

Part V: Code Scanners

Preface

Everyone who has an interest in a business or works with computers that need to process dates correctly after midnight on December 31, 1999, should read this book.

The book starts with common scenarios that illustrate the tremendous impact that non–Year-2000 compliant computers, programs, and peripherals will have on the population as a whole, and on IT-related activities in particular.

The book is divided into phases: awareness and detection, planning and conversion, and implementation. It includes a rudimentary but completely functional code-scanner and reporter. The technical components cover programming languages, operating systems, and hardware. The managerial perspective includes templates for project plans, reports, and fiscal and legal considerations. There are densely packed sections on date-manipulation routines for many common languages, PC hardware and packages, and a very useful reference section on the most affected language—COBOL.

The book does not dwell on simple concepts; rather, it is a concise, factual reference work covering the widest possible range of major issues relating to the biggest obstacle in computing history.

There are two distinct groups of conditions that influence computer-related Year-2000 activity:

- Storage, input/output, transport, and programmatic manipulation of dates with invalid centuries.

- Hardware that is unable to correctly roll-over date-storage and presentation to the next millennium.

Once the magnitude of the problem is appreciated, the bulk of the book concentrates on a top-down, problem identifying-and-solving approach. Throughout there are references to other chapters and sections which provide deeper technical information on the topics discussed.

The actual technical solutions to most Year-2000 problems are fairly simple in nature; the solution is to upgrade the hardware or software that doesn't comply. The real Year-2000 problems are time, money, management skills, and motivation. With automated conversion utilities, the programming phase of the process can sometimes be fairly routine. That being said, testing large inter-linked systems to determine non-compliance and then retesting them once converted can be a managerial and logistical nightmare, so, in addition to the technical content, this book places a strong emphasis on the management process as well.

Organization of This Book

This book is divided into five distinct parts. Part I covers everything from the Year-2000 (Y2K) overview to PCs and the Front End and provides information on all of the major aspects of the Year-2000 process. Part II contains useful templates and worksheets on Year-2000 issues. Part III is a COBOL reference that gives a quick overview of the language and provides details on all date-related aspects of COBOL. Part IV covers date functions in six different languages, and Part V provides code scanning information and an appendix containing lists of URLs for a multitude of Year-2000-related web sites.

Part I, Introduction

Chapter 1, *Year-2000 Overview*
An eye-opener—how big, how wide, how far, and where to start.

Chapter 2, *Managerial Considerations for Year-2000 Conversion*
Responsibility, approaches, and considerations.

Chapter 3, *Legal Issues*
Now and after 2000—accountability beyond the obvious.

Chapter 4, *Master Plan for Year-2000 Conversion Projects*
The phases and considerations for orderly conversion.

Chapter 5, *Technical Considerations*
Evolution of date-related issues, manipulation and options, system-bridging, and file-solutions.

Chapter 6, *PCs and the Front End*
The focus is shifting to everything that isn't mainframe related.

Part II, Templates and Worksheets

Chapter 7, *Triage*
Collate, sort, track, and report on the inventory and its status of compliance.

Chapter 8, *Inventory Database Schema*
When it becomes impossible to make everything compliant on time.

Chapter 9, *Year-2000 Macro Project Plan Template*
A generic systems-conversion task and phase list.

Part III, COBOL Language Reference

Chapter 10, *COBOL Reference*
A fast tour of the most affected language and its inner workings.

Part IV, Date Function Reference

Chapter 11, *Date Functions*
Examples of how to tackle date-related code and concepts. Provides a date function overview for Chapters 12 through 17.

Chapter 12, *Pseudo-Date Functions*
Provides details and examples of Pseudo Date Functions.

Chapter 13, *COBOL Date Functions*
Provides details and examples of COBOL Date Functions.

Chapter 14, *PL/1 Date Functions*
Provides details and examples of PL/1 Date Functions.

Chapter 15, *MVS LE Date Functions*
Provides details and examples of MVS LE Date Functions.

Chapter 16, *Visual Basic Date Functions*
Provides details and examples of Visual Basic Date Functions.

Chapter 17, *C Date Functions*
Provides details and examples of C Date Functions.

Part V, Code Scanners

Chapter 18, *Code Scanner Design and Theory*
The theory behind scanning text-based source-code.

Chapter 19, *Visual Basic Code Scanner Prototype*
A working prototype ready to customize and implement.

Appendix A, *Year-2000 Resources*

Conventions Used in This Book

Constant width
is used to indicate code fragments and code examples, registry keys, and other values to be typed literally.

Italic
is used to introduce new terms, and to indicate commands or user-specified file and directory names.

How to Contact Us

We have tested and verified all of the information in this book to the best of our ability. If you have an idea that could make this a more useful study tool, or if you find an error in the text or run into a question on the exam that isn't covered, please let us know by writing to us at:

O'Reilly & Associates, Inc.
101 Morris Street
Sebastopol, CA 95472
1-800-998-9938 (in the U.S. or Canada)
1-707-829-0515 (international/local)
1-707-829-0104 (FAX)

You can also send messages electronically. To be put on our mailing list or to request a catalog, send email to:

nuts@oreilly.com

To ask technical questions or comment on the book, send email to:

booktech@oreilly.com

Acknowledgments

My special thanks to:

My wife Cherie, a senior Year-2000 project manager, who provided a lot of practical information and support.

Michael Coughlan for the excellent COBOL reference. Michael Coughlan is a full-time lecturer in the Department of Computer Science and Information Systems at the University of Limerick, Ireland. His qualifications include a B.A. (Mod) in History (Trinity College Dublin, 1977), a Graduate Diploma in Computing (University of Limerick, 1980), and an M.Sc. in Information Technology (University of Ulster, 1988). He has taught COBOL since 1981.

Danie Cornelius and Raymond Thompson for valuable COBOL input.

Steven Brower and Warren Reid who contributed much of the legal section. Steven Brower is a litigation attorney in the Orange County, California office of Ginsburg, Stephan, Oringher & Richman. He programmed in COBOL, RPG II, and APL before becoming a litigator. His practice emphasizes litigation of claims related to technology companies, intellectual property, and insurance coverage issues. He can be contacted by email at *sbrower@gsor.com*.

Warren S. Reid is founder and managing director of the WSR Consulting Group, headquartered in Encino, California. He is not a lawyer, but acts as a litigation strategist, an expert witness, and a master of complex computer litigation matters. His firm specializes in management, technology, and litigation consulting, and Warren enjoys getting into traditional as well as leading-edge technologies such as Year-2000 solutions, RAID, Hippi switches, Interactive Multimedia, supercomputing, robotics, and smart buildings. He can be contacted by email at *consult@wsrcg.com*.

I am grateful to Hirschel Wasserman, a PL/1, LE, and Year-2000 consultant, for his input in these important areas. Chris Waddell provided important assistance on the PC programming, specifically VB and C/C++. David Roger gave the book a thorough tech review. Many thanks for his many insightful and useful comments. Thanks also go to Ben Lampracht for tech reviewing the book.

In addition to those who contributed material for the book, I would like to especially thank the dedicated professionals at O'Reilly & Associates. Without their patience and know-how, this book would never have gotten off of the drawing board.

From the outset, Tim and Troy approached the project with a clear vision of the finished project and every step needed to ensure its success and appeal. They diplomatically screened, vetted, and coached until a huge volume of raw material and macro-concepts took on an orderly, workable form with tremendous value. Also, thanks goes to Troy for his efforts in putting together Appendix A.

Mitzi skillfully applied her distinct and enlightened expertise to further enhance the readability and clarity of heavy, technical passages, while Katie tirelessly formatted the very challenging content into neat, presentable material.

Last, but not least, Rob managed to interpret difficult charts and plans and make sense of very complex subjects.

On the production side, Robert Kern of TIPS Technical Publishing provided project management, and Karen Brown of Scriptorium Publishing Services, Inc. wrote the index and worked on composition. The copy editor was Rachel Anderson of Archer Editorial, and the proof readers were Angela Daley and Melinda Allen.

Sources

Additional sources, whose discussions, papers, and articles proved an invaluable source of inspiration and information are:

- The META Group Inc.—an independent market assessment company that provides research, analysis, and advisory services pertaining to information technology developments and trends. Serving more than 1200 clients worldwide, META Group Inc. distinguishes itself with broad service coverage and highly personal service. The company is based in Stamford, Connecticut.

- EraSoft Inc.

- Data Dimensions (UK): Millennium Journals

- Peter De Jager/Tenagra: *http://www.year2000.com*

- ComputerWorld

- The Gartner Group

- Microsoft Corporation: *http://www.microsoft.com/year2000/*

- IBM (The Year 2000 and 2-Digit Dates: A guide for Planning and Implementation): *http://ppdbooks.pok.ibm.com/cgi-bin/bookmgr/bookmgr.cmd/books/y2kpaper/contents*

- Jerome T. Murray and Marilyn J. Murray (Year 2000 Computing Crisis – Millennium Date Conversion Plan)

- Letter to the editor of Communications of the ACM (CACM, volume 11, number 10, October 1968, page 657), written by Henry F. Fliegel and Thomas C. Van Flanderm

- "Julian Day Numbers" by Peter Meyer, dated 21 November 1997, published on the Internet: *http://www.magnet.ch/serendipity/hermetic/cal_stud/jdn.htm*

- Source: IBM Language Environment for MVS & VM: Programming Reference (SC26-3312-02)

PART I

Introduction

CHAPTER 1

Year-2000 Overview

Picture a day less than two years hence.

On the way to work, you stop for breakfast. The point-of-sale terminal at the counter of your favorite diner won't print a receipt, since its date has automatically been reset to 1900/01/01. It beeps vigorously, flashing "**Invalid Date!**" on its LCD display.

You stop for gas, but the gasoline pump won't work because the date set by the company's back-office computer is invalid.

When you get to work, the parking boom won't open because its logic has been reset. The turnstile in reception reads your card but doesn't permit access—same problem.

The elevator buttons are all flashing simultaneously, since routine service appears to be about 100 years overdue; you decide to walk the eight floors. (You're already an hour late, so what's another five minutes?)

When you finally reach your desk, the first thing you notice is a message blinking on your PC..."**Network Failure - Error 23157-45, NOVRAM Date Invalid.**" You decide to call the Help Desk, but the phone won't accept your code because it automatically expires extensions that haven't been used for a year or more.

You re-boot your computer and choose the **work offline** option.

The CMOS on your PC doesn't roll over properly, and suddenly the machine starts beeping emphatically as the legend "**Invalid System Date!**" appears on the screen. Your old version of the operating system won't accept a date of "00" from the CMOS, as it is designed to accept *valid* years only.

The phone rings. Well, at least there's still life out there. The new switchboard operator sounds a little hysterical. "We have had to deactivate all security on the phone system until further notice—it's the only way to use the phones until the EPROMs are upgraded," she says.

In three seconds, the phone rings again. "George in dispatch says the terminal won't print delivery notes, and there are hundreds of urgent consignments to go out!"

Alan rushes in. "There was a small problem with the salary run. Checks were printed with the year as '1900,' and the banks won't honor them."

Then comes the last straw. Your long-overdue holiday reservations, flight plans, and itineraries are totally confused and invalid.

But you won't have time for that vacation anyway, because the worst is yet to come. Interest payments, amortization programs, savings and retirement accounts, maturity dates, account payments and receipts, payrolls, email, spreadsheets with date calculations, databases with automatic date-stamping and limited field sizes, mail-merges with embedded dates, schedules and service reminders, and telephone and microwave transmitters are all about to blow up in your face... The list of problems that you will face over the next few days, weeks, and even years is apparently endless.

The Problem

All of the errors in the disaster scenario above are collectively referred to as "**The Year-2000 problem**." Hard as it is to believe, this entire hornet's nest has been stirred up by the simple inability of poorly-designed computer programs to properly handle the transition to the next century. Not only are most computers and applications suspect, but electromechanical equipment, networking and process-control hardware, and operating systems are also widely affected. Unless all systems are checked and converted, there will be serious global repercussions.

The Year-2000 problem's root cause is easily explained. The earliest computer programmers had so little memory to work with that any trick for saving two bits was worthwhile. In 1950, who was even worried about how computers would handle data in 2050? The chances that a year entered into corporate records would need to begin with anything other than "19" seemed quite remote, so dropping the century digits was adopted as a memory-saving method. As computers became more powerful, this abbreviated dating convention continued to be the standard, mostly out of habit.

But here we are at the end of the twentieth century, a time when the inability of our machines to answer the simple question "is it the twentieth century or the twenty-first?" could result in the collapse of the communications, financial, filing, monitoring, security, and manufacturing systems that our entire economy relies upon.

Year-2000 errors are already occurring. For example, recently a computer program determined that a prisoner's release date, 1/10/15, had passed, and he was almost released after serving only a few days. The program assumed the date in question was 1915, not 2015, because the century had not been stored. On a lighter note, a few very old people have reported the receipt of letters assigning them to their new primary schools.

But compared to the huge financial and security systems that may suffer Year-2000 confusion, these cases seem minor. In fact, CNN has reported that the NYSE wants to close on the 31st of December in 1999, because its managers fear that all prior dealings could be accidentally invalidated due to Year-2000 errors. Malfunctioning programs will cause many businesses to lose track of critical systems, affecting production and cash flow. For organizations in the health and safety fields, repercussions could be dire, even life-threatening. Year-2000 confusion will also trigger legal witch-hunts, as companies and governments try to pin the blame on someone.

The Cost

While at first it may seem almost preposterous that two missing digits can wreak so much havoc, it becomes clear just how large the problem might be when you think about the many places that dates are used and referenced within computer programs. Obviously, the problem is real, and something must be done—but what? And how much will it cost?

Luckily, we do know how to prevent Year-2000 fiascoes, although it's not easy. First, you have to find all the hardware and software that might be affected. Then you have to decide whether to replace it or fix it. Then you have to make sure your fixes work by testing and integrating new software with code that may have been written before many of your existing staff were hired.

The actual cost of achieving Year-2000 compliance will go far beyond analysis and conversion costs, however. Production delays, reduced market share due to poor PR and media reports, and the loss of profitability or important data will all affect companies. Once the dust has settled and everyone is compliant, another ugly chapter will unfold: the search for culprits within companies, and the search for corporate accountability by shareholders and victims of accidents or other losses.

Reports indicate that the U.S. government is budgeting $30 billion for conversion, and Fortune 500 corporations have earmarked between $20 million and $200 million each for Year-2000 conversion projects. The vast majority of these budgets exclude the cost of litigation, which could exceed that of conversion unless there is government intervention.

In small- to medium-size companies (those with between 5 and 100 DP staff), minis and PCs form the bulk of hardware inventory. However, the impact of Year 2000 will be as great at these firms as in mainframe environments, although the problems will often be more difficult to address. Apart from the widespread, decentralized nature of PC computing, many small to medium companies run older software and hardware. In some cases the presence of pirated software is also an issue. These companies are reluctant to upgrade, or even to acknowledge the problem, especially since Year-2000 issues are perceived by many as *mainframe-related*.

It is estimated that only 30 percent of these companies will be even close to fully compliant by the big day. Among those that have a head start, the chain reaction of upgrading software, then the operating system, and then the hardware as well, is occurring much more often than originally anticipated because of overlooked PC programs.

Often, smaller companies have the oldest PC hardware, and the least compliance with four-digit dating in the CMOS and operating systems. Many accounting and spreadsheet packages probably don't comply either. Some estimates put the cost of PC compliance at around $200 per machine, apart from new hardware. This figure includes a scanning and software-inventory process, but it excludes the cost of converting user-developed programs, spreadsheets, and databases.

Even well-informed IT managers at large corporations are struggling to justify Year-2000 conversion expenditures, especially when only 15 percent or so of the costs will provide visible performance increases or advantages. Many decision-makers are hoping they will retire or be promoted before the crunch comes; others are minimizing estimates in a desperate attempt to get financial approval now—with the intention of revising their budgets later. It's likely that many companies will experience serious financial difficulties due to delayed or partial solutions to a very real problem.

Experts continue to be amazed that the financial directors of many companies are still looking at individual cost to their organizations, assuming that they can wait now and absorb the expense in existing maintenance budgets later on. However, at that late stage the industry's ability to supply staff may be outstripped. Truth-fully, 1997 was probably the last year when larger companies, especially those in the financial industry, could commence work on their Year-2000 compliance projects and emerge unscathed. For the rest, triage management will come into play, often calling for some very tough decisions.

The following chart gives a very rough idea of how compliant a typical company's hardware and software inventory might be. It's important to note that although the graph tends toward 100 percent compliance by 2000, this does not imply that the inventory will be 100 percent compliant if one purchased all new software and hardware in the year 1999. In fact, many problems will still occur at such sites due to lack of testing or poor integration—but at least the situation will be closer to satisfactory.

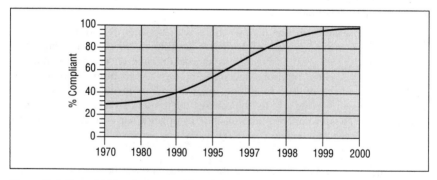

Figure 1-1: Year-2000 software and hardware compliance

Management

In companies, responsibility for the Year-2000 project shifts upwards as the overall impact becomes fully appreciated. Initially, some under-worked middle-manager is assigned an impact analysis role. Once this task approaches completion, however, the magnitude of the problem and its influence on company viability are brought home. The project priority is then upgraded, and senior project managers are incorporated into the process. These individuals begin to document the tasks and deliverables, and soon discover that there is even more to be done than they originally thought. Senior management are now drawn in, primarily on a financial and decision-making level, with day-to-day project management still in the hands of project staff and a growing hierarchy of sub-project managers.

The distinction between general management and project management responsibilities is more obvious in larger corporations than it is in smaller businesses. Deciding where the macro project interfaces with discrete conversion projects associated with business units or products is the responsibility of general management, as is part of the *start-up* phase for a Year-2000 project. (See Chapter 4, *Master Plan for Year-2000 Conversion Projects*, for a full explanation of Year-2000 conversion phases.)

Even mature IT departments often lack the necessary short-term project-management infrastructure to coordinate such a tight, yet wide-ranging, project. New initiatives are unsettling to legacy infrastructures with established methods, and it takes time to implement new lines of communication, set and agree on priorities, establish standards and procedures, allocate or redeploy staff, and synchronize schedules.

Without positive leadership from senior management, a surge of denial and re-delegation of responsibility will be a common reaction.

Solving your Year-2000 problem involves making tough choices, improving procedures, meeting deadlines, and automating routine tasks. It is an opportunity for staff to take a constructive look at all aspects of operations, and an opportunity to implement up-to-date techniques. As a result of Year-2000 projects, new design approaches, such as automated modeling and business-rule repositories, are being introduced to established DP departments that haven't seen change since COBOL was invented. Legacy staff suddenly have to lead small teams of new programmers with fresh methodologies and ideas. Although the overall effect of the Year-2000 issue is likely to be negative, there are positive aspects as well.

Year-2000 solution-providers in the code-conversion component of the project will have a tremendous advantage after the crisis is resolved, when their roles and relationships to the company will be reviewed. These firms and individuals will have access to user code, design and database schemes, and they will have the staff at hand to maintain these systems. Inventory and system knowledge will have transferred to them because of the Year-2000 crisis, at least in part. This may shake up the hierarchy in some organizations, to the benefit or detriment of individuals involved.

Staffing

The single largest factor affecting timely Year-2000 compliance is staffing. Good intentions, money, and time aside, the project will still fail without competent staff. Not only are programmers versed in older languages required, but expert project leaders and managers capable of coordinating the complexities of simultaneous multisystem conversion will be needed at all levels.

Most large companies determined Year-2000 conversion budgets before 1997. The demand for staff increased rapidly, and availability of third-party personnel for Year-2000 work has declined accordingly. As a result of this growing shortage of programmers and project staff—not to mention the increase in salaries and retention packages offered due to the shortage—some large Year-2000 conversion outsourcing firms are providing conversion facilities to only those users who sign 5- to 10-year maintenance, re-engineering, and/or integration agreements. This saves outsourcers from personnel cutbacks when the rush is over, but it ties their clients to long-term commitments that they may come to regret.

The later a Year-2000 conversion job starts, the smaller the pool of available resources will be. This situation is compounded by the fact that the later the job starts, the more staff will be required to do the same work. You'll need extra hands not only to meet the looming deadline, but also to overcome redundant, duplicated activity due to the late start. The law of diminishing returns definitely applies: Every new person on a project adds another group of communication links, and every new developer compounds version control and testing.

A typical staffing situation for Year-2000 conversion follows in Figure 1-2:

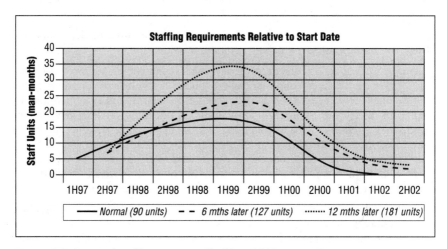

Figure 1-2: A typical staffing situation for Year-2000 conversion

Resource requirements increase quickly once decisions are reached, peak at testing, and then gradually fall off. Unfortunately, in the case of Year-2000 projects, the completion date is as fixed as the earth's orbit around the sun. Moving the project completion date ahead will not be an option when staff shortages occur.

Timing

It can take as long as a year for a large company that recognizes the need for a conversion project to actually begin work. The date manager who starts investigation today could easily find that he or she has less than a year to complete conversion, testing, and migration by the end of 1999.

To make timing even more difficult, some vendors are behind schedule on Year-2000-related changes, including revisions to systems software. Fully compliant versions may not appear until 1998 or 1999. If an enterprise is wholly focused on its own conversion project, it may have insufficient staff left over to test and implement new software from vendors, especially if revised versions are full of additional features and functions.

Rules imposed by regulatory agencies will also affect Year-2000 project planning. In the United States, the IRS* is expected to set a date (probably in 1998) on which all dated records sent to the agency must include the century. U.S. Electronic Data Interchange standards have required all transactions to be century-dated since July 1, 1997.

Finally, many financial organizations are linking advanced stages of conversion and compliance to new loans. Organizations in search of funding will have to take such completion deadlines into account when setting up Year-2000 timetables.

The Solution

The first step to solving Year-2000 compliance problems is identifying the programs, hardware, and storage components that will need revision.

The next step is determining the most cost-effective way to make each item on that list compliant. Often software upgrades will be dependent on hardware upgrades, and some short-term solutions will only be cost-effective for a brief while.

They may be keeping it to themselves, but when it comes to Year 2000, the general opinion of many system vendors is "upgrade or you're on your own." Although they do have a vested financial interest in this argument, in many cases it is also valid. *Upgrade-ripple,* where a new version of software requires new operating system and hardware upgrades as well, is going to be a reality for most sites.

Approaches to the Year-2000 Problem

Upgrade-ripple aside, most companies start their Year-2000 planning by looking at software conversion. They must first decide whether to expand data files, or to leave them as they are and try to solve the problem by coding. These two methods are often referred to as the *data* or *logic* approaches.

The data approach starts with expanding any date-related data field, then modifying all code, screens, and reports that use the newly enlarged field. This solution is the most robust and durable, but it can also require more work.

The logic approach is sometimes called the *window* approach, because it tries to define logical windows within which the century must be either 19 or 20. This

---

* Recently, a "Request for Comments" (RFC) from major contractors dated May 15, 1997 appeared on the Web site of the U.S. Internal Revenue Service. The IRS clearly admits that unless they are bailed out by private-sector partners, their computer systems probably will fail in 2000!

method attempts to minimize the amount of conversion in a system by only working with expanded dates in localized sections of the system.

Some of the questions that must be answered when choosing a software conversion method are:

- Can the database or file be expanded without bringing down the system or corrupting the data?

- Is there sufficient storage and MIPS for testing?

- How will displays and reports handle the additional data?

- What data definitions and structures have to be changed?

- If the field-size increases, can the communications message accommodate the additional data?

- What changes to programs have to be implemented?

- Who will make, test, and migrate the new programs, databases, and interfaces?

> Further discussion of this topic can be found in Chapter 2, *Managerial Considerations for Year-2000 Conversion.*

The range and repercussions of date-related problems make preparing for Year-2000 compliance a unique exercise, so there are no previous examples or case studies to emulate. The Year-2000 project forces an exploration of unfamiliar methods in all of the following areas:

- Cataloging programs and identifying redundant or obsolete files and data.

- Scanning code and hardware to determine the scope of the problem.

- Converting programs to different languages, platforms, and versions.

- Changing systems-management programs, file resource management, performance monitoring, archiving, service subroutines, and communication utilities.

- Coordinating vendor compliance, upgrade and performance undertakings, and obligations.

- Revising and redesigning data formats and storage techniques.

- Redesigning or replacing hard-coded processes in equipment and devices (for example, POS equipment, ATMs, PBXs, hand-held scanners, access-control terminals, remote-monitoring devices, etc.).

- Accommodating data import and export requirements outside the control of the enterprise.

- Revising user interfaces for both data-capturing and reporting processes (forms, reports, screens, etc.).

- Changing hardware, such as BIOS and CMOS, that cannot store dates correctly.

- Purchasing and implementing new tools, methods, and systems.

Input and Display Issues

Before getting down to the nuts and bolts of devising a Year-2000 solution, there are a few basic issues that must be taken into account. One of the most important of these, especially for organizations with an international presence, is the fact that dates are displayed differently across the globe. Some are in the format MMDDYY, while others are displayed as YYMMDD. In some European countries, they appear as DDMMYY. Within the same country the format sometimes varies between corporations and government departments. Mixing formats already causes confusion, and the year "00" will make it worse. Add to this the completely different dating systems sometimes used in Asia and the Near East, which must be adjusted for if they appear in some of an organization's records.

In other words, when designing a Year-2000 solution, it isn't enough to ask only if the year should be preceded by 19 or 20. Programs and computers will also have to be smart enough to answer questions like, "what is the correct interpretation of 020304?":

> Feb. 3, 2004,
> 4th March 2002,

or

> March 2, 2004?

During the years 01 through 12, there will be additional confusion—does 011201 denote January 12, 2001 or December 1, 2001?

Embedded Dates

One of the more ubiquitous contributors to the Year-2000 problem are *embedded dates*. These are *hard-wired* or *constant* identification data, field-layout masks, or components of larger alphanumeric fields. Embedded dates are difficult to detect, analyze, and convert: first, it may not be immediately obvious that these numbers contain dates; second, the dates within these numbers are probably essential to program function.

Embedded dates could appear in formats such as:

```
YYMMXXXX (Invoice #),
XXXXYYMM (Policy #),
XXYYMMXX (License #),
YYMMDDHHMMSS.SSXXX (Comms. Control and Transaction stamping)
```

Embedded dates will also impede efforts to comply with international standards, such as International Standards Organization (ISO) standards. Organizations that believe all date problems can be eliminated by conversion to a millennium-compliant platform must scrutinize their in-house and outsourced software and data records for the presence and use of embedded dates. Those developing new software should, if possible, avoid embedding dates altogether.

Date-stamping

Sometimes an embedded date (often with a time stamp as well) is employed to uniquely identify a particular item or event, such as a telephone call logged to a digital list. This convention is commonly used in serial-number algorithms, such as account numbers, license numbers, and invoice numbers. Date-stamps are also attached to records of communications and transactions, as well as to records kept by backup and recovery programs. Errors in the format and processing of these date-stamps due to Year-2000 roll-over could have widespread implications.

Date-stamps often create problems when their formats change, such as when old dates are not recognized by new recovery routines. If changes are not made, the transactions or records could be processed out of sequence.

Many IT departments rely on a truncated (YY) format rather than the standard date-stamp format. They do so for reasons as varied as storage savings, legacy-program compatibility, and visual continuity for displays and reports. One should never assume that default (century-compliant) date-types were used throughout a system that relies on date-stamps.

In situations where dates appear at the beginning of a field, one encounters another challenge. Some software automatically suppresses leading zeros when they appear in numeric fields. This probably went unnoticed when the year had two valid digits, such as 98, but the whole program could go haywire when the digits 00 appear in the year field and are removed.

This type of suppression can also cause serious program crashes. For example, a year label of 00 could be treated as NULL and rejected, causing mathematical functions to abort with calculation errors or to divide by zero errors. Most operating systems and processor instruction sets generate errors when requested to perform an instruction that exceeds the capability of the device.

When dates appear at the beginning or end of a field, they are often used to group or differentiate information. Encapsulated dates are not always as important as prefixed or suffixed dates, although their presence makes it evident that this information was considered important by the business at one time, and makes it likely that the date is used somewhere in the system. Birth dates used on drivers' licenses and personal ID cards may also cause problems, because other systems often use these numbers to derive birth dates automatically or to double-check information supplied by the client and typed by an operator.

Embedded dates create several challenges for Year-2000 analysts, because they widen the code-scanning process beyond the occurrence of "date" or "dte" in code. For example, the fields POLNO, POLNUM, POL_NO, and POLICY could all contain embedded dates derived from "start date," "DOB," or "termination date." To avoid problems caused by encapsulated dates, all code must be scanned for every possible occurrence of variables and constants that contain dates or date-related data.

Event Horizons

The Year-2000 problem will not suddenly catch up with the world at midnight on December 31, 1999. Many business applications look ahead months or years to create expiration dates, due dates, and other future dates.

A Year-2000 *event horizon* is the date when a system could, or will, fail due to an inadequate or invalid date.

The table below gives a few examples of how far ahead you can expect systems to fail, and when they should be converted.

Table 1-1: Event Horizons and Action Dates

Examples	1995	1996	1997	1998	1999	2000
5-year prison parole review	*					
48-month vehicle lease		*				
3-year university syllabus			*			
Credit card expiration date				*		
One-year contracts					*	
Age calculations (compared to today's date)						*

Embedded Systems

Embedded systems differ from embedded dates. They often appear as firmware on ROM and EPROM, which hold the programs for starting or running greater systems. They may also be present within compiled Dynamic Link Libraries (DLLs), where date-handling is abstracted from the internal workings and hidden from the programmer. It is difficult to locate the source code or original programmer, so problems with embedded systems can be especially serious. Many peripherals warrant extensive analysis for embedded systems.

A few examples of hardware (apart from computers) that should be inspected are:

- Switchboard logic processors
- Elevator controls
- Building security systems
- Environmental control units and air conditioners
- Motor vehicle electronics
- Bank safes with time-locks
- Videocassette recorders
- Domestic devices with timers

Once an embedded logic problem has been detected, the options are replacing the chip or control logic, or replacing the whole unit. Huge orders for telephone switchboards are starting to flow, and the volume will get higher as the millennium approaches.

One area of concern is on the border of IT responsibilities, and therefore disregarded or disowned by many Year-2000 project managers. It is, however, of great importance—the millions of access control, point of sale (POS), and process-control devices, as well as other peripherals that utilize date-stamps and grouping functions embedded in firmware. A large bank in Canada tested one of its facilities and found that three out of four elevators and all three time-locked safes would fail on the big day.

Telephone corporations are deeply disturbed by the expected failure of older exchanges. The cost of replacing them, even if replacements were readily available, will be high. These systems also link into all sorts of accounting and charging services, which will have to be converted to new hardware as well.

Thousands of remote monitoring sites for railways, meteorological services, mines, forestry concerns, electrical installations, and other purposes may fail if the date is part of their reporting, sampling, or summarizing functionality.

Archiving Systems

Most organizations store data for a minimum of seven years, as dictated by IRS rules and other statutory reasons. Existing archives must be recoverable after a Year-2000 update.

Stored data must be available for auditing and historical-inquiry purposes, as well as for emergency backups. It is vital that archiving systems be inspected early in the project, since existing material may need reformatting. If a system writes an expiration date of 20/20/00 on a tape, it's possible that this tape will be recycled (and reformatted) when the system deduces that the data has expired, or that the tape has never been used at all!

This problem will be compounded by each new archival cycle, so Year-2000 strategists must ensure the synchronized conversion of both systems and archived data.

Testing

For Year-2000 conversion, testing will be doubly challenging. Existing systems must be proven compliant, after which all converted systems must be tested again, in all stages of integration—unit, integration, and user. If the first tests are methodical and well-documented, the second test sessions should run more smoothly.

Often a unit works when tested in isolation, yet fails when connected to external systems. Bridge testing (both bidirectional and unidirectional—see the following section for a full explanation of bridging) is incomplete until all systems have been integrated and tested as a whole.

Where dating files are used instead of direct queries to hardware or operating systems, additional configuration and testing will be required for the dating file and supporting code.

If a large section of the non-compliant inventory is hardware, previously compliant applications and operating-system configurations will have to be tested again on new platforms.

Bridging

When systems or programs are in the process of conversion, the unconverted programs must still interface with the converted ones. Temporary programs called *bridges* can be written to accommodate the difference in data format between programs. For example, a bridge program could correlate between 6-digit and 8-digit date fields until the system is fully converted. When conversion is complete, the bridge is decommissioned.

Bridges will be particularly essential in organizations where tape-based and electronic data transfer takes place continuously, such as banks. It is almost impossible to convert and migrate all interfacing programs simultaneously, so version-activated interface-definition switches can be built into bridge programs to ensure smooth operation during the Year-2000 transition.

PCs

Because many frontend operating systems and hardware will be replaced by 2000, the Year-2000 focus at most sites is on mainframes. This is dangerous, because roughly **85 percent** of all PCs (and their user-generated applications) are not fully compliant due to deficient or redundant combinations of hardware, applications, or operating system software.

PC problems need to be approached separately from mainframe issues. They are more widespread, and will be more difficult to deal with than mainframe problems because of the distributed nature of PC installations. Within a single organization the variety of operating systems, packages, versions, and makes of hardware is alarming. That makes assessing potential problems very difficult.

In 2000, there will still be literally millions of non-compliant XTs, ATs, 386s, 486s, and Pentiums in operation. File and directory listings on PCs can display all sorts of strange date derivations, depending on the BIOS date, display-options, and O/S version. Some display YY without a century date, while others show the full date as ":0" or "19:0" depending on the view option selected. Some files may be properly sorted, while others are not.

Applications that use the system-date, such as scheduling, version-control, delete-protection, and file-management programs, may have a variety of reactions to Year-2000 events. Some will hang, others will exit without saving, and many will just treat 00 as 1900.

Millions of small but vital spreadsheets, accounting programs, and PC databases are essential parts of day-to-day activities such as payrolls, production, distribution, leave, and cash-flow. Most of the original authors have disappeared and won't be available to assist with the conversion. These utilities must be evaluated and detailed fully in the inventory phase.

Although many vendors suggest that the solution is to upgrade all desktop machines, this isn't always feasible. Additionally, even after hardware upgrades, the arduous task of inspecting and converting all of the user-developed spreadsheets, databases, and source code will remain.

Cooperation may be elusive. Some users are happy with the performance and reliability of their old accounting package running on DOS 3.0 and will be reluctant to face the expense and downtime that comes with a simultaneous system and software upgrade. End-users or group managers may argue that their PC problems can be resolved through variations in usage (date-formatting), patches, or third-party filters, but these short-term solutions merely delay the inevitable.

A complete guide to addressing PC-related Year-2000 problems is provided in Chapter 6, *PCs and the Front End*.

The Millennium Bug Approaches

No matter what electronic equipment your organization relies on, there is a Year-2000 problem lurking somewhere in your installation. Some companies will be more affected than others, but no one can afford to ignore the issue. This book illuminates what may be the most-discussed topic in computing history, and will help IT professionals detect and destroy the Millennium Bug before it wreaks havoc.

This is one case where it will be infinitely better to be safe than sorry. Year-2000 projects will be expensive and time-consuming, and they will offer little tangible return on investment. As a result, it may be hard to get management on board. However, heads will roll in organizations that do not address the issue. Keep yours intact by being proactive.

CHAPTER 2

Managerial Considerations for Year-2000 Conversion

The Year-2000 issue can start a civil war within a company, with managers caught in the middle. Those who are aware of the size of the problem battle bean-counters who deny expenditures that will generate no return... apart from survival, an issue they can't seem to comprehend. Meanwhile, those responsible for results clamor for the authority to redirect activities and procedures to squeeze optimum performance from diminishing resource pools. The ebb and flow of liability, accountability, and responsibility ripples all the way down to programmers, users, and even customers and bank managers.

This chapter provides the tools and concepts you need to bring the rest of the organization in line with your Year-2000 plans.

Influencing Executives

The success of this project—in some cases, the survival of the business itself—will depend on how well management prioritizes, and on how thoroughly it supports staff tasked with ensuring compliance. In too many cases the impact of non-compliance has been under-assessed and Year-2000 resources under-allocated, creating unnecessary pressures.

A general rule of thumb: the higher (and sooner) the authority given to Year-2000 management, the more successful the outcome. Normal business procedures must be streamlined to give the exercise the best chance of success. This requires understanding, approval, and full cooperation from the top down.

Analysts predict that less than 50 percent of companies will be close to full compliance by 2000. Many unconverted systems will be critical to cash-flow, and therefore to viability. Various 1996/1997 surveys of mainframe users showed approximately 60 percent are actively pursuing Year-2000 compliance, while 10 percent felt there was no problem. The rest were still evaluating the issue, or just starting to address it. This situation is changing rapidly as the end of 1998 draws near and most will attempt compliance. How effective this late flurry of activity will be is debatable.

At a recent Year-2000 seminar, this key point was made: "Money is not the issue, time is." Hard as it may be in bottom-line-fixated organizations, you must make this your Year-2000 motto. Determine what has to be done, and commence work as soon as possible. If you need to justify your emphasis on time, use the old saying "time is money." In the case of Year-2000 projects, that's literally true—the longer your compliance project takes, the more it will cost. In fact, some corporate estimates foresee costs doubling roughly every six months.

Do whatever you must to ensure that CEOs and directors comprehend the worst possible extent of non-compliance, and be wary of anyone who minimizes the issue. Corporate management must drive the initiative as if their very survival depends on it.

And it does: many reports suggest that large numbers of accountable executives will be held liable for poor performance due to inadequate Year-2000 conversion efforts. This could be a powerful motivating factor. If you need it, use it.

You have other ammunition for bringing the accountants over to your side. While it's true that few immediate financial returns will accrue from massive investments in Year-2000 conversion, there can be substantial indirect returns. If you can quantify these items for your organization, they may prove persuasive. Some of these include:

- Revisiting the whole inventory enables system architects to assess and plan development directions and strategies.
- Conversion to client-server platforms as a Year-2000 solution also facilitates long-term efficiency, and reduces hardware and software costs.
- Outstanding and overdue updates can be addressed while code is made compliant.
- The system can be infused with new methodologies and skills during the Year-2000 compliance project.
- Up to 20 percent of mainframe code over five years old is unused and obsolete. Locating and removing it can immediately free extra storage.

Year-2000 Planning

Inventory Database

- Programs and packages
- Hardware (including switchboards, access-control devices, etc.)

- Solution and system vendors
- Staff (users, project, analysts, programmers, etc.)
- Personnel responsible for ensuring compliance

Not only will it keep critical information on hand, this database will help you identify lost or invalid code, and track update ripples to other linked programs. It is the primary source for determining the state of compliance within the organization.

MIPS and storage

Experts estimate that up to 10 percent of mainframe MIPS (Million Instructions per Second) will be required to address Year-2000 conversion and test requirements. Since roughly 10 percent of the content of most systems is date-related, a similar amount of mainframe storage will also have to be dedicated to the project. These additional MIPS and storage requirements will vary according to application type, proportion of parallel conversion, age and size of inventory to be converted, and other factors.

Testing multiple systems during the final countdown can generate surges of up to 25 percent, heavily impacting hardware performance and storage needs. During the critical development and integration testing phases, much of the high-demand activity will have to be conducted after hours. This may translate into overtime wage costs.

Project management

In addition to senior management, the Year-2000 project will require significant project management expertise. Coordination and scheduling will make up approximately 25 to 35 percent of total effort expended on this endeavor. On a positive note, a well-managed project can cost half as much as a project undertaken in a haphazard, ad-hoc style (this estimate excludes abstract costs, such as litigation), with great improvements in efficiency and control.

Tools

With the correct use of tools, the cost of the conversion can be reduced by another 5 to 35 percent. It all depends on how tools are utilized; if the composition of the portfolio allows them to be used advantageously. A project that involves mainly COBOL will require a less-complex toolkit than one requiring a mix of many packages and languages.

There were only about 10 Year-2000 solution vendors in 1995, but now there are over 200. Buyers must choose between relatively unknown vendors selling new and unfamiliar tools.

The best places to acquire the latest product- or platform-specific information are dedicated Year-2000 sites, such as the list of URLs in Appendix A, *Year-2000 Resources*, in the "Year-2000 Tools" section.

Other important sources are the *independent* consulting firms such as Gartner Group, Meta Group, or Giga Group.

These sites are updated regularly, and they provide a wealth of information. There are literally hundreds of Year-2000 sites, so don't limit your search. Just be aware that those sites with something else to sell may have that objective in mind when solutions are discussed. Often upgrades are unavoidable, but sometimes there are more cost-effective solutions.

If you need information from vendors not listed in Appendix A, it would be wise to call them directly for pointers to online or printed data. All major hardware manufacturers and most software vendors have Year-2000 compliance liaison offices in place. In many cases, these individuals can provide you with specific advice, software patches, or bridges, or tools to further your project. Remember, if you can make your current vendor's product compliant rather than switching to something new, that's to the manufacturer's (and user's) advantage. You can probably use that fact as leverage to win assistance if it's not immediately forthcoming.

Systems integrators and resellers that you already work with may also have Year-2000 information and tools on tap, and can be particularly helpful in handling cross-platform problems.

COBOL

While surfing the Net, I came across an interesting COBOL site. CobolTexas (*http:// www.coboltexas.com/*) claims to scan at "a penny a line of source." On the day I looked at this option, its home page also contained the words "Y2K Converter/ Validator"—could this be one-stop e-shopping?

Registering with CobolTexas is a relatively simple process. Either call the phone number displayed, or select the hyperlink at the bottom of the Web page and follow the instructions. Once you have your *Control Number*, you attach your files to an email and send them off for scanning.

I downloaded this company's one-page sample report, and it was readable and succinct. It quoted "105 hits" in 28,567 lines of code (LOCs) and a minimum conversion estimate of 59.8 hours, which equates to 478 total LOCs/hour, or 1.75 date LOCs/hour.

Total man-hours will obviously be a lot higher when project management, administration, testing, and so forth are added, but at least one can get a handle on the cost of core activities. Before choosing a scanning methodology one should also determine the ratio of *hit* accuracy to *miss* probability, and decide if the price per LOC scanned varies with *mesh* size, which is proportional to miss rate.

AS/400 - RPG

Although there are probably other RPG conversion suites available, INTO 2000 from INTO 2000 Inc. (453 Big Canoe Jasper, GA 30143, *104762.2306@compuserve. com*) provides a serious alternative to manual AS/400 RPG/CL conversion.

The tool is both a scanner and a converter, and offers many useful features. These include:

- Generation of route maps for work breakdown
- Ability to handle up to 999 users simultaneously, all working on PCs

---

- Generation of detailed Microsoft Project templates, as well as Microsoft Access databases and reports

- Analysis and conversion of both RPG and CL files, and database rebuilding

- Testing and data-migration planning tools

Although there are never any guarantees in Year-2000 conversion, INTO 2000 is supported worldwide, with many successful implementation sites. The company's sales department claims that larger corporations have realized six-figure savings by using its product.

Staff

In 1997 industry pundits forecasted that wages for experienced mainframe staff would escalate at rates approaching 60 percent per year. Although automation has offset this escalation, it is still around 40 percent in many regions of the industrialized world.

The following chart illustrates the demand for different categories of staff across the project. Understanding staff requirements in advance can significantly enhance deployment efficiencies.

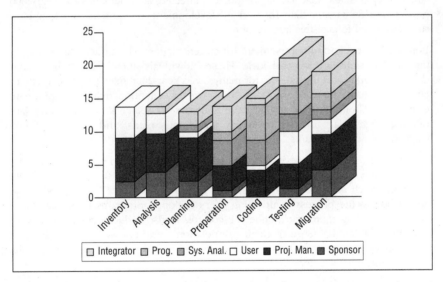

Figure 2-1: Proportional staff participation by phase of Year-2000 project

As the figure above shows, the ratio of project-management staff to development, testing, and implementation staff is roughly 1:3. This figure will vary from site to site, but it emphasizes the need for a substantial management complement.

Apportioning Duties to Minimize Expert Requirements

It is important to minimize application-expertise requirements. Application experts will be in the greatest demand. If the process depends on them, changes will drag out when they are called away to fix bugs, design enhancements, or just answer questions.

Reducing work into manageable chunks makes it possible to assign specific tasks to more junior staff. These people can work from standards, slowing only when unusual cases reveal themselves. It's hard to freeze a system while performing date updates, so do the updates in parallel with other ongoing maintenance and merge the two at the end. This is simpler than combining them into one complex project.

You can reduce the resources required for code-conversion by up to 20 percent in areas of common functionality simply by using clearly defined repeatable cycles (RCs) or processes.

Recruitment and Retention

Recruitment of staff needs to commence as early as possible, if you want to get the best. Typical company recruitment time now is as long as six months to fill an opening for full time staff, and two to three months to fill a contractor position. This will be one of the most frustrating aspects of the project.

Since every business that uses a computer is affected, staff demands for Year-2000 projects are far greater than for normal development: recruitment and long-term strategies need to take this into account.

Bonus programs and tuition payment for current staffers who undertake training in the needed skills are a good idea. These individuals already know how your company works, and the skill-set for many basic Year-2000 fixes is rather rudimentary. As demand for their skills grows, however, retention may be a problem. Companies should formulate incentive schemes to retain key staff. Some are offering huge salary increases, holiday and bonus plans, and all sorts of tax-exclusive expense accounts.

You may also be able to leverage on a surprising source of internal expertise: the much-maligned end user. In some cases, end users can upgrade their own programs, such as custom databases, with tools provided by IT managers. As an added bonus, the process of updating user-developed programs formalizes these systems, bringing them back under IT control. It also reduces competition with end users, builds the sense of client co-operation, and improves functionality and durability of the system as a whole. These user-modified applications must be fully tested before they are deployed, however.

Most companies will need additional hands to complete their Year-2000 plans, however. A number of entrepreneurial organizations have established training centers to produce entry-level programmers in advance of anticipated demand. These graduates handle mass updates within pre-determined guidelines and under the supervision of senior staff. Unfortunately, these companies are mainly producing COBOL programmers—for other languages, personnel will still be in short supply. In addition, experienced project managers and large-scale systems experts can't be created overnight.

And despite the competition for talent, there are still reservoirs of potential hires that can be tapped by savvy managers. Your own company's retired or *downsized* employee—perhaps even the very programmers who once worked on the systems you're converting—are an obvious pool.

Downsizing over the past two decades at large companies, particularly IBM, has created a rather large cohort of experienced computer professionals who remember COBOL with fondness. Many of these people took early retirement, but would be happy to supplement their pensions with a finite project like your Year-2000 effort. Big Blue Alumni International (*http://www.bbai.onramp.net/bbai/*) is a good place to find ex-IBMers.

At Unix-heavy sites, you might want to call on the expertise of former phone-company programmers. In some areas, and for some projects, former military computing personnel or Reservists may be an appropriate source of permanent or project hires.

Outsourcing Issues

Of course, all of the usual sources for high-tech contract workers have ramped up their delivery system for Year-2000 talent, and many managers will be forced to avail themselves of these resources.

By using outsource personnel, managers may be able to better utilize their most knowledgeable internal staff as team leaders. It is also easier to minimize over- and under-staffing if contractors are used as staff-buffers. The lack of knowledge or experience brought in by new staffers can be remedied through better tool utilization, such as the use of expert systems, and by strengthening process monitoring and mentoring.

There are also drawbacks to using outsource Year-2000 staff, however. Many firms have decided against off-site conversion services in particular, due to the security issues inherent in either allowing remote access to internal systems or transmitting sensitive data. Banks have been particularly leery of going down this path, as they fear that their internal data could be copied and disseminated for illicit purposes by programmers in India, Pakistan, or Eastern Europe. These concerns are justified.

In addition, off-site projects can be notoriously difficult to manage, even if corporate IT managers are physically present at the remote site. Communications problems, translation issues, and the possibility that outsource staff skills may be misrepresented by unscrupulous *body-shoppers* are also legitimate worries. The old adage, "you get what you pay for," is often true. Foreign programmers are well aware when they are being underpaid and overworked, and the best of them have already taken advantage of the rather liberal work-visa programs available to highly skilled programmers.

As for contracting to bring foreign programmers in to staff your Year-2000 project, make sure to check out your labor source carefully. Some companies have experienced legal problems when firms bringing in these workers neglected to obtain all of the proper papers. Others have found the conditions under which these programmers are employed to be unacceptable. The worst of the firms in this business keep their stables of coders practically under lock and key, putting them up in cheap motels that they are not allowed to leave, and transporting them *en masse* to the work site and back. Often the workers are being charged a great deal for this hospitality against the low hourly rate they will be paid on completion of the job, while the body shop keeps the lion's share of what your firm pays per worker. Whether or not these *digital sweatshop* conditions give you pause for ethical reasons, it seems likely that work performed under duress, on an impossible schedule, and by underpaid workers, will not be of the highest quality.

An unfortunate tale I heard last week comes to mind: a Canadian consulting company hired and transported a group of middle-eastern COBOL programmers at considerable expense. These people worked for three weeks before leaving *en masse* for the United States where salaries are higher and the U.S. dollar is stronger.

That said, foreign programmers brought in by reputable firms or via direct recruitment, who will comply with the terms and conditions of their employment contracts, can be an excellent resource.

Figure 2-2 illustrates the time ratios between phases of a Year-2000 project. Consider it in conjunction with Figure 2-1.

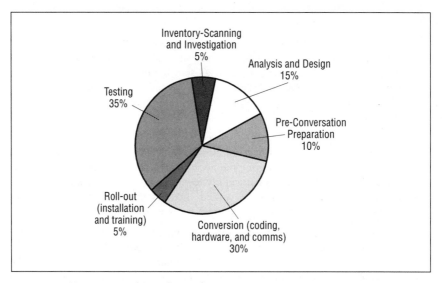

Figure 2-2: Time required per phase of a Year-2000 project

Recent statistics from noted academics and research firms show figures for the conversion/coding effort moving closer to 30 percent, and testing closer to 50 percent, while for mainly hardware-type projects the ratios are even more pronounced.

Budgets and Costing

The additional cost of physically storing and transporting a four-digit date rather than a two-digit date is small, usually less than 5 percent more per transaction or record. However, the cost of ensuring that those two additional bytes are processed correctly can be astronomical.

A conservative estimate for complete conversion (analysis, modification, testing, and migration) ranges between $1.50 and $2.00 per *line of code (LOC)*. Pure assessment and conversion costs are currently estimated at $0.40/LOC. These costs are expected to increase by an average of 30 percent before the end of 1998. An interesting observation is that fourth generation languages, specifically database applications, have far fewer lines of code per date incident (sometimes only 15 percent). However, it is more difficult to automate the conversion process for this code, so conversion time per incidence is only slightly less. The more business rules and actual code behind the *bound* (record-related) screens, the more conversion effort required.

As 1998 budgets become available and time/liability awareness increases, there will be a huge surge in demand for Year-2000 conversion services. This could deplete the resources of major Year-2000 solutions vendors, potentially driving up the cost of both tools and direct services. By mid-1998, the availability of third-party personnel will decline significantly, and conversion prices will increase 25 to 35 percent. The intense competition for rapidly diminishing numbers of available (and competent) programmers in older languages such as COBOL, PL1, Assembly, and RPG will push salaries to the limit in 1999.

> When faced with alarming budgets, remember that for every dollar spent on the conversion process, fifty cents may be returned in the form of better inventory and efficiencies. On the other hand, for every dollar not spent, a cost as high as $10 can be expected from damages and litigation.

How Year-2000 exercises are financed will depend on internal strategies, but the issues of disclosure and accountability are paramount. With respect to liability, whether the process is treated as a three-to-five-year investment or as an unforeseen running cost is debatable, as long as all concerned parties are in the picture.

Indirect Costs

As Year-2000 budgets take shape, two indirect cost factors are often overlooked:

- The cost of software version updates linked to Year-2000 constraints and migration demands
- Increased hardware costs for additional MIPS and storage requirements, as well as upgrade ripples caused by resource-intensive versions

These costs won't surface during the initial phases of assessment and conversion, but they will rear their heads during the testing and commissioning process.

Delivery time for hardware is a big concern. Assuming that 20 percent of mainframe users require significant upgrades, the time between placing an order and actually taking delivery could easily be between 6 and 18 months. PC delivery times won't be affected as much—and this could even be an incentive to distribute processing and change architectures. Since PCs are upgraded more frequently anyway, most of the additional cost will be absorbed in operating budgets.

If you order the machine in 1998 but have only allowed six months for code conversion, testing, and migration, that's a potential problem. Going external for MIPS won't help; solution vendors will already be suffering from the same problem.

There are two ways to develop Year-2000 conversion cost estimates for 1998 budgets:

- Hire one of the many third-party conversion/assessment firms to prepare independent cost estimates

- Develop internal estimates using one or more of the many tools and methodologies available

Third-party solutions may require many months for a thorough impact-analysis, including contracting, application review, program inspection and assessment, and report preparation.

Large companies using external solutions providers for Year-2000 conversion have standardized on three cost structures, which could help you determine your yearly costs. These approximate figures may continue to rise as the millennium approaches:

- A $50,000 to $100,000 charge for assessment and strategic planning

- Code-conversion costs of roughly $0.30/LOC (COBOL) or $1-$1.50/LOC (non-COBOL, such as Assembler, PL1, etc.) The price for code conversion will vary based on the following factors:

  - Proportion of COBOL to other languages

  - Home-grown code versus standard COBOL code supplied with off-the-shelf systems

  - Level of maintenance and documentation of programs

  - Variety of languages and programs

  - System interdependence

  - Availability of staff

- Testing, integration, and migration costs of $0.20–$0.50/LOC

These cost structures let corporations derive broad quantitative figures and time frames, information that can be used by senior management to create realistic cost assessments.

For example, conservative estimates for a corporation with 10 million COBOL LOCs and 2 million non-COBOL LOCs can approximate maximum overall conversion costs (see Table 2-1).

Table 2-1: COBOL Conversion Costs

	COBOL	Non-COBOL	Total
Assessment	$50,000	$50,000	$100,000
Conversion	$3,000,000	$3,000,000	$6,000,000
Integration, Testing & Migration	$2,000,000	$1,000,000	$3,000,000
Total			$9,100,000

These costs might be lower in organizations that have adequate internal personnel and tools, or in companies that can negotiate volume discounts with external solutions vendors. Large Year-2000 conversion customers (those with 30 million or more LOCs) who sign five- to ten-year general maintenance agreements will not feel the cost-escalation in the short term, but they will eventually pay for the service.

Offshore groups claim that they can perform Year-2000 code scanning and conversion at about half of in-house costs per LOC, but start-up and familiarization times will delay actual conversion, and you might incur hidden costs. These groups are forming partnerships with local solution providers to create wider service offerings. There are data-confidentiality, access-control (firewalls), trade, and business security issues involved when releasing systems to third-party organizations, as discussed in the Recruitment section earlier in the chapter.

Don't forget that increased MIPS requirements are usually followed closely by similar software-budget increases. Users might have to migrate to newer system software versions (such as CICS, ESA, IMS, or NT4) and newer application releases (such as SAP R/3, Office 98, and so on). Although companies must deploy adequate tools, time, planning, and personnel during the analysis and modification phases of any Year-2000 project, the testing, integration, and error-handling phase could easily consume the majority of the Year-2000 budget.

Internal Assessment and Conversion Costs

Where insufficient time exists to implement a third-party assessment for the 1997/98 budget planning cycle, the following cost estimates can be used as a rough guideline. These estimates are also useful for double-checking quotes from third parties.

Estimates for *complete conversion* (analysis, modification, and testing) range from $1.00 to $2.25 per LOC. The lowest rate is for standard COBOL, and applies to the total number of non-repeating LOCs. Users can acquire assessment tools and services from many of the companies listed in the appendixes.

Pure *assessment and conversion costs* ($0.40 per LOC) increased by an average of 30 percent by the end of 1997, and a 50 percent price jump to over $0.75 per LOC is expected in 1998. In other words, assessment and modification costs may double in a single year. The fully loaded conversion costs, which include extensive testing and full implementation, will be approximately $2.00 per LOC in 1998.

Another assumption you can use to get rapid, broad assessments for conversion is that each date-occurrence on a screen, process, output-form, report, database, file, or data-communications definition will take one man-day to identify, one to assess, one to convert, and one to test, for every stage. For example, an invoice date is probably captured (or automatically assigned) to a screen, transported, then processed, printed on a cash register slip, stored, and later printed on the customer statement and sales report. That makes 7 stages at 4 days each, or 24 man-days. This is an over-simplification and does not take into account acquisition and setting up of new (upgrade) equipment, establishing testing facilities and tools, reporting structures and procedures, staff recruitment, and so forth. It also does not consider the platform, state of documentation, and ease of actual conversion. At least one can get the big picture fairly easily.

Evaluating Solution Options and Benefits

In 1995, The META Group, Inc.* listed five types of solutions vendors, although there may be overlaps in services between the types. The range of vendors and products is changing so rapidly that this list should only be used as a starting point. See also Appendix A, *Year-2000 Resources*, for a list of vendor URLs to start from. One can also assume these organizations have accumulated considerable experience and expertise since 1995. Most vendors also offer management, personnel, and assessment services. Since many vendors have only been in business for a year or two, one should check references carefully.

Automated or Expert Systems Conversion:
Cap Gemini America, Inc. (New York, NY) and Peritus Software Services Inc. (Billerica, MA) offer automated or expert systems-based scanning and conversion systems, coupled with personnel teams that tackle the rest of the project. Both companies will set up on- or off-site factories where code can be shipped, tested, and corrected. These firms claim that their processing methods (e.g., logical code analysis or rules-based processing) can achieve 25 to 35 percent productivity gains and 25 percent cost savings as compared to typical internal Year-2000 efforts. Computer Horizons Corp. (Mountain Lakes, NJ) also offers an automated code-conversion service, and has recently signed an agreement to build offshore applications development services.

Life-Cycle Tools:
Adpac (San Francisco, CA) and ViaSoft (Phoenix, AZ) have offered applications life-cycle development tools and Year-2000 code-testing and assessment tools for several years. In addition, these two vendors have branched out into assessment and strategic implementation services—Coopers and Lybrand uses ViaSoft's tools. Another major applications-development tools vendor, Compuware Inc. (Farmington Hills, MI), has built Year-2000 code-recognition testing and assessment features for its Expeditor and Playback products, and has offered a similar life-cycle tool suite with associated services since 1995. Micro Focus (Palo Alto, CA) recently entered the market with an acquired tool and its own services.

---

* META Group, Inc. (based in Stamford, CT) is an independent market assessment company that provides research, analysis, and advisory services pertaining to information technology developments and trends to more than 1200 clients worldwide.

Outsourcing/Services:

Data Dimensions (Bellevue, WA) has been the market leader in providing external or Year-2000 conversion outsourcing, focusing solely on this market for years. Clients supply up to 90 percent of the personnel and all of the tools, with management services by Data Dimensions. This firm also provides assessment studies and implementation plans. Several Big Six firms have initiated offshore development sites for outsourcing services, with Data Dimensions, Coopers and Lybrand, and Arthur D. Little being the most notable. IBM has also initiated a service business based in Chicago, Illinois, aimed at code refurbishment and Year-2000 conversion.

Testing Tools:

Two vendors supply testing tools for internal user testing, assessment, and validation efforts: Mainware Inc. (Minneapolis, MN) and Isogon Corp. (New York, NY). Similar frontend testing and validation tools can be obtained from Adpac, Compuware, Micro Focus, and ViaSoft.

Offshore Development:

Hexaware Technologies (Princeton, NJ) supplies methodology, some tools (Hexaware partners with Micro Focus), and offshore personnel. The firm employs on-site personnel to manage the project, and then beams code via satellite to India, where two shifts of personnel perform much of the labor-intensive work at 50 percent of American personnel costs. Any financial testing is performed on-site. Other firms with offshore development centers include Service 2000, Visionet, Data Dimensions, and Computer Horizons.

With the number of Year-2000 date conversion vendors now well over 200, buyers should negotiate for end-to-end services. You'll also want to make sure that there is compatibility between larger, full-service vendors and smaller, niche vendors working on the same project.

Program Updates Done as Maintenance

Experts believe that it is unwise to attempt Year-2000 conversion as part of normal maintenance operations in mid-size to large companies. Normal maintenance only addresses internally developed software—meanwhile, operating systems, external I/O, off-the-shelf packages, and hardware still have to be updated. The smaller the company (and the more PC-based it is) the less difficult this approach will be to manage.

Client/server applications are amenable to the maintenance approach, since they are modular and layered by nature; however, many applications converted to client/server systems still contain date problems. Identifying what to look for, and where to look, is often sufficient to correct these problems during maintenance.

Chapter 6, *PCs and the Front End*, on PC applications, provides much detail on analyzing frontend applications, databases, and spreadsheets in potential problem areas. Much of the communications layer is handled via TCP/IP and the latest versions of network operating systems, so we can expect fewer compliance problems in this area. Network hardware, accompanying firmware, and switching devices must be checked thoroughly if any date-stamping historical storage is present.

The conventional approach must be applied to scanning source code for business layers and graphical user interface (GUI) processing, but at least the assessment and conversion will be segmented and relatively easy to appraise.

CHAPTER 3

Legal Issues

Legal liability is the most volatile and far-reaching aspect of the whole Year 2000 process. Legal realities vary from country to country, and potential liabilities are evolving as new aspects of the Year 2000 problem come into general awareness.

Y2K Liability and Risk

Managers and planners need to take into account four types of potential liabilities:

- Suits filed by clients whose savings or investments have been misplaced or affected adversely, or who have been charged unfairly for financial or other services due to computer error.

- Death and injury casesattributable to non-compliant systems, such as elevators, access-control devices, environmental control and security systems.

- Group or class-action litigation filed by companies affected by non-compliant software.

- Suits from shareholders of companies that sold non-compliant software to third parties.

From a direct IT perspective, these issues can also be classified as either users or vendors liabilities or responsibilities.

User responsibilities relate to the goods and services provided to clients — specifically, the responsibility for ensuring the validity of reports, amortizations, interest calculations, expiration dates on packaging and other time-dependent documents or calculations

Vendor liabilities are more complex. There is a balancing act between having the comfort of legal security and still being able to acquire services and solutions from vendors. Supply-and-demand pressures in the Y2K arena are increasing by a factor of two every four to six months, so the suppliers of hardware, software and solutions appear to have the upper hand.

In general (and unless specifically stated in a contract), older computer systems do not have to comply with new demands, such as Y2K compliance. For companies with non-compliant equipment, this means that when the vendor says upgrade, buyers have little choice than to comply with this demand. If a hard-line approach is taken, the vendor might adopt an unsympathetic attitude and leave a company in an even worse predicament. Vendors may consider dropping clients rather than getting bogged down in legal and technical obligations. One has to balance the element of trust in an agreement with the procurement of a valuable service. There is far less risk when dealing with a large, reputable company.

When preparing contracts with vendors, consider the following:

- Timeframes
- Costs
- Penalties
- Maintenance and support
- Full date-handling functionality and approach
- General undertakings (staffing, etc.)
- Virus-free installation
- Permissions from original vendor and, if applicable, agreements with third parties, such as other vendors or outsourcing firms

Ten Legal Issues

At this point, you probably wish that you could ask a legal expert many questions about Year 2000 legal liability issues. This article, kindly provided by Steven Brower and Warren S. Reid, should provide many of the answers you seek.

Introduction

In recognition of an extensive body of earlier works, this article does not attempt to rehash the historical precedents, or analyze the technical options. Instead, we address new issues and issues which we believe have not been adequately addressed by the prior literature. (For one example of the prior literature see the seminal "2001: A Legal Odyssey", written by Warren, published in The Computer Lawyer and on the Year 2000 web site.)

For clarity, we have utilized the following terms throughout this article:

Year 2000 Problem
> The potential for a computer (hardware or software) to fail to function correctly at, or near, January 1, 2000.

Year 2000 Compliant
> Hardware or software which doesn't have a Year 2000 Problem any more (or never did).

Solution Provider
> A company which offers to take computer systems, which do have a Year 2000 Problem, and to make that same system Year 2000 Compliant.

Vendor

Seller (licenser) of computer hardware of software, whether or not there is a Year 2000 Problem in that product.

1. **Who will be the most likely defendants in Year 2000 litigation?**

From my perspective as a former programmer, and 15+ year litigator in computer cases, substantial Year 2000 litigation will not be limited to the obvious defendants, software vendors of non-compliant systems (see questions 2, 3, 4 and 5).

I expect that the substantial cases will also include the following:

Year 2000 Consultants/Solution Providers

There are a growing group of entities which offer to provide software solutions and/or assistance with Year 2000 issues. That group is, in my opinion, undertaking perhaps the most substantial risk of litigation (see question 6 and 7).

Directors and Officers

A substantial amount of litigation may involve corporate management either for failing to address the Year 2000 problem or for failing to disclose the financial impact of compliance (see question 8).

Year 2000 "certification" entities

The provision of a "certification", which is being done for a fee, potentially creates liability from two different sources: those who purchase a product from the "certified" entity, in reliance on the certification and those vendors who obtained the certification without being advised that it would potentially increase their liability in litigation (see question 9).

Software Acquisition Consultants

The consultants were retained to ensure that the system, proposed by the vendor, complied with the business needs of the customer. Huge RFP's were created, and software vendors responded. Did the RFP ask about Year 2000 functionality? Did the consultant explain to the customer the difference between a sliding window, a fixed window, encapsulation and four-digit date functionality? With the advent of electronic commerce and other expansion of data sharing, will the system really be functional?

Vendors of Computer Systems and Software Which Are YEAR 2000 Compliant

Many vendors are, or will be, selling computer products which are truly YEAR 2000 Compliant. However, like any other computer products, they will have their own deficiencies. Many customers rushing to acquire a new system which is YEAR 2000 Compliant will lack sufficient time for planning, investigation, acquisition and testing, just as those vendors may lack sufficient infrastructure to handle the increase in business. The net result will be an increase in the rate of suits arising out of a failure to meet the customers expectations.

2. **How can software sellers (licensers) limit their potential liability resulting from Year 2000 problems in new sales/licenses of their goods and services?**

The first line of defense for cases arising out of breach of contract, breach of warranty, or fraud, is clear contractual terms, with documentation of any intended limitations in the product. Hopefully your defense will not be limited to talking about the fact that other competitors also failed to take reasonable precautions, and failed to honestly advise customers of the potential problems, even if true.

It would seem that for any system being sold today, or currently under warranty and/or maintenance agreement, the vendor should already know that either: a) the system will continue to function in the Year 2000; or b) the system will be upgraded, sometime in the future, to function in the Year 2000; or c) the system will not function in the Year 2000. This is especially relevant from a legal perspective because the statute of limitations on breach of contract and/or fraud (for systems which are being sold and/or maintained today) will not have expired prior to 2000. In other words, you can still be sued then, for what you do wrong today.

If a system, in its current incarnation, is expected to run properly in the Year 2000, no action is necessary on this topic of contract disclosure. However, if the system will require an upgrade, and if there will be any cost to that upgrade, new customers should be advised that they will be required to upgrade, and you should be able to produce or demonstrate when and how you gave that notification. They should also be provided with some information about the anticipated date of delivery of such modifications, and the estimated cost. For the purpose of this section, the "cost" of a maintenance agreement must be considered a cost to obtain the upgrade.

Some vendors will object to these potential disclosures, saying that they will be put at a disadvantage because their competitors have similar problems and aren't disclosing similar information to their customers. A business decision can always be made not to disclose information to customers. However, a business decision not to disclose potentially material information, information which is known to the vendor, must consider the potential cost of fraud claims by customers.

3. **Are vendors obligated to make systems Year 2000 Compliant under existing warranties and/or maintenance agreements? (i.e.—Is the Year 2000 Problem, for Vendors, avoided by the force majeure clause in the agreement?)**

Most warranties and maintenance agreements promise that, during the term of the agreement, the system will continue to function in accordance with the specifications.

Some agreements do provide the vendor an option of charging additional money for a new version, with new functionality. However, it would not appear that the ability to continue using the old functionality into the Year 2000 constitutes new functionality. Further, the change in dates is not an "Act of God," or otherwise an external force beyond the control of the vendor, any more than a leap year is. Thus, I expect that any vendor with a continuing support obligation will be required to provide continuing functionality into the Year 2000.

What about a system which was installed 10 years ago, where the vendor has had four major updates to its system, but has a customer on the old version, still paying for maintenance? Whether or not litigation can be avoided will depend, in part, on the status of customer relations. Perhaps some vendors will simply provide the newest version of the software for a nominal fee in recognition of the revenue received over the past 10 years under the maintenance contract. However, if the customer has a substantially customized system, that solution will generally not be economically feasible.

4. **If a customer's warranty period has already expired, does the vendor still have potential liability?**

The answer is a qualified "Yes." In some circumstances such vendors still have potential liability. In fact, I predict that the outcome of this question will constitute one of the major battlegrounds of Year 2000 litigation.

Many vendors might assume that since the warranty period has expired, and since, in many cases, the customer "chose" not to pay for maintenance, they have no further obligation to customers with non-compliant systems. However, it must be remembered that warranty periods are generally for a limited duration, such as 90 days or one year. The statute of limitations for fraud, on the other hand, is generally several years, often with additional time for delay in discovery. In other words, as of 1998, the statute of limitations will allow litigation by customers who purchased systems since at least 1994, and, in many cases, much earlier. Thus, there may be a need to address the needs of those "former" customers.

There will be many issues. For example, who had an affirmative duty to raise the subject of Year 2000 compliance, and when did that duty arise? Vendors will point to huge RFP's, prepared by the customers and their consultants, which don't mention Year 2000 compliance issues. They will state that common business practice, and competition, require that they only respond to customer concerns. Customers will point to the expertise of the vendors, and the vendors unique knowledge of the capability of their own products. Customers will argue that the Vendor had an affirmative duty to mention that the product wasn't going to work properly in "xx" years. They will argue that this isn't the same as, for example, a change in operating systems, because that is something which the customer can control by staying with old technology, by emulation, etc. Here, the change to the software is mandatory, in order to continue use of the program. Vendors will reply that they had no way to foresee that the customer would buy a system in 199x, and fail to purchase upgrades and/or maintenance, thereby continuing to use "old" technology. Customers will point out that the industry has long been aware that some customers don't buy the newest versions, and that the vendors failed to send any notification about the necessity to purchase an upgrade.

The outcome will vary from case to case, but in many cases the vendor will be held responsible.

5. **Should vendors attempt to limit their liability to previous customers by advising them how to obtain Year 2000 Compliance?**

This is a question which each vendor will need to discuss with their own legal counsel because of the differing factual circumstances and business risks. That is, if the vendor has a strategy for Year 2000 Compliance in its products, and if it has good relations with its customer base, it would probably be wise to send notification to the customers saying something like: "Our products, beginning with version "x.x" will be fully functional on and after the Year 2000. We expect to release version "x.x" in the third quarter of 199x. The cost for upgrade will be $$$$."

However, there are several risks in that strategy. First, some customers, especially those who are otherwise dissatisfied, may use such notification to initiate legal action against the vendor, prior to the expiration of their individual statute of limitations for fraud or breach of contract. Second, if the date is too far in the future, it may cause concern among existing (and prospective) customers about the stability of the product. Third, if there really isn't a solid strategy for a fully-functional Year 2000 product, questions directed to customer support personnel may result in unsatisfactory responses.

Warren's Comments:

An interesting question regarding Vendor-promised due dates for their Year 2000 solution is to what extent user companies and their Officers and Directors can rely on such promises. For instance, if a vendor says it will provide the Year 2000 solution for your platform on 9/1/99, is that good enough? 3/1/99? 1/1/99? 6/30/98? 12/1/97? 6/30/97? Each of these dates are significant and propose different challenges and risks to the user company and its Officers and Directors.

To effectively perform their stewardship responsibility, and help avoid potential liability, Officers and Directors must assure that the developer company promising to provide the Year 2000 solution on the former group's platform will be able to do so in a timely manner. This is just plain good business sense. This will require that the developer has the resources, methodology, know-how, and incentive to provide that solution on a timely basis.

If the developer company is a large company, does it have the appropriate management support and plan, project management, tools, resources, etc. in place to make that performance date reasonable? What other strategic initiatives are fighting for those resources? If it is a small company, does its management really have the resources and wherewithal to make such a commitment? The Officers and Directors must do their due diligence to determine whether the promised date is reasonable-given that so many promised dates on large systems projects are typically missed. They must take the same care they would when acquiring a company in terms of asking the right questions about the people, policies, financial stability, strategic plans, procedures and technology, resources, technical know-how, and their specific solution to resolve the Year 2000 problem (four digits, sliding windows, encapsulation, etc.). This is essential so that they can determine whether the risk of waiting for the promised solution outweighs the risks of moving forward with alternatives. If automatic interfaces are required, it is important to inform suppliers and customers of your Year 2000 requirements. In any event, the user company must provide for some contingencies at known "drop dead" dates to enable starting on an alternative path if a promising vendor is unable to deliver for any reason.

Given my opinion that Year 2000 Problems will affect software on January 1, 1999, I don't believe that any promised fix to be delivered after the first of 1999 will be acceptable under any circumstances. Also, you must get periodic (no less than once per month) progress reports from the vendor which, at least, includes:

- progress made
- problems encountered
- how problems were resolved
- actual and expected changes in staff, budget, tools
- steps to be completed by next report

6. **What liability is potentially being assumed by Year 2000 Solution Providers as a result of agreeing to make changes to the customer's computer programs?**

Solution Providers are generally offering to identify date specific code, to modify the date specific code to operate properly (whether by direct change, sliding/fixed window and/or encapsulation), and to test those modifications. This is being done with a combination of automated tools, contract employees, off-shore programming (whole towns are reputedly being assembled in India), and project management. In most cases it means that the solution provider will have "examined" every line of source code for the customer, and will have actually changed a significant percentage of that source code.

The most obvious source of liability is for problems directly related to the intended scope of work, date-related items. Whenever you change thousands of data items, and thousands of lines of code, you introduce a statistical likelihood of errors. However, such errors are presumably well within the scope of risk which was understood by both the solution provider and the customer at the time they decided to do business together. Courts are likely to accept the allocation of risk in the contract between the parties.

What obligation does the solution provider have to fix non-date related code, where the solution provider became aware (or "should have" become aware) of a "bug" in the course of its date related work? Those expectations should be established in the contract between the parties, generally noting that the solution provider is not being paid to fix non-date bugs, and is therefore not responsible for those bugs.

Additionally, what obligation does the solution provider have to identify bugs in date related code, where such bugs are not directly related to Year 2000 functionality? For example, assume that the Solution Provider finds a line of code, used for the calculation of interest in a bank, which incorrectly calculates the amount of interest (that is, the error existed prior to any Year 2000 change). Again, the contract should specify how that information will be transmitted to the customer, and how the solution provider will be compensated for making those extra changes.

Another challenge (challenges are potential sources of alleged liability) is the customer's management of its own computer system. For example, does the customer have adequate backup of data files? This becomes especially relevant during testing. There have already been reports that "advancing" the system date, for testing purposes, can result in expiration of limited time software, accidental erasure of "permanent" data, and other unexpected outcomes.

Finally, the solution provider will certainly be in the middle of any litigation between the original software provider and the customer. Even if the solution provider has a good relationship with the customer, if the customer has reason to sue the original software provider (whether or not related to Year 2000 issues), there is a high probability that the solution provider will be brought into the litigation on a cross-action by the defendant/vendor. How can they ignore someone who just reviewed every line of code, and who changed substantial portions?

Warren's Comments:

Training is another area of potential liability and I am very concerned about what I hear of the training being given to programmers to resolve the Year 2000 problem. In addition to India which is using many unemployed Ph.d.'s, Ireland, and the Caribbean are creating entire organizations of people with minimal COBOL training to solve this problem. It is my understanding that the quality of the training at many such firms is minimized because the owners of the off-shore programming companies believe that fixing the date problem doesn't require a knowledge of appropriate operating systems, compilers, and more complex data, environmental, procedural and algorithmic functions, data definition alternatives, efficiency options contained within COBOL, recovery factors, etc. In the U.S. one outfit advertises that they will give you all the training you need in COBOL to fix Year 2000 Problems in ten days-not bad but not good either! I believe this short-cut type of training will cause problems because more than a cursory knowledge is needed! Other organizations are pulling together work teams with four inexperienced programmers and one experienced lead programmer. I believe the amount of turnover, standardization of solutions, and use of tools will make a big difference in the quality of the solutions that these work teams will provide.

In addition, for CIOs of user companies, managing multiple sites, new off-shore staff with new skills, on old code with unknown (at least to the programmer) business requirements, on outdated platforms using old operating systems, will be a very difficult task at best. I suspect that in more than a few cases, the CIOs will just get/take what is given to them and have to keep their fingers crossed. That situation and approach of course is fraught with risk.

In Steve's second paragraph under this issue, regarding the likelihood of errors when you change thousands of lines of code, I would like you to think about this as well. It has been a long standing rule of thumb that if a programmer makes one fix to a program that is 100 lines of code long (not data definitions, but logic) that he/she has studied, there is a one in six chance that a new error will be introduced. This is like Russian Roulette! Even more interesting, if the code is shorter in size, the likelihood of errors actually increases as the fix is given less care because it is considered trivial. Also because of this attitude it is more casually tested. Then, More regression type problems are not caught until the program is back in production. Counterintuitive but true!

In the old days, cash may have been king, but "regression testing" is king in the Year 2000 solution game. Regression testing is testing which assures that not only has the error been fixed, but that no new errors have been introduced inadvertently. A good regression scheme requires that the rules for determining how far to go back and retest already approved functions (ergo the word "regression") should be documented beforehand so that inevitable tempting shortcuts won't be taken as time becomes short.

7. **What might happen to Year 2000 Solution Providers, and their customers, after Year 2000 changes are completed? (i.e.—Do customers have the right to use consultants to perform Year 2000 changes?)**

Some of the Solution Providers will become experts in a certain application. That is, they will have completed a conversion of the ZZZ package for one company, and then they will get a referral to other customers who are also running ZZZ software. Once the Year 2000 conversion work is completed, and they begin looking for other consulting work, they might decide to specialize in "support" (maintenance and/or enhancement) of ZZZ software.

ZZZ, which was acquiescent during the Year 2000 conversion, because it was besieged by other customer demands, now objects to the fact that the Solution Provider had access to source code, proprietary information, etc. Both the Solution Provider, and the customers who granted access, find themselves in litigation.

Companies, as a part of their Year 2000 planning, must review whether they have the legal right to use non-employees. Perhaps the software license gives that right, but the customer is required to obtain a signed non-disclosure agreement.

Even internal use of the source code may cause long-term problems. There will be instances in which the customer has a right to use the source code, but loses all future warranty service by use of that source code to change the system.

8. **What responsibility do Directors and Officers have to: 1) ensure that Year 2000 Problems will not materially disrupt their business; 2) disclose the potential cost of conversion?**

As a result of the Private Securities Litigation Reform Act of 1995, and the rejection of Proposition 211 in California, Directors and Officers have an opportunity to make reasonable business decisions. But the failure to disclose material information can still result in liability.

Significant emphasis has been placed on "forward-looking statements", which now have a safe harbor where they are accompanied by "meaningful cautionary statements identifying important factors that could cause results to differ materially from those in the forward-looking statement."

Just as the Year 2000 is not a force majeure, it is not an unknown circumstance. Warren has already begun documenting this subject as you will see from his comments on this issue below. Companies will be required to undertake some level of expense in order to avoid Year 2000 problems. Companies which do not undertake such expense will encounter some interruption of business. And, depending on what occurs in the next two to three years, all companies may encounter some interruption of business when third-parties, which haven't made adequate preparation, are unable to support the company. (If you are a manufacturer, for example, and if one of your parts suppliers is unable to deliver just-in-time parts for a period of time, your quarterly results are likely to be impacted.)

Moreover, under the current standards, the costs to an individual company of making their system Year 2000 compliant, must be expensed, not capitalized. The estimated costs, which have been discussed by several experts, will be "material" to the bottom line of many companies. Using Lexis I did a scan of annual reports. I was able to find very few references to any disclosure about the potential impact of the Year 2000 on the companies listed.

I have already received information from individuals, within the information systems portions of companies, indicating that there are "smoking gun" memos discussing the need for the company to become Year 2000 compliant, and documenting management inaction on that subject. Companies which make "forward looking projections," without reflecting the known, material cost of Year 2000 compliance, may put themselves outside of the safe harbor provision.

Even if management is addressing the Year 2000 Problems, there are some questions about the duty to supervise vendors. Assume, for example, that a vendor supplied a mission critical software package which is known to have Year 2000 Problems. Assume further that the vendor, which is relatively small, promises to have the revisions ready by June, 1999. Finally, assume that the vendor has never, in fact, delivered any of the promised modifications in a timely manner. What level of scrutiny must be applied, by management, in order to avoid a significant impact on the business?

Warren's Comments:

I believe that when all is said and done, the courts will judge against vendors who fail to provide a promised Year 2000 solution, who did not make it known to the client that there would be no solution, or who entered into a faulty contract or one contemplated in bad faith. I do, however, believe that those judgments will be in line with the amount originally charged to the customer for the system and not tied to other business losses-especially if the contract between the parties specifically disclaims/limits express and implied warranties and excludes recovery of consequential, indirect, incidental, and special damages.

Therefore, a turnkey system of three million dollars for hardware and software, or a software development project that cost a user five million dollars, which are not Year 2000 Compliant, will probably involve a three or five million dollar judgment in favor of the user. Or, the court might award reimbursement to "cover" costs to make the system Year 2000 compliant. While it is possible in the area of failed vendor systems to find judgments against vendors of several hundred percent more than paid for the system, this is quite rare. That's the American way! Of course, a poorly drafted contract that does not provide adequate vendor disclaimers and liability limitations may prove particularly harmful to a vendor in such cases.

I believe that the big-ticket settlements and judgments will come down against Officers and Directors. This is because if a multi-billion dollar annual sales company loses 300 million dollars of sales, or market share, or stock market value, etc., the finders of fact will want to impose a judgment that is in line with that loss, ($300,000,000) which really isn't directly proportional to the cost of the system solution (perhaps only $3,000,000). My experience is that this, too, is the American way!

Looking at the Director and Officer liability issue more broadly, I believe that Officers and Directors have never yet been held responsible for big computer failures, per se. The scapegoat was always the project manager, or perhaps the CIO. On a big enough and obvious failure, maybe even the CFO would have been fired. Because of the potential impact of a company not being Year 2000 compliant and the known or knowable affects of such a situation, I believe Officers and Directors will be held liable for the first time for systems failures. It is a combination of the magnitude and visibility of the issue, and the fact that computers now are such an integral part of the on-going functioning of a business that Officers and Directors, as "stewards of the assets of a company," need to take responsibility and be held liable.

On September 17, 18 and 19, 1996, the popular newspaper cartoon "Dilbert" had three cartoons on the Year 2000 problem. These were published in the business section of newspapers all over the U.S. and, perhaps, worldwide. No explanation was given as to how to interpret the jokes, why they were funny, why there were timely, and why the reader should care. Rather, it was rightfully assumed that, as of that date, executives and business people reading the paper would have a knowledge of what the Year 2000 problem is sufficient enough to appreciate humor regarding the significance of the problem. I believe that no Officer or Director will be able to avoid liability for that problem in his/her company, after that date, using a defense of ignorance. (i. e., can't say, "I was not aware of the problem, its significance, magnitude, or its affect on my organization"). The Year 2000 had already been mentioned or analyzed in virtually all major business mediums. Thus, Officers and Directors that had not already done so should have begun to address the problem beginning September 20, 1996 at the latest-and that something should have included: planning for the resources, and overseeing the successful correction to that problem within their organization.

Based upon my knowledge of Officer and Director liability, from doing consulting/expert witness work in other matters, I believe that the Officers and Directors would have to go beyond simply relying upon a plan put together by their CIO. Having an outside expert, consultant, or quality assurance person reviewing the plan, the priorities set, the resources needed, and the schedule, is certainly in order. The smart company will even hire a second expert to look at the first expert's work to make sure the job can be done, on time, and adequately tested before the turn of the century. The opinion of the two experts will, particularly if the expert's agree on the plans for moving forward, help almost any board survive a legal challenge, even if they don't, in fact, achieve Year 2000 Compliance on time. The business judgment rule and other laws associated with Officer and Director liability will hold sway in these matters.

Furthermore, it is likely that a 500 million or three billion dollar company which relies upon a two million or 20 million dollar vendor of mission critical software to get the problem fixed will find itself in trouble if the fix doesn't occur. Adequate contingency plans must be made and implemented if it looks like the vendor will be late, won't be able to fix the problem, or otherwise can't deliver the fixes. After all, the shareholders never voted for the under-capitalized software company as the management of the company. Lastly, under SEC rule 6835, Officers and Directors are supposed to report known future events, that may have a material impact on the company, in their reports to the SEC. I am not aware of any companies who have made a report regarding their Year 2000 Problems.

9. **What are the potential pitfalls in Year 2000 Certification for software vendors?**

Some organizations are offering Year 2000 "Certification." However, the scope of investigation being undertaken by the certifying entity, in many cases, would appear to be too narrow. At least one organization offering Year 2000 certification doesn't even examine the actual computer products/tools of the Solution Provider. Instead, the certification is actually for the "process and method" which the vendor claims to apply in the course of delivering its products and/or services. Indeed, one major certifying organization specifi-cally offers to provide essentially the same certification process to any software project, even if it isn't related to Year 2000 compliance.

It is not clear whether the purchasers of products from "Year 2000 Certified" vendors will be advised that the certification has nothing to do with the actual functionality of the products, only with the design and management method-ology claimed to have been applied to development of the products. Since the only market value of a certification is to support sales by reassuring customers, the purchasers of such "certified" products may have a direct cause of action against the organization providing the certification.

Further, a company obtaining a certification may be increasing its own poten-tial liability in at least two aspects. First, a court could find that the "certification" constitutes an express warranty, thus making the vendor liable for failures in performance far in excess of what was contemplated by the vendor's counsel when preparing the vendor's limited warranties. Second, no published opinion has applied a "malpractice" standard to computer profes-sionals, generally because computer programming is not a licensed profession. However, if an industry wide organization claims to be "certi-fying" software methodology, a court may find that those holding such certification are "voluntarily" assuming a "professional" obligation, and thus have liability for "malpractice," notwithstanding the terms of any contract between the vendor and the customer.

Warren's Comments:

Before you rely upon a certification, do a little homework about the certi-fying authority. Make sure that it is not funded by the companies it is certifying. I think any certification program that does not include a fair amount of on-site interviewing with the developer, including surprise, on-the-spot requests for specific documentation on alleged Year 2000 compliant programs or projects in process, is deficient. Lastly, any program that relies upon affidavits from executives indicating future compliance to a certified process should be looked upon askance unless there is a capability of future follow-up and surprise audits by the certifying entity regarding the actual processes used within the developer.

I have spent substantial time testifying against some of the world's largest and most famous systems developers, who, although they have a great methodology on paper, did not use it on a particular, critical project. That's why they were in court in the first place, and it's why they lost!

10. **What kind of insurance will be involved in these cases?**

I am unaware of any "first-party" insurance for this issue. By "first-party" I mean insurance which will cover "your" costs for the Year 2000 problem. For example, Business Interruption won't help you, even if you need to close down for a few months, because "computer failure" isn't one of the covered causes of loss.

In regard to "third-party" insurance (liability to others), perhaps the most obvious coverage for some of these claims will be Directors and Officers Liability insurance. No matter how much effort they invest, some executives will find themselves with critical Year 2000 Problems that will have a material negative impact on their company's financial results. Others will fail to deal with the issue until late in 1998, and when they do make an effort they will find substantially increased prices for labor, computers, testing, and all other components, and they won't have disclosed the material effect on their 1999 bottom line. It will be contended that they are liable for a substantial, previously undisclosed, negative result, about which they had actual knowledge.

Another coverage, for vendors, is Computer Errors and Omissions insurance, commonly described as "computer malpractice" insurance. Although it has been generally available for a number of years, there is reason to believe that the Year 2000 problem is receiving substantial scrutiny from the specialized underwriters involved with such coverage. Existing policyholders may find restrictive endorsements proposed at renewal, and new applicants may find that they cannot obtain this insurance if they are deemed to be at particular risk.

Steven Brower can be contacted by e-mail at sbrower@gsor.com.

Warren S. Reid can be contacted by e-mail at consult@wsrcg.com.

CHAPTER 4

Master Plan for Year-2000 Conversion Projects

In corporations with more than a million lines of code—which isn't very much—Year-2000 compliance projects will fail and deadlines will be missed unless a formal, disciplined project management (PM) approach is implemented. The implications of large financial and other mission-critical systems failing impacts shareholders, the community as a whole, and total corporate viability.

The project manager's scope of responsibilities varies significantly according to the size of the operation and the type of business. He or she could be entirely in charge of the project, overseeing many sub-projects that each have a project manager, project leader, and team. In a smaller organization, the project manager may be solely responsible for the Year-2000 effort. Many companies use the terms *project manager* or *project leader* in place of *systems analyst* or *team leader*, in which case a more technical role is played.

Most professional PM organizations emphasize management, co-ordination, and fiscal characteristics, and tend to exclude more junior or very technically oriented activities.

Whatever the definition your company uses, in the case of Year 2000, the project manager's role is specific: to get the site compliant in time.

The Seven Stages of a Year-2000 Project

The Year-2000 exercise has seven significant sub-projects or stages:

1. **Start-up.** Define project-management roles, structures, and lines of reporting. Allocate responsibilities and demarcate ownership boundaries. Agree on formal project-management standards and procedures.

2. **Inventory.** Perform a detailed portfolio analysis, identifying applications that will be redundant or replaced in a few years. Be sure to take trends toward client/server systems and downsizing into account.

3. **Analysis.** Draw up Value to Business and Cost of Conversion charts. (See the section "Prioritizing and Triaging," later in this chapter.) Compile a prioritized list. Managers need to analyze the impact of all applications and develop a strategy and sequence for fixing each one. Where systems and programs share data, your analysis will indicate where bridges between converted and non-converted systems need to be built.

4. **Planning.** Sequencing, bridging, purchasing, and prioritizing all require serious planning. Setting up a workable, efficient, coding development and testing environment (with automated workbenches) will minimize unexpected delays in the next stage. Conversion strategies must be quantified with regards to logic-to-data ratio. Establish procedures for replacing code and verifying changes by updating databases and altering files well before actual coding commences. Users must agree on standard date-code formats.

5. **Coding and Conversion.** This is a separate, large-scale project. Managers must track and measure both personnel resources and conversion sequences. They must also prepare contingency plans to address unscheduled hitches. These plans must anticipate natural attrition (and poaching) of key personnel, events that may necessitate multiple revisions and start-up sessions. Since third-party agencies will probably perform part of the work, external progress should be monitored closely.

6. **Integration** and **Testing.** Up to 25 percent of mainframe MIPS will be used for testing, especially in advanced stages of integration and bridge decommissioning. The recursive testing process (regression testing) should be done during off-peak hours, if possible. The testing process requires effective auditing and tracking of all changes and revisions. In addition, projects may have a second major change-testing project due to unsynchronized external conversion schedules.

7. **Quality Assurance, Migration, and Feedback Reports.** The importance of training, orderly migration, and follow-up reports is often minimized, much to the detriment of complex projects. Accurate and timely feedback followed by appropriate fine-tuning should resolve glitches before they become major incidents.

Each of these steps is explained in greater detail below. You can use this section as a blueprint for creating a Year-2000 conversion plan for your organization. Address the points listed under each of the seven steps to customize these procedures. You may also think of issues that are unique to your company or agency as you read this chapter—take note of these as they occur to you, and ensure that they are taken into account as your plan evolves.

You may want to revisit this chapter midway through your Year-2000 project, as it's likely that the plan you create now will need to change over time to fit real-world conditions. You'll want to make sure that all of these steps are undertaken in sequence, however. Take the time to reassess your plan periodically, with special attention given to synchronizing each phase of the job. A delay in completing one step of the process will affect deadlines and duties in all subsequent steps. Project-management tools, such as task-diagramming and scheduling software, can help you predict scheduling conflicts and avoid snafus.

Start-Up

Define project-management roles, areas of responsibility, structures, and lines of reporting. Identify product (or business unit) ownership boundaries. Agree on formal project-management standards and procedures.

RCs and MRPs

Year-2000 conversion projects can be broken down into a series of Repetitive Cycles (RCs), which are sometimes called Modular Repeatable Processes (MRPs).

These cycles can be repeated sequentially or in parallel, depending on where in the conversion process they lie.

The idea is to break the whole effort into a series of manageable units, each of which can then be modified and repeated as necessary. Each RC must be clearly defined, with a specific scope, and guidelines for input and output. The RC concept is similar to the Object-Oriented Programming paradigm, where managers break a programming task down into discrete parts (objects) that can be assigned to individual programmers and that can be reused as needed in other programs.

Although the RC concept can be applied to every stage of a Year-2000 project, **Inventory** and **Analysis** are two activities that immediately lend themselves to the concept.

Inventory

Although the task is laborious and repetitive, companies learn a lot from the inventory process. Just finding and cataloguing the code yields major benefits. Eliminating redundant or duplicated code and data can free up huge amounts of storage space. *Sometimes up to 30 percent of the code in libraries is obsolete or unnecessary.* This is an excellent opportunity for housekeeping, as well as an essential part of the Year-2000 project.

The inventory phase is one of the most staff-intensive parts of the Year-2000 project. It can be broken down as follows:

1. Hold an awareness and responsibility seminar for inventory officers.
2. Generate and distribute questionnaires.
3. Locate and compile a list of systems, files, and dependencies.
4. Collect and collate data concerning all items on this list.
5. Determine event horizons, importance to business, and difficulty of conversion for each of these items.
6. Map dependencies and relationships between these items.
7. Collect vendor and external interface compliance data for all items.
8. Create and disseminate reports that summarize what you have learned in the inventory process.

Chapter 8, *Inventory Database Schema*, includes a questionnaire, which adds some detail to the inventory report layout. You can use this document as a template for your own report.

To ensure compliance, assume that every computer, peripheral, program, file, and database is affected.

Information can be gathered via user surveys, maintenance-staff interviews, and perusal of documented maintenance costs. These methods are inexpensive and quick, but they are also subjective. Supplement data gathered from individuals with objective sources whenever possible to avoid being influenced by personal (and sometimes ill-informed) views.

Well-designed documentation of the data-gathering process is essential. Generic examples can be found in Chapter 8. A database should be used to store inventory information, which should include:

- Dependencies
- Business units
- Overlapping and sharing of files, peripherals, etc.
- Vendor information and maintenance contracts
- Importance of system (both impact and scope)
- Fields for progress indicators, milestones, and contact people
- Undertakings and obligations repository

Some companies use the inventory database as a monitoring and reporting center. A sample database can be found at the end of Chapter 8.

Using a large insurance company with a COBOL-based back-end environment as an example, an approximate ratio of affected systems is as follows:

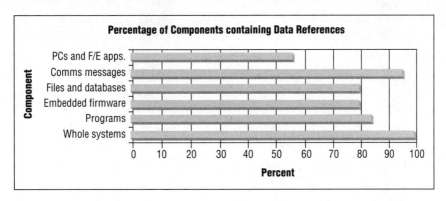

Figure 4-1: Approximate percentage of components containing date references

Note that the number of PCs and F/E applications with Year-2000 problems will decline at a faster pace than mainframe problems as newer PC hardware and software are commissioned. Even so, many PC databases, spreadsheets, and source code will still need to be converted to full compliance.

The following areas must all be ascertained in the inventory stage:

1. The size and number of programs in mainframe, PC, and other systems.
2. The size and number of databases and repositories, including back-up files.

3. All hardware and firmware (BIOS, ROM, etc.).

4. All time-dependent or time-based peripheral systems (security, telephone switchboards, time-locks, elevators, etc.).

5. Business units and responsibilities.

6. The importance (and priority) of the programs to your organization at user level—sometimes users believe the system is more important than senior management thinks it is. Sometimes they are right.

Although it should be confirmed in writing with individual vendors, using a document similar to the one found in Chapter 8, it is reasonable to assume that most reputable off-the-shelf packages and PC hardware/BIOS issues will be resolved in versions released after 1998. All user-generated programs and files, however, must be tested. Most will need to be converted.

Analysis

Reports made in 1997 indicated that fewer than 30 percent of IT departments have successfully implemented change and configuration management as a business practice.

Well-run Year-2000 conversion processes will change this statistic dramatically. Configuration management is recognized as an absolute necessity in a Year-2000 project—without it, there is no way to effectively roll out components on complex platforms. Automated configuration-management control has been employed by many organizations to oversee distribution of systems software, development, tools, and vendor application packages.

The success (or failure) of Year-2000–compliance projects pivots on the thoroughness and detail of the Analysis phase. Sufficient time, process control, and project management must be embedded in this phase. Rough guidelines on timeframes and metrics can be found in the Management section "Metrics and Statistics."

The Analysis stage requires a top-down approach. You will need to analyze, in this order:

• Value of the program to the users and the business

• Program/data dependencies

• Vendor/development/outsourcing dependencies

• Degree of difficulty of maintaining the program

Once a list of all systems (products) is available, charts similar to those below can be used to represent inter-system dependencies on a macro level. Detailed data-flow diagrams should be studied to ensure that conversion covers all components.

Relationship and data-flow mapping is vital. Knowing how data moves and what it is used for is essential when weighing the merits of expanding the date field to four-digit year fields versus windowing. Mapping may seem like an extra layer of work, but it isn't. Even if you retain two-digit years in the data, you will still make changes that could affect data integrity. Letting people know that changes are being made is more than just a courtesy.

For example, upstream or downstream applications may also need to change to four-digit years. It will require additional labor to intercept and assign century

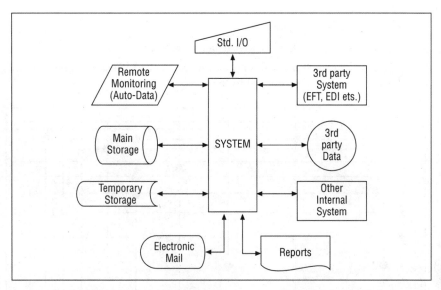

Figure 4-2: Generic input output diagram

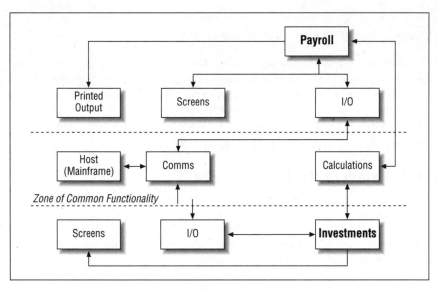

Figure 4-3: Examples of system dependencies

values via bridging each time these programs look at a date. In addition, sort-sequences and other logic may be impacted.

Prioritizing and Triaging

An important part of the decision-making process is prioritizing the systems and programs to be fixed. You will need to determine:

- Importance to business mission or finances
- Importance to staff (utility)
- Degree of technical difficulty to maintain or replace

The following graph illustrates the prioritizing process (the first two points above have been averaged to derive Value to Business).

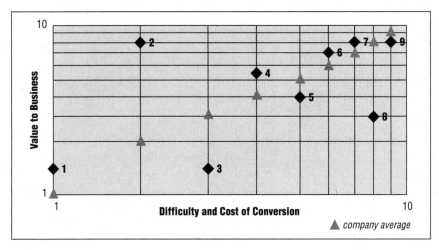

Figure 4-4: Cost of conversion versus value of system to business

From the chart, one can see that systems 2 and 7 are critical to business success, and that system 7 will require approximately four times the resources that 2 needs to convert. This is an over-simplification of the usual situation, where dependencies, bridging, MIPS requirements, and sequencing are all additional factors, but it does quantify the relationships and assists triaging decisions where necessary.

The triaging process is expanded in Chapter 7, *Triage*.

Automation in the Analysis Phase

Date occurrences in job-streams, databases, files, applications, and source code are found accomplished in this phase, an activity that is vital to the conversion and planning effort. Done manually, this process borders on the soul-destroying. Scanning tools are available for both mainframe and workstation environments that can review the code and determine dates. However, output from these tools must be checked manually, since strings such as *update* will also be reported when searching for combinations that include *date*.

It goes without saying that the more sophisticated the tool, the greater its price, and the higher the need for senior technical staff to employ it. Sometimes it's better to embrace an automated scan with a manual *fix*, since the *fixing* tools tend to cost more than the *scanners*. A balanced approach takes resources and time into account.

When the logic is reviewed (if a standardized set of date-routines will be used for the conversion), a specification indicating the appropriate date routine calls is prepared for the actual changes to the system. In addition, the range of date use requires that all logic identified in the *Analysis* task be reviewed on a line-by-line basis. Automating this type of task is difficult, and usually is best addressed by tools like code-splicers and maintenance workbenches. The final result of this resource-intensive job is a specification for change that is utilized in the actual change of code and files, as described in the "Coding and Conversion" section.

A full suite of tools in the hands of competent operators can provide a net benefit of as much as 35 percent over fully manual conversion projects. Languages such as COBOL are well-supported, and some platforms, such as MVS, have attracted a large number of third-party software development tool vendors. Others rely on the manufacturer's built-in tools.

Logistical Estimates and Resources

To estimate costs, start by sizing up the job. How many LOCs does a company own, and what is the date incidence? Scanners often report date incidence in 10 percent of the code, while a manual scan could reduce this to less than 5 percent.

File Expansion or Code Solution

The decision to expand the file or leave it alone must be made early in the process. If the date fields in permanent storage currently hold six digits with no century, the options include:

- Packing (compressing) the dates into existing byte storage

- Encoding the dates to include the century

- Expanding the date field(s)

- Adding extra fields (duplicate date fields for converted and unconverted systems)

- Windowing

> Expanding fields or adding columns increases total storage, and requires re-formatting all archive data; packing leaves the storage size alone, but requires type changes, and sometimes conversion algorithms. Some organizations have encoded the century by substituting alphabetic or symbolic characters for year or month, but this approach limits future functionality, and stymies ad-hoc sorting and querying.

Resource Drain Due to Existing Application Failures

As time progresses, failure of existing (and newly converted) applications will reduce the resources available for work on updates. This increasing curve of demand for resources as the big day approaches will stress the infrastructure tremendously. An organization in this predicament will find more and more of its energy going into short-term solutions—until it reaches a point where it cannot cope.

It is critical that sufficient resources are available to service the project—this is one case where late-night shopping isn't a satisfactory option.

·Function Points per Date Incident

Many consultants base cost estimates on the rough correlation of one function-point per each business-date incidence. From this figure, it's possible to derive a very rough estimate of *man-days* and *code-conversion costs.*

An average of 100 LOCs (COBOL) and up to 300 LOCs (Assembly or other) per function point is common. Every date instance is associated with an approximate number of LOCs. Only a few will need to be converted, but most should be checked.

Although COBOL programs generally have the largest conversion requirements, they will be simpler to convert than others because many tools and solution vendors are available. Scanning tools will pick up the date instances, but conversion staff must explore the ramifications of that information.

The most expensive languages to convert (per function point) will probably be PL/1 and Assembler, due to low staff availability.

Cost for converting object-oriented code is difficult to assess. Theoretically, it should be easier due to the inheritance and polymorphous characteristics of the paradigm. On the other hand, because it is relatively new, much object-oriented programming (OOP) code has been written by people still mastering the minutiae of programming. Maybe you will need to add a staff-assessment section to your staffing formula.

The chart below summarizes 1997 research on the proportion of *approximate* LOCs per development language for the total inventory. Note that the "Other" block is substantial, and includes RPG and at least 50 other languages.

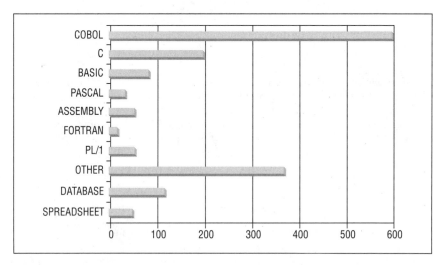

Figure 4-5: Approximate code ratios

The following chart provides a general indication of cost in cents (conversion only) per function point. Supply of and demand for staff will drive the figures upwards over the next two years.

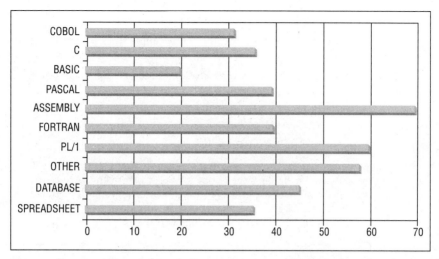

Figure 4-6: Approximate cost to convert (per function point, by language)

The next chart indicates the ratio of conversion costs per stage for COBOL- and Assembly-based programs. This ratio will vary considerably according to tools and staff availability. "Other" refers to management, testing, and distribution.

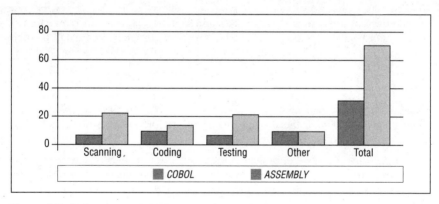

Figure 4-7: Code cost comparison

Many consultants believe that the cost of code-conversion will be comparable to the cost of database conversion, allowing estimates to be reliably based on cost per incident of date fields. In some data-intensive situations, however, the cost could be even higher.

For projects with more than 500,000 LOCs due for conversion, the use of automated costing tools (COSTAR, for example) is imperative. Often smaller projects will also benefit from a formal costing process.

Once the effort required to renovate or update software has been estimated, you can place a value on systems and plot the Business Value/Conversion Difficulty graph (see the Analysis section earlier in the chapter). This valuation may have interesting results that go beyond the Year-2000 project at hand:

- Organizations may decide to retire the whole application because it is too expensive to replace or renovate.

- Alternatively, they may reduce the processing burden by eliminating marginal or exceptional functionality or reports.

WARNING

Beware of getting sucked into piggy-back projects during your Year-2000 conversion project. By limiting the scope of the work to the date-change only, added efforts are curtailed. If other functional changes are undertaken at the same time as date-changes, delays can be introduced—or exacerbated—by workshops and think-tanks involving clients.

Projects usually grow as people become aware of the ramifications of the original change or discover other problems in the code, such as incorrect data or processing logic errors. IT staff must resist the temptation to rewrite code just because they don't like the original author's style, or because the logic is too complex and hard to maintain.

The Year-2000 project manager must have the authority to reject requests for code enhancements, no matter how minor. To appease those clamoring for other changes, keep a record in the database of additional problems as they are noticed. You'll probably develop a fix-it list that will keep staff busy for years once the Year-2000 scramble is over.

Planning

Once the Inventory and Analysis phases are complete, and all dependencies have been fully documented, the program manager can present one of the following options for each entry on the list:

1. Discard the program or system completely. If the system is due for replacement, now is the time. Replace it with an off-the-shelf solution. There are many powerful alternatives to general financial, design, and inventory applications, among others, and it may cost less to integrate one of these than to rewrite an in-house app.

2. Convert to a different environment. You can use existing downsizing or client-server directions to motivate this migration. At the same time, include a little Business Process Re-engineering where indicated.

3. Outsource the solution. Although outsourcing costs more than in-house work, resource limitations may impel it.

4. Convert the program in-house. In-house knowledge and loyalty are important factors in this process. Cross-training can fill the short-term need for COBOL staff, who can then be re-oriented once the conversion pressures are off.

Business units and senior general management will decide the course of action taken, and you can then move on to conversion-related technicalities.

Coding and Conversion

The coding conversion process can be broken down into a series of easily manageable Repetitive Cycles (RCs). These can be repeated sequentially or in parallel, depending on where in the process they lie. These RCs must be clearly defined, with specific scopes, input, and output.

Some experts say the most durable, cost-effective approach to conversion is to expand programs and data to four-digit years. This method is consistent with all standards, allows maximum flexibility in exchanging data with outside sources, and minimizes long-term maintenance costs.

However, strong business reasons may make expansion to four-digit dates impossible. In this case, the use of two-digit centuries and fixed/sliding-window logic is applicable. If two-digit dates are used in programs, you may still find situations where two-digit dates will be required in code. The logic approach is certainly the fastest, and it will have the least impact on hardware or stored data.

Usually a combination of both approaches will be required.

Master Plan

Standards

One would hope that standards would clarify the situation, but unfortunately, most standards permit both two-digit and four-digit solutions. There are two primary international standards that specify how dates should be represented:

- ANSI X3.30 - 1985 (American National Standards Institute), *"Representation for Calendar Date and Ordinal Date for Information Interchange."* This standard was adopted as FIPS 4-1, Federal Information Processing Standards.

- ISO 8601 - 1988-06-15 (International Standards Organization), *"Data Elements and Interchange Formats (Information Interchange and Representation of Dates and Times)."* The Canadian Standards Association as CAN/CSA-Z234.5-89 has adopted this standard. Most countries use the ISO standard as a basis for their own set of standards, usually overlaid with national format and presentation.

Both ANSI and ISO standards agree that the date-layout YYYYMMDD (all numeric with no separators) is the preferred Gregorian format. For ordinal (Julian) dates, the form is YYYYDDD, where DDD is the day of the year. If you use either of these forms, your systems will comply with both ANSI and ISO standards.

Embedded Dates

The project team usually consults with the application owner to resolve the issue of embedded dates. Business concerns commonly associated with embedded dates are inventory, accounting, prioritization, expiration, and accessibility. How the client uses dates determines whether the century is significant. If the century is required, support staff must be prepared to answer questions about the number, nature, and complexity of date-processing routines.

Unfortunately, involving the application-owner or sponsor often opens a can of worms. You may get requests for other changes, as long-dormant issues come up. Now that the application requires modification, those changes may appear justified. Refer to the Analysis section earlier in the chapter for the ammunition you need to resist these requests.

Parallel Conversion

Only small installations will be able to convert everything at once and then begin multiple parallel testing. Usually one system at a time will be converted, then bridged to unconverted systems. This step is necessary not only for proper testing, but also to generate the Year-2000 simulations you'll need for the QA phase.

> The Coding and Conversion phase of a Year-2000 project is highly technical. This chapter presents an overview of the issues only. General technical details can be found in Chapter 5, *Technical Considerations*, while language-specific information is presented in Chapters 10 through 17.

Determining the Ratio of Data to Logic Approaches

Both the data and logic methods have to deal with expanded display fields and mechanisms. When determining which will be used and where, the real issue is whether expanded fields in stored or transported data will result in too many problems with display and report fields. If they do, then the logic route could be a better solution. Potential problem areas include fixed storage and transport blocks, row-by-row conversion of all stored data, and rebuilding indexes.

The decision-making process can be formalized using the following inputs, mostly from the technical project staff:

- Cost and time to change code
- Cost and time to change data storage and handling
- Variation on processor demand (machine cycles)
- Quantity of additional storage required
- Cost of testing, distribution, and maintenance

Since the answers they provide will be influenced by the potential level of automation, consider the optimum solution that each solutions provider offers when determining how much of the process can be automated, and at what cost. It will be very difficult to evaluate outside vendors and their products, since not all have references or track records. Their projected productivity levels (cost per application, module, or line of code) are untried. By the time ample references are available and vendor strengths have been fully established, most users will already have been forced to choose.

Code Conversion

The following is a framework for a *code-conversion* RC. Remember to monitor progress all the way through this process.

1. Study the code-scan report for trends, volumes, and functional usage.
2. Select applicable programming and conversion tools and platforms.
3. Determine which files, copy-books, and shared modules should be updated.
4. Document the impact of these updates on other systems.
5. Determine resource requirements and availability.
6. Create a timeline for the project, and obtain agreement from all parties.
7. Commence conversion.
8. Commence unit testing.
9. Document changes.
10. Collate observations, and feed these back to generate the next cycle.

The code conversion stage is usually managed by a team leader or systems analyst. Programmers and technical staff need to be closely involved in all steps to ensure the efficiency of evolution of the RC.

Usage of code-conversion resources can be reduced by up to 20 percent when RCs are properly implemented in areas of common functionality.

Chapter 10, *COBOL Reference*, and Chapter 11, *Date Functions*, provide plenty of background for the *logic* approach, as well as generic solutions.

Integration and Testing

Almost all applications will be affected by Year-2000 conversion in some way, and many of them are interdependent. Now the magnitude of the integration process comes into perspective!

In projects that are under pressure to deliver on time, it is common to find integration-testing left to (or incorporated with) user-testing. The developer is directly responsible for testing and delivering units of the system, but it does not readily accept responsibility for testing the assembled product. Project leaders and managers need to concentrate on alterations to the system and how these could affect the interfaces between units, especially client/server or external (third-party) interfaces, where the impact of inadequate testing also becomes the concern of business-unit leaders.

Each converted module or unit added results in a testing ripple across all previously tested sub-units, calling for regression testing. A version upgrade can influence date-format configuration files and settings, which in turn alters screen and document presentation. A well-planned conversion project can help reduce the number of cycles in this process.

Clearly, documented interfaces and impact scenarios are important to the generation of test scripts, helping to prioritize and highlight potential problem areas. Checklists of current and historical test points, with proper sign-offs, are essential to minimizing the possibility of something slipping through.

Estimating Testing Requirements

About half of all project resources will be needed for testing. Unit testing will require 40 percent of that amount, while integration and full-system testing take the rest.

Capacity, facility, and staff planning efforts can begin as soon as preliminary estimates are complete. The highest MIPS and DASD capacity surges for testing could be 50 percent where one extremely large, primary database servicing the bulk of transactions shares logic with hundreds of integrated programs.

Fortunately, fewer than 10 percent of users will experience this type of growth. Normally a large organization with multiple databases, installations, and divisions will experience MIPS surges of up to 25 percent. If that organization presently allocates 15 percent to testing and the focus of that testing activity shifts significantly to Year-2000 projects, the additional increase in testing-based MIPS and DASD may be as low as 10 percent.

Test Script Development

Since the Year-2000 update involves almost all systems and files, testing becomes a major part of the process. The development of detailed test scripts is necessary for quality assurance and completeness.

The process of creating test scripts, test databases, and comparison files will define frameworks for RCs. While these processes increase storage requirements and machine cycles in testing, they also increase the potential for improved efficiency in applying changes to the system.

Test scripts can take on a host of different forms depending on the author's interpretation, type of system, and tools available. In its simplest form, the script is just a list of things to test—usually based on changes that have been made. After internal and external dependencies and platforms have been converted, this list is expanded to include regression and integration testing.

Automated testing requires the configuration of more complex test scripts that include specific data and variations thereof, operational sequences, ranges and limits, and relationships. Stress testing is another script component. It has to be able to drive the tool to test the volume limits of the system components. Fortunately, the vast majority of Year-2000 conversions will not include major architectural or transport-layer alteration, and hence will not need total-system testing. These projects will focus on date-field presentation and manipulation instead.

All output or valid random samples, even when screened by the tool, must be checked against input from the script. Sometimes a simple merge-field in a document or report can be overlooked, and result in widespread confusion.

Testing Tools

Proper tools can certainly make the testing process easier, but none can provide a total solution. Planning is the key to productive use of tools.

Regression-testing and integration-testing tools are necessary. These are often available in-house. Date simulating test software that can replace "current date" systematically across the required range is an important tool. It is recommended that testing include the years 1997 through 2001—and even 2005 and beyond, if indicated by event horizons.

The range of testing tools grows daily. Try to avoid products that work around the symptoms rather than providing a permanent solution, and shun software that does not follow industry standards. Automatic code conversion has to be carefully monitored and the results tested thoroughly. Testing tools such as test-data generators, data-agers, and key-capture (for generating macros) are available for most environments.

References to specific tools and vendors occur throughout this book, but every system in every company has its own unique peculiarities and dependencies, and will still require unique treatment and in-house expertise. Contact your solutions vendors and consult up-to-date lists of tools on Year-2000–related Web sites for more information.

Quality Assurance, Migration, and Feedback Reports

Accurate and timely feedback is a very important stage in the Year-2000 exercise, and shouldn't be overlooked. Glitches can be resolved by proper use of this stage, thus preventing major incidents from occurring.

Quality Assurance

As the clock ticks, the reality of the impact of unconverted systems begins to question the structure of classical Quality Assurance (QA) and control systems.

In the ideal world, an application is bug-free, complies to the company GUI standard, and is totally robust. In the months leading up to the new millennium, focus will shift toward maintaining business revenues—at the cost of almost all traditional QA principles. This is another ugly facet of triaging, and it will result in friction between the established order and the Year-2000 project manager. Parking issues till after the Year-2000 event and possibly agreeing on a phase-2 roll-out are workable strategies; often, very senior management have to overrule QA staff and heighten tensions. Absolute diplomacy in the project office is vital to the objective—remember, there will be life after the Year 2000, and you would like to retain your position to enjoy it.

You will have to review and prioritize the current QA process. Critical issues of data security and integrity must preside over aesthetics. Sign-off procedures have to be streamlined, regression-testing optimized, and migration planned very carefully to conform with the new *priority A principles of QA*.

Migration

Migration of systems into production requires a change-management process and effective documentation, which should cover change and installation procedures. The tools and infrastructure for this phase are generally available in most large companies.

If your organization has field sites that use the software, effective training will be needed to make users aware of how important valid century dates are, as well as to familiarize them with new screen and report layouts. Ideally, validation windows should be embedded in converted programs to make the system more robust.

Migrating systems with modified frontend components will require additional planning, expenditures, and strategic staff deployments for installation and training.

Remote sites and groups of end users will need to be part of the loop via feedback reports to the Year-2000 project team.

Important Factors for Year-2000 Planning

As your master plan for Year-2000 conversion takes shape, remember that the severe penalties that could arise from a poorly-managed project dictate that only the very best staff should be in charge of implementation.

Only the most experienced and highly skilled employees will be able to understand and accommodate the massive testing and integration requirements that characterize the final stages of a Year-2000 conversion project. Most companies planned to complete code-conversion by year-end 1997 or mid-1998, leaving 18 to 24 months for testing millions of lines of code. If you have gotten a late start, your coding and testing schedules may approach the realm of impossibility.

Doing the impossible is a tall order. You can help your top Year-2000 team members by providing a well-thought-out structure for the project, and by ensuring that they will find support for their efforts at all levels of the organization. As you create a master plan for carrying out the seven steps listed previously, be sure that it includes these essential elements:

- Enterprise-wide planning, including formulation of standards and practices and relationship mapping

- Project managers who maintain high-level awareness and who have the ability to reschedule priorities

- Efficient communications

- Detailed working processes for completing the entire Year-2000 compliance project

- Assignment of adequate and well-trained Year-2000 conversion specialists

- Access to tools that reduce tedious tasks by automating simple update practices, such as date-field expansion and data changes

If these elements are built into your master plan, it will have a high probability of success. If any one of these elements is missing, failure is very likely.

CHAPTER 5

Technical Considerations

This chapter compares the logic/windowing approach and the date-field expansion approach in depth. It also covers bridging, and probes issues surrounding the storage, conversion, and processing of dates.

Although many believe these are primarily mainframe topics, any system that accesses files must be analyzed and, if necessary, made Year-2000 compliant. This applies to PC databases, spreadsheets, and other files used for initialization and control of programs. Chapter 6, *PCs and the Front End*, addresses PC-specific problems in more detail.

Historical Dates and Leap-Year Theory

Early date systems worked on the assumption that the earth took a whole number of days to rotate around the sun (365 days, to be exact). This resulted in a shortfall of approximately one day every four years, which Julius Caesar decided to remedy by creating a new calendar. His Julian calendar added a day every four years, creating what we now call leap years. Unfortunately, he over-corrected slightly, and every 128 years his calendar was one day ahead of reality.

By the thirteenth century this problem was apparent to astronomers, who recommended a variety of solutions. Finally, almost two hundred years later, Pope Gregory XIII decided to remedy the situation once and for all. He used the Lilian solution, which was provided by the physician Aloysius Lilius. In 1582 a Papal decree was issued stating that the ten days that had accumulated since the time of Julius Caesar be dropped immediately. According to this decree, the day after the 5th of October 1582 would be the 15th of October 1582, not the 6th.

An adjustment was also made to the method of calculating leap years. Every fourth year would still be a leap year—except for any century-ending year (a year ending with two zeroes) that was not divisible by 400.

The following rules can be used to determine when leap years occur:

The year YYYY is a leap year if:

YYYY MOD 4 = 0 AND YYYY MOD 100 <> 0

or:

YYYY MOD 400 = 0

Therefore:

2000 MOD 4 = 0 AND 2000 MOD 100 <> 0 (false)

or:

2000 MOD 400 = 0 (true)

If you do the math, you'll find that while the Year 2000 is a century-ending year, it is also divisible by 400. Therefore, it will be a leap year. This observation is important because some programmers only accommodated the century condition (and not the 400-year one), which would make 2000 *not* a leap year.

WARNING

The Julian calendar is very different from the *Julian day* or *Julian period*, and should not be confused with them.

The Julian period was devised by French scholar Joseph Justus Scaliger (1540–1609), who wanted to assign a positive number to every year in a long series without having to concern himself with BC and AD. The Julian period is not related to the Julian calendar—it was named after Scaliger's father, the Italian scholar Julius Caesar Scaliger (1484–1558).

Scaliger's Julian period starts on 1 January 4713 B.C. (Julian calendar) and lasts for 7980 years. A.D. 1997 is year 6710 in the Julian period. After 7980 years, the cycle starts from one again.

The terms Julian Date and Ordinal Date are often used to represent a date format, such as YYDDD or CCYYDDD, where YY or CCYY could be any year or century and DDD is the day offset from that year. This concept forms the basis of date arithmetic, and is found throughout Chapter 11, *Date Functions*, and beyond.

Logic/Windowing versus Date-Field Expansion

In simple terms, when you use the logic or windowing technique, you leave the two-digit (stored) years alone and add code that determines the century *on the fly* (while the data is being processed). There are several ways to do this.

One windowing method is based on parameters, either hard-wired or derived from input files. A base year, such as "50" for 1950, is selected. Then every year between 50 and 99 is treated as a 20th-century date (1950, 1951, etc.) and any year between 0 and 49 is treated as a 21st-century date (2000, 2001, etc.).

Where CC is the century and YY the year, the code might look like:

```
CC = 19                          //default
YY = input data
if YY < 50 then CC = 20
```

In addition, logical operations based on the contents of another field in the database can be used to determine the century. Here are two examples:

If the code returns a current age (based on *current year* minus *birth year*) of 09, this could mean the client is either 9 or 109 years old. If the life-insurance premium the client has been paying lately is relatively high, then one can logically assume that the age is 109.

The calculation of the *maturity century* of a ten-year term investment plan can be determined by looking at the start date. If the start date is "94," the "04" maturation century date must actually be 2004. If the plan commenced in "85," the maturation century date "95" must be 1995.

In Chapter 12, *Pseudo-Date Functions*, this concept is demonstrated using the WindowCentury function. Chapters 13 (*Date Functions*) and 14 (*PL/1 Date Functions*), which cover COBOL and PL/1 date functions, respectively, explore variations on the logical operations theme.

Considerations for Comparison

As explained above, the windowing or logic approach seems so simple. Why would anyone want to take the much more difficult and time-consuming route of changing both the actual date data and the applications, when simple code tricks could suffice?

As you probably deduced from the examples provided above, the real world just doesn't allow for simple, one-size-fits-all solutions. There are some excellent arguments for using the date-field expansion approach:

- There is usually more programming associated with the two-digit approach than with a four-digit year. You'll have to convert formats before doing simple comparisons or calculations.

- When storage is expanded, code should still be checked to ensure that the whole four-digit year is being processed, not just the YY part. Data structures and definitions must also be scanned, and sometimes modified, to store the extra two bytes within the code.

- Windowing processes continue to work even when deriving realistically incorrect output. With a four-digit system, invalid input data will trigger instantaneous notification.

- Routines for sorting and validating two-digit years will require additional modification to handle *windowed* derivations. Since extra code must be added to nearly every program to handle dates, the project size doesn't diminish—it may even increase.

- Data input and output to third parties may not match their data definitions, standards, formats, or conversion timing when two-digit dates and windowing are used.

Technical
Considerations

- Some date ranges, such as those found in scientific data, span more than 100 years. A windowing approach would be impractical in these cases.

- The logic approach usually adds processing cycles (MIPS) and reduces throughput. Sometimes windowing-driven performance requirements minimize the resources saved by avoiding bridges and conversion.

- A logical date-derivation operation (window) developed for one date may not fit each type of date that the program handles, resulting in poor maintainability and proliferation of *base* dates.

- Fixed windows can leave logical time-bombs in programs that are used beyond their life expectancy (a common scenario).

- Expanding all stored dates to four-digit years and correcting the code to match is certainly the cleanest solution, and it's easiest to understand and manage.

- Zoned or packed-decimal dates in the YYYYDDD format take up the same amount of physical space as the YYMMDD format stored as numeric data.

- Four-digit dates must still be carefully reviewed to ensure data integrity. Sometimes the century digits are not initialized; they could contain anything.

- For seldom-used archived data containing two-digit years, conversion programs will need to be written to ensure compliance with new programs.

- Expanding the date fields uses more storage, and some database designs are not conducive to expansion. For example, you'll have problems if the date is also an index or key, or if expansion would overwrite adjacent data.

- When expanding files and databases, automatic population routines based on windowing have to be written and run to fill the additional two bytes with valid data.

Date Storage and Packing Options

PC applications tend to use (and store) dates as displayed and formatted by the operating system, unless told to do otherwise. All tables, spreadsheets, and other documents created with these applications must be checked for manual and automatic input. In addition, all files in storage should be reviewed, especially if date-storage types are not type *date*.

Mainframe storage and packing options can be more complex. The data types mentioned below are explained in detail in Chapter 10, *COBOL Reference*.

The COBOL *Packed Decimal* or COMP-3 data types use one byte of storage for every two digits in the PICTURE clause. The right-most byte contains only one digit and the sign. The number +456 is represented in hexadecimal notation as "456F."

A six-digit date in packed decimal format can be stored in four bytes: four bits for each digit, four bits for the sign, and four unused bits. If this date is expanded to the ordinal date CCYYDDD, no additional storage is needed when four bits are used for each of the seven digits and the sign in the remainder.

Although this method saves storage space, the date might still need to be converted to a six- or eight-digit date format, depending on application requirements. Data-expansion benefits could outweigh date-transformation benefits in cases where performance is critical.

Numeric fields on databases, such as the DB2, are usually in COMP-3 or COMP-4 COBOL format. Most DBMSs provide DATE types that store the century portion of dates. Check to determine exactly how your DBMS stores dates, and whether they are Year-2000 compliant.

- Date compression—in older systems where storage was a major consideration or where the Year 2000 was over the horizon, other date-storage techniques are often found. Sometimes these compaction methods were used for obscure reasons, which need to be explored thoroughly before conversion. The year value was stored as the year subtracted from 2000 (for example, 1995 is stored as 5, and 2005 is stored as –5).

- The year value is stored using the *9's-complement* method, in which the value stored is the difference of the year subtracted from 99.

- A one-digit code was used for century where "0" = 1800, "1" = 1900, and "2" = 2000 (087 would be 1887, 198 would be 1998, and so on).

Sometimes it is possible to store the century without physically changing or expanding data storage. Table 5-1 gives a few examples.

Table 5-1: Retaining Data Storage

Field Description	Format	Field Length
YYYYMMDD	PACKED UNSIGNED2	4
YYYYDDDS	PACKED SIGNED	4
0YYYYMMDDS	PACKED SIGNED	5
YYYYDDD	CHARACTER	7
YYYYMMDD	CHARACTER	8

Some organizations choose to minimize the impact on data-entry procedures, report and screen formats, and century-loading procedures by retaining old storage formats and extending the year fields as shown in Table 5-2.

Table 5-2: Using Old Storage Formats

Field Description	Format	Field Length
MMDDYYYY	PACKED UNSIGNED2	4
0MMDDYYYYS	PACKED SIGNED	5
MMDDYYYY	CHARACTER	8

Technical Considerations

Dealing With Single-Digit Century Dates

In rare situations, space considerations and computational time requirements prohibit or prohibited full-century storage on older mainframe systems. Some common storage formats for single-digit century are:

Table 5-3: Common Storage Formats

Field Description	Format	Field Size (bytes)
CYYDDD	CHAR	6
CYYMMDD	BINARY	2
CYYMMDDS	PACKED (SIGNED)	4
CYY/MM/DD	CHAR	9
MMDDCYYS	PACKED (SIGNED)	4
MM/DD/CYY	CHAR	9

The use of the single-digit century dates does not often reduce update work, since logic windows must be added to interpret the data and then pour the full century information into output and display fields.

Bridging

Bridging is the term used for programs and modules that provide temporary interfaces between data and applications that have been converted to Year-2000 compliance, and those that have not.

Programmers can build a whole set of bridges to patch together converted and unconverted systems, then dismantle them as soon as both sides of the bridge are converted. As the clock ticks and pressure grows, there is a tendency to leave some bridges in place, treating them as an ad-hoc windowing solution. However, if the windowing is hard-wired this approach can leave time-bombs in the system. If data and structures are re-defined in the bridge, it also confuses the DDL- and copybook-maintenance process.

One bridging technique that's gaining popularity is the temporary use of additional fields in tables: one for the original date, and one for the converted (expanded) one. This involves expanding the database and changing copy-books, but it significantly reduces bridging requirements. The old code continues to run without bridging until the conversion is complete, including batch data updates. At that time both extra storage and redundant programs can be unplugged.

Before this method can be used, storage-requirement analysis must show sufficient space and sequencing of both development and testing storage. Since most systems have up to 10 percent date content, an additional 5 to 10 percent storage capacity is required to use this type of bridge. A more accurate assessment can be obtained from the detailed inventory.

File and Database Date Conversion

Changing dates in files and databases is usually a straightforward process, once the decision to use the data approach has been made. Programmers can often rely on products that automatically expand files and databases. This activity usually requires an online data dictionary and repository. If dates are keys (indexes) or system-assigned, some systems will disallow attempts at field conversion. In these cases the database itself will have to be redesigned.

Date expansion in files and databases involves the same approach as expansion of other fields, such as fields for Branch Number, Account Number, or Address. However, expanding fields via program-logic is obviously more difficult, since sub-strings of dates are commonly used, and dates may be embedded in compound fields. Both code and data will need thorough testing to ensure that all dates have been properly converted without reducing functionality.

Storage limitations are a major concern when using the data-expansion method. Changing code itself adds minimal storage demands. However, databases may have to be duplicated, at least temporarily, to facilitate access by both converted and unconverted programs. Duplication may also be required when testing auto-population algorithms and bridging modules. Duplicated files could easily fill available storage and force a change in conversion plans. If you only need space for a short while, temporary storage can be obtained from service bureaus or Internet Service Providers (ISPs).

CHAPTER 6

PCs and the Front End

At many corporations and smaller sites, Year-2000 issues involving PCs and frontend applications have been overlooked. Now this part of the inventory is getting the attention it deserves. This chapter is dedicated to helping you identify Year-2000 frontend and PC problems at your site, and to helping you fix them.

There are three main areas of concern:

- User-developed or externally written applications

- Operating systems and desktop applications

- BIOS and other hardware

Ideally, these system components should be inventoried at the same time to minimize disruption of operations, and to make the magnitude of upgrade ripple more visible.

Although many of these applications and products will not be problematic or can be made Year-2000 compliant with relative ease, incorrect or inadequate usage plays a far more influential role than originally thought. Processing, capturing, or importing two-digit centuries can cause systems to malfunction when ambiguity between centuries arises, even if the underlying application is perfectly robust— and we all know that's not always the case.

How big is the frontend Year-2000 problem?

In the course of carrying out their Year-2000 inventory duties, intrepid investigators have suddenly started uncovering all sorts of spreadsheets, desktop databases, and programs that are critical to the organization, yet not documented or listed anywhere. These discoveries are coming at a late date in the Year-2000 project, and it may be hard to fix these problems in time at some sites. In addition, it can be difficult to determine whether the problem (and the responsibility) lies with the package itself, or with the design of the individual spreadsheet or database.

At a recent meeting on this very subject, a giant Canadian firm disclosed the discovery of a non-compliant, PC-based database program within its computer system. As the company's staff soon found out, this was not a minor application; instead, this was the very software that controlled the packing, consignment, and routing of millions of dollars worth of materials and finished products daily. The firm estimated that if it hadn't discovered and converted the database, which used ambiguous six-digit date fields, its whole regional distribution and shipping process would have collapsed. The ensuing $40,000-a-day crisis would have taken weeks, if not months, to unravel.

The company then conducted a scan of over four thousand PCs via a network-based maintenance system, in search of files ending with *.mdb*. Indeed, more than 2,200 machines had Microsoft Access installed, and on those machines they found 11,379 files fitting the description. When they excluded the sample databases supplied with the application, they still had almost 5,000 user-created databases. Even if only 10 percent of these played a useful role in the organization, there were still around 500 databases that should be looked at closely, despondent IT staffers learned.

These databases were spread across Mexico, the United States, and Canada, often in remote sites where the engineers and workers were a law unto themselves when it came to hardware and software acquisition and development. Telling them to hold everything and fix some obscure problem right now was a tough call. The whole process had to be handled carefully.

Deciding how to ensure the Year-2000 safety of thousands of spreadsheets, databases, and applications written in a host of three GLs, such as VB, C++, and Pascal (not to mention the specialized little monsters created with Prolog, Lisp, and Fortran), is a daunting task.

Before you can even start to fix these problems, you must convince someone with a budget that they do exist, and that they're important to the company.

Finding Frontend Problems

A Year-2000 project manager must first create a sense of awareness among decision-makers, without generating panic or unnecessary expenditures. You could call this engendering a state of *positive alarm*. Once this objective is achieved, requests for finances and conversion resources should follow.

To ascertain the extent of the problem at your site, complete the following steps:

1. Undertake an inventory of the following:

    – Types, makes, models, and BIOS versions of all hardware that has embedded software, including telephonic, access control, and environmental control software and devices

    – Desktop packages and operating systems, including network software, running on these machines

    – User-developed or externally-sourced applications and files

2. Scrutinize databases, spreadsheets, and other user-generated files, checking last-edited dates and names. Attempt to associate them with business processes.

3. Determine the state of Year-2000 compliance in hardware and packaged applications.

4. Scan the databases, spreadsheets, and user-generated source code to determine the degree of compliance. Effective tools for rapid scanning and reporting are available. These can automate or supplement the business-process method of ascertaining business value of systems.

5. Summarize the problems found. Prioritize them by level of severity, and illustrate (with user assistance) the impact of non-compliance.

6. Present this list to managers, auditors, and financial staff. This information will support the need for a full, unfettered conversion process, and help staff to asses the priority of the project and its components.

In large organizations, the frontend compliance process can be broken into two stages: a pilot project, followed by a full compliance effort. Often managers need to be carefully convinced before they will allocate sufficient resources. It is an unfortunate characteristic of the Year-2000 issue that the person responsible for conversion is almost always responsible for raising its importance, and for securing funding and resources. If that person has insufficient resources to make a case for the problem's magnitude, he or she is faced with a classic *chicken or egg situation.*

Inventory

Determine types, makes, models, and BIOS versions of all hardware that has embedded software, including telephonic, access control, and environmental control software and devices.

In smaller installations, it is sometimes easier to ascertain compliance while taking stock of inventory in general. If this is so, test all machines for compliance rather than cataloging varieties and versions of hardware and then conducting random tests across the range.

Other types of hardware (PBX systems, elevators, security, etc.) and related software will still need to be certified as Year-2000 compliant.

Finding the make and model of a machine is easy, but getting the BIOS version can sometimes be a problem. The BIOS program runs before the operating system loads, so it is possible to read these details off the screen as the machine is cold-booting. Small text messages like "AWARD ver. 2.3e" or "AMI 1.8 ver 4.7" will flash on the screen before the operating system loads.

You can also open the box to get the BIOS details. Look for one or two large integrated circuits, on which you should find labels featuring the word *BIOS* or a BIOS vendor's name. Often the version and release details will be on these labels. Be sure you are not voiding any warranty conditions when opening the box, and don't even attempt it if you aren't familiar with the inside of the PC.

Locate desktop packages and operating systems, including network software, running on these machines

Derive a list of products and version numbers by examining the files on each machine. This list should include the operating system version. All user-acquired products must also be detected and evaluated.

Most large companies have an approved list of desktop software, so it should be relatively easy to locate these suppliers and determine how compliant their products are. Most vendors can also help you figure out what to do with packages that aren't compliant.

Identify user-developed or externally-sourced applications and files

These packages fall into various categories, including:

- Software developed by a central IT department as part of a client-server system or network—hopefully, these applications of recent vintage will comply with design and testing standards

- Specialized software developed by a central IT department for individual use

- Files or programs developed by end-users or associates for localized use

- Custom programs written by third parties for any of the above categories

A list of these packages must be compiled, and each item should be prioritized according to both impact (fatal/critical/important/other) and scope (corporate/department/individual/other). A *fatal* rating applies to those applications whose failure could be life-threatening, such as building-maintenance or security. *Critical* programs are those whose failure would immediately disrupt major processes.

When scoring these applications for conversion-sequencing, triage, or backup, attach numerical *weights* to the matrix. Multiplying the Impact and Scope columns (Total) indicates priority. Table 6-1 illustrates this concept.

Table 6-1: Impact and Scope

Program	Impact	Scope	Total
Carol's birthday list	0	0	0
Shipping and routing	3	3	9
Test database	0	0	0
Insurance frontend	3	3	9
Elevator maintenance system	5	3	15
Jim's team's time-sheet spreadsheet	1	1	1

Associate Files with Business Processes

Scrutinize the database, spreadsheet, and other user-generated files, checking last-edited dates and names. Attempt to associate them with business processes.

There are literally thousands of programs designed to run on PCs, so it's very important to determine which files belong to which application. A full list of file extensions, the suffixes appended to file names by various programs, can be very helpful. For example, typical spreadsheet and database files end with suffixes like *.wks*, *.wk5*, *.xls*, or *.mdb*. Table 6-2 lists some common file extensions; your user documentation should have product-specific lists. Be sure to check for program and project files as well as for databases.

Table 6-2: Products and File Extension

Product	File-Extension
Access	.mda, .mde, .mdw, .mdb
Dbase 1.4	.dbf
Excel	.xlt, .xlw, .xls
Foxpro	.dbf, .dbc, .pjx, .prg, .spr, .dbc
Lotus 123	.wk1, .wk2, .wk3, .wk4, .wk5, .wks
Paradox	.db
Quattro Pro	.wq1
Symphony	.wrk

You can save time by deleting the sample applications and files that come with almost every package from your list—or from the machines themselves. This is a good job to give end-users. These files are not important to the business, will cloud scanner findings, and should be excluded from the analysis process as early as possible.

Organization is important at this stage, because you will be working with huge lists of files. You could track everything with a database of every file found in the index. You could then associate each indexed file with its application or with a redundant indicator to ensure that nothing slips through.

Once inventories are complete, the assessment stage begins. At this time, degrees of compliance are ascertained and added to the database.

Determine the State of Year-2000 Compliance in Hardware and Packaged Applications

Most personal computers use two date systems:

- The BIOS clock, which is found on the motherboard and maintained by a small battery

- The operating system clock, which is held in RAM and lost when the machine is switched off

The BIOS date can be updated during a cold start, during which you can access CMOS settings (this is the hardware memory area where drive types and system configurations are stored). You can also update the BIOS by changing OS dates, which usually updates the CMOS at the same time. The firmware programs used for maintaining the CMOS are on a BIOS chip or chips on the motherboard.

WARNING

Don't fiddle with the CMOS unless you are suitably qualified and all the settings are backed up.

The OS date is volatile, and is stored in RAM. It's usually a copy of the CMOS date that's set when the OS loads. This date can be changed from within the OS, but occasionally this change is not written back to the CMOS and is subsequently lost when the machine is turned off. This is rare in newer systems.

The CMOS date-format sometimes differs from that of the OS date. Often it's based on the number of days elapsed since 1980, or some other arbitrary date related to the BIOS program.

One must experiment to detect and accommodate differences in how different dates are stored and calculated.

If a PC date is set when the PC logs onto a network, the network machine must be tested first. In these cases, the network OS automatically updates the local OS. The PC can be set to local operation for individual testing.

General tests of PC dates should follow the sequence listed below. Using specially designed utilities from reputable vendors can minimize the risk, and will also help you illustrate results.

There is always a possibility of a system crash. Everything must be backed up—including CMOS settings, which should be written in the service documentation for the machine. A workable fallback plan must be written before changes commence.

Mail and Scheduling applications could easily auto-delete old transactions, so these should be shut down prior to testing. Version control related to last edit date is another potential problem area.

Certain BIOS will not permit re-booting with dates larger than 2000, so the system will have to be initialized and completely reset. Usually this is done by bridging the relevant motherboard jumpers. Make sure you have recorded all settings and read the motherboard (BIOS) documentation before embarking on the tests below.

Test A:
Set the date and time of the OS close to midnight on the big day (31/12/1999 23:58) and ensure that it rolls over by watching the clock display, or by requesting date and time if they are not automatically displayed.

Test B:
Determine if the CMOS date was updated when the OS date was changed. To do so, cold-boot the machine, re-load the OS, and check the OS date. If the

PCs and the Front End

date is incorrect, either the CMOS didn't accept or store the new date, or the OS couldn't read or display the CMOS date it found.

Test C:

Cold-boot the machine, then stop the boot process before the OS loads by hitting the CMOS Setup key. Usually there is a screen prompt to push ESC or F1 to Setup. Then set (or attempt to set) the CMOS year to "2000." After saving your changes, exit the CMOS, let the system complete the load, and check to see if the OS year is correct.

Test D:

(Software) While the machine is running, change the OS year to 2000 and investigate the effect this date has on all applications used. Be sure to check editors and file date-stamping. A table of applications like Table 6-3 should be used to document your findings.

Table 6-3: Item/Input/Output

Item	Input Year-2000 Date	Output Year-2000 Date
Spreadsheet	Accepts and stores all eight digits	Derived/displayed correct date
Accounting program	Accepted valid transaction date	Report prints valid transactions for the specified query period
CAD program	Accepts eight-digit update date	File stored with correct edit date
Shipping database	Assigns shipment date	Is shipment documentation printed correctly, on the right date?
File manager	N/A	File stored with correct date

Chapter 8, *Inventory Database Schema*, provides some blank forms that can be customized as needed.

In large companies where computer literacy varies considerably between users, the need for automated processes and utilities is increased. Just explaining how to follow and interpret the results of the steps above to five thousand users would take more time away from doing the actual work than you can afford.

In a limited evaluation of a representative suite of products from Calgary, Canada-based EraSoft* disclosed that these Year-2000 automation tools, at least, performed well and located all the problems they were designed to find. (This is not to say that a double-check isn't important.) There are many more Year-2000 tools available, for example, Check 2000 (see GMT—*http://www.gmt-2000.com/gmt-2000/bombsquad/bombsquad_pc.html*).

The EraSoft tools tested include:

* EraTest PC, which finds hardware/BIOS problems

---

* At the time of going to press, EraSoft was about to be acquired by ViaSoft, of Phoenix, Arizona. Product names, functionality, and components could change, so use the relevant chapters purely as examples of the process and considerations.

- EraScan PC, which finds potential problems in most desktop databases, spreadsheets, and source files

Products like these can help you work faster and more efficiently. For example, when EraScan examines a spreadsheet, it color-codes and highlights affected fields to help you prioritize potential problems. For volume-scanning, a program like this beats manual attempts hands down.

A third EraSoft utility, EraFix PC, is intended to solve the problems found by EraTest. This product was not evaluated. As this book went to press, EraSoft was generating updates and enhancements to its existing products, and adding new tools. This is the case for all Year-2000 utilities vendors.

You can find contact information for EraSoft and many more companies, as well as information about specific tools, in Appendix A.

In addition to products available from commercial vendors, you can find many Year-2000 related shareware programs on sites like *http://www.year2000.com*. The effectiveness of these tools will need to be determined by the user.

When you test the system manually, as in Tests A through D earlier in the chapter, there are some inherent dangers. These include:

1. Even if the user boots from a normal DOS boot disk and works on hard drives, invalid dates may appear in the file system, because DOS can still access the hard drives.

2. Some software licenses are associated with date-sensitive configuration or *.ini* files, and may expire when the license program checks these files. Re-activation of the license may require correspondence with the vendor or even fees.

3. Date-related software, such as calendars and scheduling applications, may permanently delete or archive current data.

4. There will always be strange BIOS and peculiar systems that do not conform to conventional testing and configuration—be on the lookout for these.

5. When the OS date on some older OS versions is set to 2000, newly created files are century-stamped to "00" or "19." This has a major impact on version-control algorithms and manual procedures that look for the latest date. Sorted directories can get scrambled, and programs won't know which file is current. This is especially true in cases where automatic backups or temporary files are used. Email software and other network applications can also *lose* data that is set to automatically archive or delete old files.

Packages, Files, and Other Programs

It's relatively easy to determine where potential problems lie in most off-the-shelf packages—all you need to do is scan Year-2000 and vendor web sites, and read related documentation distributed by major vendors. On the Internet, you can find literally thousands of articles that detail problems experienced with specific products.

A few of Microsoft's products have Year-2000 related bugs, most of which are documented in the Microsoft Technical Support Knowledge Base. This support database is available on CD-ROM as well as on the Microsoft Web site (*http://www.microsoft.com/kb/*). In addition to bug information, the Knowledge Base also contains advice related to Year-2000 issues in general. For example, it offers Visual Basic and Visual FoxPro articles that provide Year-2000 advice and tips for software developers.

Microsoft also has an excellent Year-2000 site on *http://www.microsoft.com/year2000/*.

Table 6-4 is a list of Microsoft Knowledge Base keys that can be used as the search criteria in the Microsoft Online Help system, speeding up your query. Their presence does not imply problems with the applications listed; often the articles are purely informative in nature. In the case of date-input and storage, it's important to understand the century-defaulting and cusp-ranges applicable to each version of a program.

Table 6-4: Products with Year-2000 Related Articles (Source: Microsoft Year-2000 Web Pages)

Product Name	Knowledge Base Article(s)
Exchange Server 4.0	Q152874, Q153655, Q152858, Q158263, Q158699
MS Access, all versions	Q162745, Q155669, Q132067, Q92816, Q161345
MS Excel, all versions	Q106339, Q118923, Q164406, Q73673
Exchange Server 4.0	Q152874, Q153655, Q152858, Q158263, Q158699
MS Project 4.0	Q161089, Q125305, Q160677
MS Works 1.x and 2.0	Q50679, Q100822
Visual Basic	Q162718
Visual C++ 1.5–4.2	Q110719
Visual FoxPro	Q162388, Q156009, Q169471, Q148873
Windows 3.x	Q85557
Windows for Workgroups	Q85557
Windows 95	Q85557
Windows NT–J 3.51	Q163915
Word 5.0 (for MS-DOS)	Q68181
Word 6.0	Q171286

Knowledge Base is continuously updated and should be checked regularly. You can learn a great deal about various issues in this database. For example, Knowledge Base article #Q85557 documents a problem in a particular version of Windows 95, in which the File Manager displays an incorrect date for files created with a date of 01-01-2000 or later, and points you toward a software patch that will fix it.

This is just one of many PC-based Year-2000 glitches. Fortunately, the ones affecting Microsoft are well documented. For example, when you search for a document in Microsoft Word 6.x using the "Find File" feature, the search will fail if you search for dates later than 12/31/1999.

This is because Word 6.x only uses the last two digits of the year when using the "Find File" feature: when you enter a year of 2006, Microsoft Word 6.x assumes the year is 1906, not 2006.

> This is a limitation of the "Find File" feature only. Internally, Word 6.x uses a four-digit representation of the year. Note also that in the "File Searching" feature for Microsoft Word 7.x and 97, all four digits of the year are used.

To work around this problem, use the search feature from the operating system itself and follow the steps below:

Windows 95 and Windows NT 4.0

1. On the Windows task bar, click Start, point to Find, and click Files Or Folders.

2. Click the Date Modified tab.

3. Enter a search date in a format similar to 1/1/2006.

Macintosh

Use the Find File that is part of the Macintosh Operating System.

Another common Year-2000 problem that is likely to crop up in PC installations involves Microsoft Access. Unless you explicitly enter the year in a date field as 2000 or later, Access will save the year portion as 1900 to 1999 as appropriate. In other words, if you type in a date 01/01/00, it will save the year portion of the Date/Time data type internally as 1900. If you enter the date as 01/01/2000, Microsoft Access saves the year portion internally as 2000. However, the date still appears in the date field as 01/01/00 if displayed using the Short Date format.

This automatic allocation of century-digits to dates based on the year-relationship to a cusp date or range is common in PC applications. Unfortunately, the year range varies from product to product and from version to version, and you will need to experiment with your own products. Microsoft recommends that all legacy data sources that interface with Access be updated to contain four-digit years.

Various versions of Microsoft Excel share this interpretation problem with Access.

The 32-bit Windows operating systems, Windows 95 and Windows NT, contain a software library with functions that can convert dates with two-digit years into four-digit years. You can use the OLE Automation Library (filename OLEAUT32. DLL) to do standard date conversions, which can then easily be modified by updating the library in question. The rules used by the OLE Automation Library and other similar Microsoft products for date conversion are shown in Table 6-5.

> An earlier version of the OLE Automation Library in Windows 95 converted all two-digit years to the current century setting of the computer.

Most reputable system vendors will either provide specific date-conversion data, or refer callers to a web site that provides documentation. However, few vendors will accept responsibility for old programs that they no longer support—instead, they

Table 6-5: Product Name/20th Century

Product Name	20th Century
OLE Automation Library 2.10 and earlier (Windows NT 3.51 prior to service pack 4)	1/1/00 - 12/31/99
OLE Automation Library v2.20 (Windows NT 3.51 service pack 4 and later, Windows NT 4, Windows 95)	1/1/30 – 12/31/99
Microsoft Access 95 and earlier	1/1/00 - 12/31/99
Microsoft Access 97	Uses OLE Automation Library
Microsoft Excel 4.0, 5.0, and 7.0	1/1/20 – 12/31/99
Microsoft Excel 97	1/1/30 – 12/31/99
Microsoft Works for Windows, versions 2.0x, 3.0, 3.0a, and 3.0b	1/1/00 - 12/31/99
Visual Basic 3.0 and earlier (VBRUN300.DLL)	Uses current century
Visual Basic 4.0 (16-bit) (DateSerial date function uses VBRUN400.DLL; all other functions use OLE Automation Libraries)	Uses current century
Visual Basic 4.0 (32-bit) (DateSerial function uses VBRUN400.DLL)	Uses current century
Visual Basic 4.0 and later (32-bit) except DateSerial function	Uses OLE Automation Library
Visual FoxPro versions prior to 5.0	1/1/00 - 12/31/99
Visual FoxPro 5.0 and later	Determined by the "SET CENTURY TO ... ROLLOVER ..."
MS-DOS DATE command	1/1/80 – 12/31/99

may suggest an upgrade or an alternate way to use the package that gets around the Year-2000 issue.

Upgrading tends to start a cascading effect, precipitating hardware upgrades. When this happens, all the user-generated databases and spreadsheets will have to be tested again for compliance with Year-2000 guidelines.

The secret to ensuring enterprise-wide compliance is completing a detailed and accurate inventory. When the metrics are known and the suppliers identified, the process of distribution can be automated.

Scan the Databases, Spreadsheets, and User-Generated Source Code to Determine the Degree of Compliance

Once a thorough investigation of user-generated applications gets underway, all sorts of funny stuff starts crawling out of the woodwork. Formulae that generate ambiguous dates, input date-data that is truncated for processing and storage, and date-fields containing text data are just a few of the brilliant ideas you may discover in these programs. All of these mistakes can cause confusion and, ultimately, problems.

If spreadsheet macros and programs are difficult to follow, you may need help from the original author. RAD systems, such as VB, and many other desktop applications use file dates to determine whether to save files. Consequently, it's vital to address such problems effectively.

All occurrences of, and references to, two-digit dates must be located, and then these dates' ranges of influence must be scrutinized. The way programs handle *date* and *text* dates varies, so the field type is important to the scanner.

Spreadsheet data activities are often more complex than databases, and are inherently much less organized. You may find fields, formulas, and derivations scattered all over the place. Many spreadsheets contain calculations that can be affected by the Year-2000 problem.

It is possible for a working spreadsheet to implode when the software is upgraded. System vendors have attempted to resolve the Year-2000 problem by windowing, generally relying on cusp dates. The limits of window ranges differ from version to version, and from vendor to vendor.

Again, commercial scanning tools can help. There are also deployment utilities and mass-configuration/automation tools available. These will be essential at large sites.

Other files

In addition to checking over all standard software and development platforms, it's important to inspect date-input field-handling in add-ons written by third parties (for example, ActiveX controls, VBXes, OCXes, and other DLLs, etc.). Depending on how frequently user-developed programs utilize these additional components, this can be a most time-consuming and error-prone step. Many developers embed neat little calendars, spreadsheets, and text boxes in their screens, just to make your job more miserable.

Tools

Chapters 18 (Code Scanner Design and Theory) and 19 (Visual Basic Code Scanner Prototype) present the building blocks for a rudimentary source scanner, which can be enhanced for your purposes. As noted earlier, there are also many very effective commercial offerings available.

The minimum requirements for a source-code scanner are:

- Ability to select groups of files for scanning

- Ability to generate date-related reports on instances and occurrences

- Ability to customize the library of search strings (for example, "date," "1997," "dte," etc.)

- Ability to report line numbers, position, and function/procedures for each occurrence

- Ability to process all common languages

Summarize the Problems Found. Prioritize Them by Level of Severity, and Illustrate (with User Assistance) the Impact of Non-Compliance

A report clearly listing all of the following should be presented to senior management:

- Affected applications

- Range or scope of usage

- Impact and severity levels illustrating (with user confirmation) the effect of non-compliance

- Conversion budgets and potential losses

- Priorities

- Staffing, testing, and other resource requirements

- Time scales

Alternatives to upgrading or changing hardware, rewriting software, and other expensive fixes should be explored prior to presenting this report.

To get user input on how the failure of specific applications would impact the company, use a questionnaire or personal interviews. Keep careful records, and account for differing views. See Chapter 8 for a sample questionnaire that you can customize.

Present This List to Managers, Auditors, and Financial Staff

Senior managers, auditors, and financial staff must all be aware of the problems if you want them to give the project high priority. Pay careful attention to how you present your report. It's easy to ignore print-outs and email, so distribute printed information in person.

It's best to do so at a formal, *high-level briefing* sort of meeting with all the important players present, rather than holding several small, informal sessions. Provide the most important points up front: why the problem is here, how big it is, how long it will take to fix, and how much you estimate it will cost. Once that's out of the way, you can break down the specifics.

For managers without much IT knowledge, avoid jargon. Put the problem in money-and-time terms that they will understand, and use specific examples of how the Year-2000 issues in your system could bring the organization to a standstill if not addressed.

Keep your presentation brief and coherent. Rehearse it in advance, and use slides, overheads, or other visual aids as possible. If public speaking is just never going to be your forte, consider having another employee who has the communication skills needed to do the basic presentation, followed by you fielding specific questions—with prepared answers to likely queries in hand.

Wait until the end of your presentation to take questions. What you want is for your audience to fully accept the concept of a Year-2000 problem at your site that must be fixed, and fast. Once that's established, you can diddle with the details of how much money and staff they're going to give you, and explain how and why specific systems are affected.

The initial reaction to your presentation may be mild disbelief, coupled with requests for more information or even for second opinions. You'll just have to weather these short-lived hurdles, and focus on funding, staffing, and timing problems while they slowly work their heads out of the sand.

Fixing Frontend Problems

Before you can fix your frontend and PC problems, you must prepare project plans and locate resources. To maintain momentum, these two activities can begin before funding is approved... if you dare.

If frontend systems that interface with mainframes need to be fixed, back-end staff must to be consulted on issues like date-field changes to communications layouts, datagrams, and windowing. Sometimes the windowing should be done on the server—for example, in cases where a small change would require rolling out a new version of client software for all end-users.

Because frontend development and deployment often proceeds faster than back-end changes, there may be a need for short-term bridging arrangements. You'll definitely want to hold regular discussions on timing and migration.

Hardware

If hardware is not Year-2000 compliant, explore issues like long-term strategies and 16-to-32-bit conversion when choosing your strategies. Sometimes the hardware is okay, but application upgrades will need more RAM or disk space. You'll need input from various departments, not to mention an element of clairvoyance on the topic of future PC technology, when deciding whether to upgrade or replace hardware as a result.

A number of shareware and budget-priced products, such as EraFix PC, claim to patch or bridge the problems of non-compliant hardware. These options need to be investigated.

Software

If spreadsheet or database applications have intrinsic design limitations, you can choose to either work around problems via windowing, or upgrade to a later version. As noted earlier, a version upgrade usually triggers an upgrade ripple, as associated programs must be adjusted, with a new operating system and additional hardware requirements in hot pursuit.

Unfortunately, PC hardware and software are not assets—they're consumables with very short life-spans. At the end of complex Year-2000 project deliberations, you will often find it's better to bite the bullet and get on with it.

If you need help from the original developers of user-generated code and files, part of your planning process will be identifying and locating these individuals.

Try to find all design plans and notes, as well as developer contact data, and keep this information with your scanning-utility reports.

Visual FoxPro

Sometimes it doesn't cost an arm and a leg to make a database program compliant. Recently, I was asked to give a second opinion on a quote for making a Visual FoxPro system Year-2000 ready. This system had about 40 screens and 20 tables, with about 110 date-occurrences in the screens alone.

The quotation was for 25 days at $400 a day, or $10,000 total; plus an open-ended cost for the testing and migration phase. On the surface, this seemed like a realistic figure for the number of date occurrences and the size of the job.

But then I used the code-scanner from Chapter 19 to take a quick look at the code in the program files (.prg). I also looked at the screens and tables, and found the initial date-occurrence count to be accurate. The code contained standard date-function usage, and didn't require conversion as long as valid (full) dates were used. Without spending too much more time on the freebie, I was about to concur with the quote when, out of interest, I perused the Help file for date-handling functionality.

I found a configuration switch—SET CENTURY ON/OFF/TO (see the Visual Foxpro entry in Table 6-3, earlier), which toggles date-displays between six and eight digits. In other words, assuming that eight-digit dates are available, they could be displayed in their full form by setting this single line of code. The system in question had by default stored the full dates in eight-byte format, but was only displaying six-byte dates without the century.

In addition to this simple programmatic omission, Visual FoxPro 3.0 (and probably other versions of this program as well) uses an argument to the SET CENTURY switch called ROLLOVER. This can set the century to which the program defaults when only six digits are captured.

The usage syntax for this setting is:

```
SET CENTURY ON | OFF | TO [nCentury [ROLLOVER nYear]]
```

The default ROLLOVER year is zero, which means that all years greater than zero are assigned to the current century as derived from the system.

To facilitate the correct display and storage of centuries by way of this setting, add:

```
SET CENTURY ON
SET CENTURY TO 19 ROLLOVER 25 .
```

to the startup program or configuration. I was unable to determine from the documentation whether both statements are required, or whether the latter would trigger the former. My interpretation of the usage syntax implies that "SET CENTURY ON ROLLOVER 25" is not valid, although this is hardly a concern.

Configuring a program this way will ensure that all dates entered with a year of less than 25 will have a century of "20," and that those above 25 will get the prefix "19." Any dates captured with only six digits would acquire a default century of

"19." Assuming sufficient screen space, the program will now display full eight-digit dates, removing any further confusion.

Where screen display space is only big enough for six characters, someone would need to spend a day or two stretching the text boxes—a relatively low-tech activity.

Although I had only spent a few hours vetting the quote, I now felt it was possibly excessive. I suggested that the company that provided the initial quote investigate this apparently simple solution, and perhaps cut its fee in half.

WARNING

If twenty-first century dates were captured and stored with the default ROLL-OVER setting, they would have been assigned a "19," and would require conversion. You would have to investigate the impact of "SELECTing" all these rows into temporary tables, then rewriting them with the valid century. The process would still be relatively simple, providing that business rules weren't impacted and data integrity remained intact.

Fortunately, no twenty-first century dates were in this system.

The PC compliance process is only just starting in earnest, and should peak in 1999. By then many more tools and solutions will be around. However, waiting for these will only reduce the time you have to fix the problem—nothing can be gained by not starting immediately.

PART II

Templates and Worksheets

CHAPTER 7

Triage

At this late date, the unpopular concept of triage—choosing the most important systems for Year-2000 conversion and putting the rest on the back burner for now—has to be taken seriously.

Triage also applies to deciding which outside suppliers and customers must be treated first. Even if there are no systemic links between them and us, if they have a system failure, can the absence of their systems hurt us? Alternatively, if our plans do not accommodate their conversion requirements, what will be their reaction?

Think of your company as a battlefield, and your Year-2000 conversion team as the medics. What systems and software are really worth saving, and which are already on their last legs? Is it more cost-effective to convert or replace specific products? Are there systems whose failure will have a greater impact than others?

Everyone in an organization will have a different view of a particular system's value. Their opinions will be based on all sorts of criteria, ranging from personal use, convenience, and job-protection, to automation and cash generation. No choice of what to keep and what to discard will be universally popular, but if everything cannot be converted in time, someone will have to make those choices.

That someone may well be you. This chapter provides guidelines that can help you make these difficult decisions.

Triage

WARNING

In addition to these guidelines, you will need strong internal support to use triage tactics successfully. Any Year-2000 project manager who does so without the full knowledge and backing of upper management runs a major legal or professional risk.

Triage Criteria

There are three primary factors to consider when prioritizing your Year-2000 activities:

- Value to business
- Cost of conversion
- Degree of difficulty

The first factor is relatively easy to quantify, but determining the cost of conversion and degree of difficulty can be complex. These two criteria are influenced by factors such as:

1. Staff requirements and availability
2. Staff costs
3. Cost to program and test hardware
4. Availability and cost of tools
5. Dependencies, and the cost of conversion or bridging to address them
6. Legal cost of not converting
7. Availability, status, and feasibility of contingencies

The following tables can be used to make costing and determining the degree of difficulty easier.

First, insert the appropriate costs in a copy of the first table below for each software system that must be converted. The left-hand vertical column is where each program or application should be listed. The horizontal column at the top corresponds to the six factors listed previously. Depending on your company's unique situation, you may need to include additional factors in this column to determine your total cost.

You should use the PCodes determined during the Inventory phase to identify each product, as well as the actual name of the application or system. Much of the information you need will also come from the Inventory database. Some items, such as the legal cost of not converting, will require investigation in concert with other individuals, including corporate accountants, legal counsel, and consultants, as appropriate.

Table 7-1: Conversion Costs

Software System	Staff	H/W	Tools	Dependencies	Legal	Total Cost
Payroll	$ 22,000	$ 15,5000	$ 9,000	$ 25,600	$ 500,000	$ 572,100
Vehicle Maintenance	$ 7,000	$ 0	$ 0	$ 0	$ 0	$ 7,000
Production	$ 45,000	$ 14,000	$ 6,500	$ 0	$1,000,000	$1,065,500
Inventory	$ 5,000	$ 3,000	$ 0	$ 0	$ 0	$ 8,000
Orders	$ 3,000	$ 500	$ 400	$ 5,500	$ 0	$ 9,400

Impact-ripple and the sequence of events associated with this conversion process are important factors. Code conversion costs are more difficult to determine than pure replacement costs. The "Function Points per Date Incident" section in Chapter 4, *Master Plan for Year-2000 Conversion Projects*, provides a simple method for making quick estimates, but the use of formal costing methodologies and tools will quantify large projects much more accurately.

Once conversion costs have been derived, however, managers will need to step back momentarily and compare them with the cost of replacing systems outright and determine which of these options is feasible. In many cases the latter option will cost less in the long-run, and in some cases it will simply cost less.

Part of triage is cutting your losses, and if replacing one system that will be particularly staff-intensive to convert frees up programmers for several other conversion projects, it's a smart move.

Dependency is usually the crucial factor in determining how difficult a system will be to convert or replace. The more products and systems it interacts with, the greater the impact of your choices will be. The triage worksheet on the following page helps illustrate how all of the products and systems in a business interrelate. To utilize the matrix, you start with an application such as Bonds and check all applicable hardware, programming languages, and external interfaces that are required to execute the application. Once complete, this will provide a birds-eye view that will aid managers in making system triage choices.

Once all data has been gathered and these charts are completed, they must be analyzed and applied to a graph similar to Figure 7-1, "Conversion costs vs. value to business." This graph plots the cost of conversion against the value to business, and illustrates the order in which systems should be converted. Value to business is very important, with considerations such as legalities, shareholder satisfaction, cash flow, production issues, and inter-dependencies all playing a part. Systems are represented on the graph by numbers, and average development costs can be added to provide an idea of relative costs and benefits.

Triage Management

When the relationship between costs and priorities is represented graphically, senior management can make faster decisions. That's essential for this type of fixed-date project.

Using the battlefield analogy again, senior managers must be the generals in this war. They will have to set the most basic priorities for triage, so you must ensure that they are working with accurate data.

The priorities set by top managers must be clearly communicated to project managers, who will have the responsibility for ensuring that their smaller choices meet these guidelines.

Finally, clear lines of communication must be set up and maintained. In medicine, triage systems break down if only the big picture gets a look—somewhere along the line, somebody has to make sure that the little stuff isn't evolving into a major catastrophe. Your front-line medics in the programming trenches may discover dependencies or special circumstances involving programs previously deemed

Completed by: _____

Date: _____

Applications

	Hardware										Programming Expertise								External I/Fs					
	Mainframe 1	Mainframe 2	Mainframe 3	Mini 1	Mini 2	Mini 3	PCs	Peripherals	WANs	LANS	COBOL	BASIC	RPG	ADABAS	C/C++	PASCAL	ASSEMBLER	PC Apps. (spreadsheets etc.)	EFT	EDI	General Bureaux (salary etc.)	Specialist Bureaux	Tapes	External Maintenance
Bonds	X							X			X	X	X			X					X	X		X	X
Insurance	X							X			X				X		X				X	X			X
Home-Loans		X						X			X	X	X		X		X					X		X	X
For. Exchange			X				X	X			X			X		X						X		
Investments				X				X			X	X	X	X		X	X					X		X	X
Leasing					X			X			X		X		X							X		X	X

Notes: _____

_____

_____

_____

_____

_____

_____

_____

_____

_____

_____

_____

_____

_____

_____

_____

_____

_____

WARNING

Testing is one of the most underestimated costs. If the cost of testing is not based on realistic budgeting and resource allocation, the result will be chaos and major cost overruns.

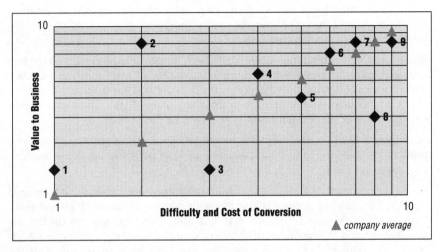

Figure 7-1: Conversion costs vs. value to business

unimportant, factors that change the whole triage picture. They may find that conversion proceeds more quickly than expected on a particular system, or that it is untenable. Project managers need to hear this information, and they need to have some flexibility to act as circumstances change.

It is essential to hold regular weekly meetings to track progress on each project, and to keep the whole team informed about emerging issues. A chart or diagram that can be filled in or colored to indicate how far each group has gotten will be tremendously useful, both for motivating the programming team and for informing senior management.

Whenever possible, end-users should be called on to perform minor duties during triage projects. Philosophically, it's important that they see how hard your team is working, which will help limit the inevitable criticism later on. Practically speaking, there may be many tasks that end-users can perform, freeing up skilled staff for more technical jobs. For example, end-users can help with, and in some cases, be wholly responsible for creation of compliance test plans and criteria. They should be doing the sign-off. Don't underestimate the role that end-users can and must play. They are key players on the team. For example, end-users can be called on to archive all essential files from their workstations. They can remove extraneous files, such as sample databases. They can check the software installed on their machines against a list of approved, Year-2000 compliant packages, and inform IT if they need to replace something. You may be able to make compliant updates for system software and popular programs available via your company's intranet, allowing end-users to perform the upgrade themselves.

Of course, your goals will include checking to ensure that all upgrades have been completed properly. But in many cases end-users can accomplish simple compliance tasks on their own, if given adequate instructions to do so.

Legal Issues

Legal implications are a subject of its own, and they are covered in detail in Chapter 3, *Legal Issues*. Consider the topics presented in that chapter carefully before and during the triage process.

When they set out on the triage trail, both senior management and project managers must be aware that they are in a position of maximum legal liability. Bad choices could be extraordinarily costly, because you are making a deliberate choice to fix some systems and not to fix others. Even if your priorities are well-chosen, failure of the less-important systems will be problematic.

Accordingly, legal counsel needs to be made aware of just what the Year-2000 project's priorities are, and why. Lawyers may spot pitfalls in advance—and that could save your skin.

Senior management will be tasked with minimizing the internal and external damage that may result from failure of minor systems or incorrect prioritization. These individuals must be proactive in this role. They will need to discuss the priorities set and the rationale behind them with the company's insurance under-writers. In publicly held companies, they may also need to consult with the investor relations department, or the business unit in charge of preparing the annual report.

Full documentation of the triage process—what was decided, and why, what was tested, and how—must be part of records retention rules drafted by the legal department.

Defending Triage

Once triage is underway, another process commences: damage control. This phase will involve your company's public relations and marketing departments.

Once you know which products or services will not be fully available at the end of 1999, your marketing and public relations employees can plan how to present the facts to clients, customers, and the public at large. Choices may include giving a positive spin to the situation, offering alternative products, helping clients line up other sources for services, or even restructuring the business around the new range.

Triage is not a pretty process, whether it takes place on a battlefield, in an emergency room, or in your company's boardroom. No matter how carefully conceived your triage plans are, the fact that you find yourself in this position indicates a lack of foresight that can damage reputations, jobs, and profits. It won't always be possible for PR departments to make it look better than it is.

CHAPTER 8

Inventory Database Schema

Formal Database Layout

Any serious Year-2000 inventory effort requires a formal database layout. Some companies work with multiple databases for storing and tracking progress of the inventory, resources, conversion, and testing. The choice of database architecture is dictated by the organization's internal command-structure and the techniques chosen for conversion distribution.

One of the primary motivations for this database is the automated and timely reporting and tracking of progress through the various stages of the project. Reports have to illustrate different views for different audiences; accounting staff are more concerned with financial impact while project managers use the detailed timing data.

Table Examples

The following tables are a starting point and should be enhanced and customized to suit particular business needs. Although the database starts in the inventory phase, it must monitor all aspects of the project and even accommodate regression testing and repetitive cycles. The Conversion and Testing table has a many-to-one relationship with the Product table, which facilitates multiple session storage. To ensure that only authorized parties can edit the Year-2000 database, build access limits and other security measures into the design.

Product

The Product table can be split between internal and externally supplied products.

Resources

People working on or associated with the conversion (developers, analysts, project managers, business unit consultants, etc.).

Table 8-1: Internally and Externally Supplied Products

Key	Description
PCode	Alpha-numeric product key
Group Name	Program, hardware , O/S, etc.
Version	Release
Type and Description	Product categories, for example, spreadsheet, payroll, etc.
BUCode	Business Unit Code (internal owner of the product)
Priority	Business priority of the product: rate function as the product of Impact and Scope
Scope	Corporate/department/individual/other
Impact	Fatal/critical/important/other
Estimated Cost of Non-Compliance	Potential cost in dollars of lost business (excluding litigation)
Unit Conversion Amount	Dollar amount in thousands to analyze, convert, and test product for Year-2000 compliance
Conversion Prime	Resource/vendor contact accountable for converting this application/product
Internal Certification Prime	Manager responsible for testing this product to Year-2000 compliance
Total Quantity	Calculated total quantity based on BU/department product quantities for the same product
License Status	Applies to externally supplied products only
Notes	Additional comments about the product
Year-2000 Impact	A derivative of impact, above; set once Year-2000 effect is ascertained
Ripple Impact	Will conversion/testing of this product impact other systems? Specify PCode
Dependencies	PCodes—Define whether co- or interdependent
Third-Party Software Used by the Application	For example, operating system, DLLs, ActiveX controls, etc.
Event Horizon	Date of first anticipated problem
Proposed Delivery Date	Confirmed delivery date of compliant version from supplier or internal converter
Current Compliance Status	Supplier's response—is this product compliant, or will it be?
Compliance Info	Supplier's information about how it determines compliance
Compliant Version #	Year-2000 compliant version number
Unit Conversion Amount	Dollar amount in thousands to analyze, convert, and test product to Year-2000 compliance
Replacement Product	Totally separate product or application that is or can replace the current product
Cost of Replacement	Total cost including H/W, S/W, O/S, training, migration, and data-conversion

Table 8-1: Internally and Externally Supplied Products (continued)

Key	Description
Latest Start Date	Latest start date for replacing the product
Planned Completion Date	Planned or actual completion date of replacement product implementation
Plan	Replacement plan description
Certification Date	Certification date on the Year-2000 certification document
Date Last Updated	Last time this product was updated
Updated By	Person who last updated this product
Original Creation Date	The date the product was created
QA Sign-Off	John Smith
Business Unit Sign-Off	Paul Martin
Migration	Roll-out
Final Sign-Off	BU acceptance

Some of the fields in this table, such as postal addresses, will only apply to multiple-site conversions and external vendors.

Table 8-2: People Working on Conversion

Key	Description
Surname	Adams
First Name	Mark
Function	Developer, manager, etc.
PCode	Product that the resource is working on
Phone Number	123-456-890
BUCode	Business Unit Code—the department that this resource is working for
City	Los Angeles
Province/State	California
Country	USA
Address	142 Appletree
Postal Code	ER1 567
FAX Number	123-456-789
Email Address	Other network/electronic mail ID
Comments	Getting there slowly
Product Familiarity	Period familiar with product (years)

Users

This table can be populated from personnel and asset data.

Table 8-3: Personnel and Asset Data

Key	Description
Surname	White
First Name	Peter
Function	Developer, manager etc.
PCode	Product that is being used, including printers etc.
Phone Number	987-654-321
BUCode	Business Unit Code—the department that this resource is working for
Employee Code	AA64
Network ID	JKGLPMN
Office Location	3D

Departments or business units

Table 8-4: Units

Key	Description
BUCode	Departments to be sub-divided into business units or teams
Name	Department description
Year 2000 Manager	Senior manager responsible for completing Year-2000 activities and ensuring the department is Year-2000 ready
City	Los Angeles
Province/State	California
Country	USA
Priority	Overall business priority of the department
Company Name	Company's name
Note	Additional information on the department

Business Unit unit products

Table 8-5: Products per Business Unit

Key	Description
BU Code	Key to BU table
PCode	Key to Products table—all products used by the unit
Quantity	Quantity owned (and licensed) department
Notes	NTR

Conversion and testing

Table 8-6: Conversion and Testing

Key	Description
PCode	Key to Products table
Test Sequence Number (Pass #)	Regression, re-test, etc.
Test Sequence Comment	Hardware very slow
Process Started	8/8/99
Conversion Status	1 - investigated
	2 - commenced
	3 - delayed
	4 - ready for testing
	5 - testing
	6 - tested
	7 - QA sign-off
	8 - migrated
	9 - final sign-off
Unit - Testing	Module
Integration Testing	Assembled
User - Testing	Whole system including interfaces and dependencies
Comment	Must do inventory one more time
External or Sub-Contracted Testing and QA Sign-Off	Shortly

Forms and Questionnaires

In the following pages you will find an Inventory Questionnaire sheet, followed by a Vendor/Product Compliance Questionnaire. These forms are meant to be used as generic questionnaires for any organization dealing with Year-2000 issues.

Inventory Questionnaire

Date: _____

Completed by: _____

Phone: _____

Department:_____

Product (accounts, payroll etc.): _____

Version: _____

General description: _____

_____

System / Module: _____

_____

Operating system: _____

Comms.: _____

Client / Server proportionality: _____

_____

Programming languages involved: _____

_____

Databases and SQL involved? (Y/N) _____

External input / output: _____

Frequency of usage:_____

Sponsor: _____

Importance to business (1-10): _____ Intended life-span: _____

Suspected event/date horizon: _____

Difficulty of conversion (1-10): _____

Storage location of source files: _____

Storage location of documentation: _____

List all shared files, DLLs, resources etc.: _____

_____

State any future plans (migration etc.): _____

_____

State any 3rd party involvement (source, maintenance etc.): _____

_____

Is the source code available? Y/N _____

Who owns the source code? _____

Is 3rd party portion of code Y2K-compliant? _____

If not, when will 3rd party code be compliant? _____

Proportion of embedded software:_____

Level of compliance of embedded code:_____

State ideal and actual response performance: _____

Vendor / Product Compliance Questionnaire

Date: _____

Vendor: _____

Product/Module: _____

Platform: _____

Please indicate the most relevant statement regarding a Year 2000-compliant version of the above software / hardware:

❏ Already released

❏ Ready but not released

❏ Under development

❏ Changes not started

❏ Never will comply, or none of the above

Please state expected date/release number of the Year 2000-compliant version:

Version/Release #:_____

Release Date:_____

Will there be an additional charge to clients for this change/update?

❏ No   ❏ Yes   ❏ Depends

If "Yes" or "Depends" checked above, please explain: _____

_____

_____

Please indicate all acceptable date formats for the Year 2000-compliant version:

_____

_____

Are any third-party interfaces embedded in this application?

❏ Yes   ❏ No

If yes, please explain:

_____

_____

Project Contact: _____

Phone: _____

Year-2000 Compliance Project

Table 8-7: Product Progress Summary Report

Milestones	Milestone Code
Certification Prime Appointed	MS 1.
Priority and Risk Assessment Completed	MS 2.
Conversion Commenced	MS 3.
Test Plan Completed	MS 4.
Conversion Completed	MS 5.
Integration Testing Completed	MS 6.
User Testing Completed	MS 7.
Migration and Deployment Completed	MS 8.
Project Signed-Off	MS 9.

Table 8-8: Mandated Completion Dates

Milestone	Priority A Projects	Priority B Projects	Priority C Projects
MS 1	06/01/98	07/14/98	09/30/98
MS 2	07/01/98	08/14/98	10/14/98
MS 3	07/14/98	09/30/98	11/14/98
MS 4	08/14/98	10/14/98	12/14/98
MS 5	09/30/98	11/14/98	12/30/98
MS 6	10/14/98	12/14/98	01/14/99
MS 7	11/14/98	12/30/98	01/30/99
MS 8	12/14/98	01/14/99	02/14/99
MS 9	12/30/98	01/30/99	02/28/99

Table 8-9: Progress—Priority A Projects

	MS 1	MS 2	MS 3	MS 4	MS 5	MS 6	MS 7	MS 8	MS 9
Payroll	−1	−4	−4						
Inventory	−2	−4	−4						
Production	0	−1	−1						
Shipping	−1	−3	−7						

Table 8-10: Progress (Average by Priority)

Milestone Code	Priority A	Deviation (weeks)	Priority B	Deviation (weeks)	Priority C	Deviation (weeks)
MS 1	06/08/98	−1	07/28/98	−2		
MS 2	07/21/98	−3				
MS 3	08/14/98	−4				
MS 4						
MS 5						

Table 8-10: Progress (Average by Priority) (continued)

Milestone Code	Priority A	Deviation (weeks)	Priority B	Deviation (weeks)	Priority C	Deviation (weeks)
MS 6						
MS 7						
MS 8						
MS 9						

Inventory
Database

CHAPTER 9

Year-2000 Macro Project Plan Template

Creating a Template

The Macro Project Plan presented here is based on an approximate project duration of 400 days (including weekends and holidays). It is a generic guideline, so every task and sub-task must be investigated and adjusted to meet your organization's particular situation.

The primary task thread in the plan concerns managing in-house software conversion, with hardware, tools, vendor management, and packages interwoven and indicated as monitored tasks. Ideally, separate plans for each sub-thread and every system should be compiled, but the necessity of this requirement depends on the size and complexity of the total IT installation. Some possible additional project plans are:

- Inventory database design, population, and compliance-process monitoring and reporting
- Mainframe, mini, networking, communications (PBX/telephony) security, and PC hardware
- System and solutions vendor management for all of the previous items, including Year-2000 tools
- Outsourced and off-the-shelf software conversion and acquisition
- Compiling legal and contractual obligations
- Listing compliance priorities
- Pilot and full roll-out
- PC packages, files, spreadsheets, and databases
- PC upgrade/replacement plans
- External partner contact and certification programs

In the Macro Project Plan, the term *resource* denotes both personnel and equipment.

Table 9-1: Macro Project Plan

#	Task / Phase	Days	Depend-encies	Start Date
1	Year-2000 System Compliance Project Plan	400		
2	Phase 1: Inventory and Scope	32		3/10/98
3	Phase 1.1: Plan phases 1 and 2 and set up project teams/primes	2		3/10/98
4	Phase 1.2: Determine and acquire investigation budget (optional)	2		3/10/98
5	Phase 1.3: List applications, H/W (including PCs), storage, networks, and comms.	15	3	3/12/98
6	Phase 1.4: Determine external interfaces (EDI, EFT, tapes, etc.)	5	3	3/12/98
7	Phase 1.5: Determine internal dependencies and business relationships	5	3	3/12/98
8	Phase 1.6: Determine event horizons	5	5	4/2/98
9	Phase 1.7: Ascertain legal responsibilities and impact of non-compliance	5	8	4/9/98
10	Phase 1.8: List vendors and establish vendor management team/prime	2	5	4/2/98
11	Phase 1.9: Determine budget for 1 and 2	5	6,7,8,10	4/9/98
12	Phase 1.10: Submit observations and primary master plan	5	11	4/16/98
13	Phase 2: Analysis and Investigation	86		3/19/98
14	Phase 2.1: Determine value of applications to business perspective	3	5	4/2/98
15	Phase 2.2: Determine H/W, O/S, and platform compliance	10	5	4/2/98
16	Phase 2.3: Formulate H/W, O/S, and platform-compliance plans	5	15	4/16/98
17	Phase 2.4: Cost H/W, O/S, and outsourced applications	1	16	4/23/98
18	Phase 2.5: Scan all source-code, files, spreadsheets, and databases	30	5	4/2/98
19	Phase 2.6: Determine conversion complexity and repetitive cycles	10	18	5/14/98
20	Phase 2.7: Contact vendors regarding compliance, responsibilities, and timeframes	5	10	4/6/98
21	Phase 2.8: Assess (and cost) tools, vendors, and solutions providers	20	20	4/13/98
22	Phase 2.9: Determine external bridging requirements	12	6	3/19/98

Table 9-1: Macro Project Plan (continued)

#	Task / Phase	Days	Depend-encies	Start Date
23	Phase 2.10: Assess resource requirements and deficiencies	10	14,17, 19,21	5/28/98
24	Phase 2.11: Determine need for external resources	5	23	6/11/98
25	Phase 2.12: Investigate availability and cost of external resources	5	24	6/18/98
26	Phase 2.13: Cost internal and external resources	1	25	6/25/98
27	Phase 2.14: Estimate total costs	5	17,21,26	6/26/98
28	Phase 2.15: Establish standards and objectives for data and code	5	18	5/14/98
29	Phase 2.16: Agree on overall project budget	5	27	7/3/98
30	Phase 2.17: Document and refine master plan	5	29	7/10/98
31	*Phase 3: Pre-Coding Activity*	*398*		*3/10/98*
32	Phase 3.1: Acquire external management tools and conversion resources	10	21,23,29	7/10/98
33	Phase 3.2: Commence and monitor H/W, O/S, and platform-compliance progress	110	16	4/23/98
34	Phase 3.3: Finalize project architecture and conversion teams	3	3	3/12/98
35	Phase 3.4: Set up interdepartmental comms. practices	3	34	3/17/98
36	Phase 3.5: Establish conversion working environment	21	35	3/20/98
37	Phase 3.6: Formulate detailed update specifications	10	34	3/17/98
38	Phase 3.7: Design bridges, MRPs, database schemas, structures, copy books, etc.	25	37	3/31/98
39	Phase 3.8: Acquire/assemble conversion resources	30	30	7/17/98
40	Phase 3.9: Assess testing resource reqs, (H/W, location, and business staff)	5	38	5/5/98
41	Phase 3.10: Formulate test plans and schedules	5	40	5/12/98
42	Phase 3.11: Acquire/assemble testing tools, H/W, platforms, storage, etc.	21	41	5/19/98
43	Phase 3.12: Duplicate databases and files	10	37	3/31/98
44	Phase 3.13: Institute change management and QA procedures	5	37	3/31/98
45	Phase 3.14: Continuously audit standards and objectives for systems	380		3/10/98

Table 9-1: Macro Project Plan (continued)

#	Task / Phase	Days	Depend-encies	Start Date
124	*Phase 4: Coding and Integration*	*253*		*4/7/98*
125	Phase 4.1: Build bridges and copy data-bases	30	44	4/7/98
126	Phase 4.2: Ensure H/W, O/S, and platform compliance	1	33	9/24/98
127	Phase 4.3: Update/convert systems (using bridges)	90	126	9/25/98
128	Phase 4.4: Unit testing	20	127	1/29/99
129	Phase 4.5: Integration (and bridge) testing	20	128	2/26/99
130	*Phase 5: QA and User-Testing*	*88*		*3/26/99*
131	Phase 5.1: Intensive user testing and de-bugging and document changes	40	129	3/26/99
132	Phase 5.2: QA and extended (final) user-testing	20	131	5/21/99
133	Phase 5.3: Install and run pilot site/client F/E component	20	132	6/18/99
134	Phase 5.4: User acceptance sign-off	5	133	7/16/99
135	Phase 5.5: Store test plans and results for technical and legal purposes	3	134	7/23/99
136	*Phase 6: Roll Out and Implementation*	*30*		*7/23/99*
137	Phase 6.1: User and support training	30	134	7/23/99
138	Phase 6.2: Set up support structures	3	134	7/23/99
139	Phase 6.3: Duplicate production data and freeze	1	134	7/23/99
140	Phase 6.4: Move code/applications to production	1	139	7/26/99
141	Phase 6.5: Project completion and feedback report	20	140	7/27/99
142	Phase 6.6: Project sign-off and champagne!	1	141	8/24/99

PART III

COBOL Language Reference

CHAPTER 10

COBOL Reference

DILBERT reprinted by permission of United Feature Syndicate, Inc.

Introduction

This chapter is intended for those programmers whose COBOL is a vague memory, and for those who don't know COBOL at all but have been assigned to the COBOL conversion effort anyway. It is not intended as a complete COBOL tutorial, nor is it a detailed reference work. Think of it as a *light reference,* intended to refresh memories or impart a basic understanding of the language.

Use this reference in conjunction with Chapter 13, *COBOL Date Functions,* which provides more specifics on date-manipulation programming and theory.

About COBOL

COBOL is a high-level programming language first developed by the CODASYL Committee (Conference on Data Systems Languages) in 1960. Since then, responsibility for developing new COBOL standards has been assumed by the American National Standards Institute (ANSI). Three ANSI standards for COBOL have been produced: in 1968, 1974, and 1985. A new COBOL standard introducing object-oriented programming to COBOL is due within the next few years.

The committee is normally known as the CODASYL committee and the current phrasing makes it sound as if COBOL was developed by the Conference.

The acronym COBOL stands for Common Business Oriented Language. As its full name indicates, COBOL is intended for developing business, typically file-oriented, applications.

COBOL is one of the oldest programming languages in use. As a result it has some idiosyncrasies which programmers used to other languages may find irritating. Three in particular attract comment.

1. The COBOL standard requires that program text adheres to certain archaic formatting restrictions.

2. COBOL programs tend to be verbose. One of the design goals was to make the language as English-like as possible. As a result, COBOL uses structural concepts normally associated with English prose such as sections, para-graphs, and sentences. It also has an extensive reserved word list with over 300 entries. The reserved words themselves tend to be long.

3. Although the 1985 version of COBOL introduced many of the constructs required to write well-structured programs, it still retains some elements that, if used, make it difficult, and in some cases impossible, to write elegant programs.

COBOL Basics

This section presents the fundamentals of constructing COBOL programs. It explains the notation used in COBOL syntax diagrams and enumerates the COBOL coding rules. It shows how user-defined names are constructed and examines the structure of COBOL programs.

COBOL Syntax

COBOL syntax is defined using particular notation sometimes called the COBOL MetaLanguage. In this notation, words in uppercase are *reserved words*. When underlined they are mandatory. When not underlined they are noise words, used for readability only, and are optional.

Words in mixed case represent names that must be devised by the programmer. When material is enclosed in curly braces { }, a choice must be made from the options within the braces. Material enclosed in square brackets [ ] indicates that the material is optional, and may be included or omitted as required. The ellipsis symbol (...) indicates that the preceding syntax element may be repeated at the programmer's discretion.

Some notes on syntax diagrams

To simplify the syntax diagrams and reduce the number of rules that must be explained, special operand endings are used. These operand endings have the following meanings:

Ending	Meaning
$i	Uses an alphanumeric data-item
$il	Uses an alphanumeric data-item or a string literal
#i	Uses a numeric data-item
#il	Uses a numeric data-item or numeric literal
$#i	Uses a numeric or an alphanumeric data-item

COBOL Coding Rules

Traditionally, COBOL programs were written on coding forms. Although most programs are now entered directly into a computer, some COBOL formatting conventions remain that derive from ancient punch-card history.

On coding forms, the first six character positions are reserved for sequence numbers. The seventh character position is reserved for the continuation character, or for an asterisk that denotes a comment line. The actual program text starts in column 8. The four positions from 8 to 11 are known as Area A, and positions from 12 to 72 are Area B.

Although many COBOL compilers ignore some of these formatting restrictions, most still retain the distinction between Area A and Area B. When a COBOL compiler recognizes the two areas, all division names, section names, paragraph names, FD entries, and 01 level numbers must start in Area A. All other sentences must start in Area B.

Name Construction

All user-defined names, such as data names, paragraph names, section names, and mnemonic names, must adhere to the following rules:

1. They must contain at least one character, but not more than 30 characters.
2. They must contain at least one alphabetic character.
3. They must not begin or end with a hyphen.
4. They must be constructed from the characters A to Z, the numbers 0 to 9, and the hyphen.
5. Names are not case-sensitive: TotalPay is the same as totalpay, Totalpay, or TOTALPAY.

The Structure of COBOL Programs

COBOL programs are hierarchical in structure. Each element of the hierarchy consists of one or more subordinate elements. The hierarchy consists of:

- Divisions
- Sections
- Paragraphs
- Sentences
- Statements

Divisions

A division is a block of code, usually containing one or more sections, that starts where the division name is encountered and ends with the beginning of the next division or with the end of the program text.

Sections

A section is a block of code usually containing one or more paragraphs. A section begins with the section name and ends where the next section name is encountered or where the program text ends. Section names are devised by the programmer, or defined by the language. A section name is followed by the word SECTION and a period.

For example:

```
SelectConfederateStates SECTION.

FILE SECTION.
```

Paragraphs

A paragraph is a block of code made up of one or more sentences. A paragraph begins with the paragraph name and ends with the next paragraph or section name or the end of the program text. The paragraph name is devised by the programmer or defined by the language, and is followed by a period.

For example:

```
PrintFinalTotals.

PROGRAM-ID.
```

Sentences and statements

A sentence consists of one or more statements and is terminated by a period. For example:

```
MOVE .21 TO VatRate
   MOVE 1235.76 TO ProductCost
   COMPUTE VatAmount = ProductCost * VatRate.
```

A statement consists of a COBOL verb and an operand or operands. For example:

```
SUBTRACT Tax FROM GrossPay GIVING NetPay
```

The Four Divisions

At the top of the COBOL hierarchy are the four divisions. These divide the program into distinct structural elements. Although some of the divisions may be omitted, the sequence in which they are specified is fixed, and must follow the order listed here.

1. IDENTIFICATION DIVISION.

   Program Details

2. ENVIRONMENT DIVISION.

   Environment Details

3. DATA DIVISION.

   Data Descriptions

4. PROCEDURE DIVISION.

   Algorithm Description

The IDENTIFICATION DIVISION

The IDENTIFICATION DIVISION supplies information about the program to the programmer and the compiler. Most entries in the IDENTIFICATION DIVISION are directed at the programmer. The compiler treats them as comments.

The PROGRAM-ID clause is an exception to this rule. Every COBOL program must have a PROGRAM-ID.

The IDENTIFICATION DIVISION has the following structure:

```
IDENTIFICATION DIVISION
PROGRAM-ID. NameOfProgram.
[AUTHOR. YourName.]
other entries here
```

The keywords IDENTIFICATION DIVISION represent the division header and signal the commencement of the program text.

PROGRAM-ID is a paragraph name that must be specified immediately after the division header.

The NameOfProgram is a name devised by the programmer and must satisfy the rules for user-defined names.

Here's a typical program fragment:

```
IDENTIFICATION DIVISION.
PROGRAM-ID. SequenceProgram.
AUTHOR. Michael Coughlan.
```

The ENVIRONMENT DIVISION

The ENVIRONMENT DIVISION is used to describe the environment in which the program will run. In the ENVIRONMENT DIVISION, aliases are assigned to external devices, files, or command sequences. Other environment details, such as the collating sequence used, may also be defined here.

The DATA DIVISION

As the name suggests, the DATA DIVISION provides descriptions of the data-items processed by the program. The DATA DIVISION has two main sections: the FILE SECTION and the WORKING-STORAGE SECTION. Additional sections, such as the LINKAGE SECTION (used in sub-programs) and the REPORT SECTION (used in Report Writer-based programs) may also be required.

The FILE SECTION is used to describe most of the data that is sent to, or comes from, the computer's peripherals.

The WORKING-STORAGE SECTION is used to describe the general variables used in the program.

The DATA DIVISION has the following structure and syntax:

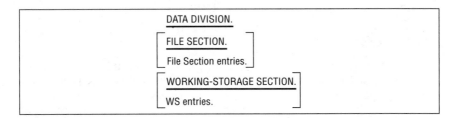

Here's a sample program fragment:

```
IDENTIFICATION DIVISION.
PROGRAM-ID.  Sequence-Program.
AUTHOR.  Michael Coughlan.

DATA DIVISION.
WORKING-STORAGE SECTION.
01  Num1          PIC 9  VALUE ZEROS.
01  Num2          PIC 9  VALUE ZEROS.
01  Result        PIC 99 VALUE ZEROS.
```

The PROCEDURE DIVISION

The PROCEDURE DIVISION contains the code used to manipulate the data described in the DATA DIVISION. The PROCEDURE DIVISION is hierarchical in structure and consists of sections, paragraphs, sentences, and statements.

Only the section is optional. There must be at least one paragraph, sentence, and statement in the PROCEDURE DIVISION. Paragraph and section names in the PROCEDURE DIVISION are chosen by the programmer and must conform to the rules for user-defined names.

Sample program

```
IDENTIFICATION DIVISION.
PROGRAM-ID.  SequenceProgram.
AUTHOR.  Michael Coughlan.

DATA DIVISION.
WORKING-STORAGE SECTION.
01  Num1          PIC 9  VALUE ZEROS.
01  Num2          PIC 9  VALUE ZEROS.
01  Result        PIC 99 VALUE ZEROS.

PROCEDURE DIVISION.
CalculateResult.
```

```
ACCEPT Num1.
ACCEPT Num2.
MULTIPLY Num1 BY Num2 GIVING Result.
DISPLAY "Result is = ", Result.
STOP RUN.
```

Minimum COBOL program

```
IDENTIFICATION DIVISION.
PROGRAM-ID.  SmallestProgram.

PROCEDURE DIVISION.
DisplayGreeting.
    DISPLAY "Hello world".
    STOP RUN.
```

COBOL Data

There are three kinds of data used in COBOL programs:

- Variables

- Literals

- Figurative Constants

Unlike other programming languages, standard COBOL does not support user-defined constants.

Data-Names, Identifiers, and Variables

A data-name or identifier is the name used to identify the area of memory reserved for a variable.

A variable is a named location in memory into which a program can put data, and from which it can retrieve data.

Every variable used in a COBOL program must be described in the DATA DIVISION.

COBOL Literals

String/Alphanumeric *literals* are enclosed in quotes and consist of alphanumeric characters.

For example:

"Michael Ryan", "-123", "123.45"

Numeric literals may consist of numerals, the decimal point, and the plus or minus sign. Numeric literals are not enclosed in quotes.

For example:

123, 123.45, -256, +2987

Figurative Constants

COBOL provides special constants, called Figurative Constants. The Figurative Constants are:

SPACE or SPACES	=	One or more spaces
ZERO or ZEROS or ZEROES	=	One or more zeros
QUOTE or QUOTES	=	The quotation mark
HIGH-VALUE or HIGH-VALUES	=	Maximum value possible
LOW-VALUE or LOW-VALUES	=	Minimum value possible
ALL literal	=	Allows a ordinary literal to act like a Figurative Constant

Figurative Constant notes

- Wherever a literal may be used, a Figurative Constant may be used.

- Where a Figurative Constant is assigned to a data-item, it fills the whole item.

- When the ALL Figurative Constant is used, it must be followed by a one character literal. The designated literal then acts like the standard Figurative Constants.

- Zero, Zeros, and Zeroes are synonyms, not separate Figurative Constants. The same applies to Space and Spaces, Quote and Quotes, High-Value and High-Values, and Low-Value and Low-Values.

Figurative Constant examples

The item GrossPay, defined here, is given an initial value of 13.5, but the whole data-item is filled with zeros when we use the command: MOVE ZEROS TO GrossPay.

```
01  GrossPay    PIC 9(5)V99 VALUE 13.5.
```

Before move	0	0	0	1	3	5	0
After move	0	0	0	0	0	0	0

The item StudentName is given an initial value "MIKE" in its declaration. The whole item is filled with hyphens when we use the command: MOVE ALL "-" TO StudentName.

```
01  StudentName    PIC X(10) VALUE "MIKE".
```

Before move	M	I	K	E						
After move	-	-	-	-	-	-	-	-	-	-

Declaring Data-Items in COBOL

COBOL's approach to declaring data-items will probably be unfamiliar to programmers used to typed languages like C or Modula-2. Rather than using types, as these languages do, COBOL uses what could be described as a *declaration by example* strategy. The programmer provides the system with an example, template, or PICTURE of the storage required for the data-item.

In COBOL, a variable declaration consists of a line in the DATA DIVISION that contains the following items:

- A level number
- A data-name or identifier
- A PICTURE clause

A starting value may be assigned to a variable by means of an extension to the PICTURE clause called the VALUE clause.

COBOL PICTURE Clause Symbols

To create the required *picture* the programmer uses a set of symbols. The most common symbols used in standard PICTURE clauses are:

9   The digit nine is used to indicate the occurrence of a digit at the corresponding position in the picture.

X   The character X is used to indicate the occurrence of any character from the character set at the corresponding position in the picture.

A   The character A is used to indicate the occurrence of any alphabetic character (A to Z plus blank) at the corresponding position in the picture.

V   The character V is used to indicate the position of the decimal point in a numeric value. It is often referred to as the *assumed decimal point*. It is called that because, although the actual decimal point is not stored, values are treated as if they had a decimal point in that position.

S   The character S indicates the presence of a sign and can only appear at the beginning of a picture.

PICTURE notes

- It is normal to use the abbreviation PIC when defining a PICTURE clause.
- Recurring symbols can be specified using a "repeat" factor inside brackets.

  For instance:

```
PIC 9(6)       is equivalent to PICTURE 999999
PIC 9(6)V99    is equivalent to PIC 999999V99
PICTURE X(10)  is equivalent to PIC XXXXXXXXXX
PIC S9(4)V9(4) is equivalent to PIC S9999V9999
PIC 9(18)      is equivalent to PIC 999999999999999999
```

- Numeric values can have a maximum of 18 (eighteen) digits.
- The limit on string values is usually system-dependent.

PICTURE examples

```
PICTURE 999    a three digit (+ive only) integer
PICTURE S999   a three digit (+ive/-ive) integer
PICTURE XXXX   a four character text item or string
PICTURE 99V99  a +ive  real  in the range 0 to 99.99
PICTURE S9V9   a +ive/-ive  real  in the range -9.9 to 9.9
```

Declaration examples

```
DATA DIVISION.
WORKING-STORAGE SECTION.
01  Num1          PIC 999      VALUE ZEROS.
01  BankBalance   PIC S9(4)V99 VALUE ZEROS.
01  VatRate       PIC V99      VALUE .18.
01  StudentName   PIC X(10)    VALUE SPACES.
```

The USAGE Clause

Every variable declared in a COBOL program has a usage, whether or not there is an explicit USAGE clause. When no actual USAGE clause is specified, the default clause is USAGE IS DISPLAY.

When numeric items have a usage of DISPLAY, they are held as ASCII characters. When calculations are done with such numbers, the numbers must be converted to their binary equivalents and the result of the calculation must be re-converted to ASCII digits. Conversion to and from ASCII digits slows down computations.

USAGE syntax

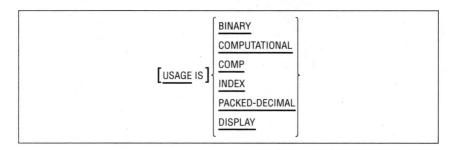

USAGE notes

- The USAGE clause may be used with any data description entry except those with level numbers of 66 or 88.

- When the USAGE clause is declared for a group item, the usage specified is applied to every item in the group. The group item itself is still treated as an alphanumeric data-item.

- USAGE IS COMPUTATIONAL, COMP, and BINARY are synonyms of one another.

USAGE rules

1. Any item declared with USAGE IS INDEX can only appear in:

   - A SEARCH or SET statement

   - A relation condition

   - The USING phrase of the PROCEDURE DIVISION

   - The USING phrase of the CALL statement

2. The picture string of a COMP or PACKED-DECIMAL item can contain only the symbols 9, S, V, and/or P.

3. The picture clause used for COMP or PACKED-DECIMAL items must be numeric.

USAGE examples

```
01 Num1        PIC 9(5)V99 USAGE IS COMP.
01 Num2        PIC 99 USAGE IS PACKED-DECIMAL.
01 IdxItem     USAGE IS INDEX.
01 GroupItems  USAGE IS COMP.
   02 Item1    PIC 999.
   02 Item2    PIC 9(4)V99.
   02 New1     PIC S9(5) COMP SYNC.
```

COMP/COMPUTATIONAL/BINARY

COMP items are held in memory as pure binary two's complement numbers. The storage requirements for fields described as COMP are as follows:

Number of Digits	Storage Required
PIC 9 (1 to 4)	1 Word (2 Bytes)
PIC 9 (5 to 9)	1 LongWord (4 Bytes)
PIC 9 (10 to 18)	1 QuadWord (8 Bytes)

Packed-Decimal

Data-items declared as PACKED-DECIMAL are held in binary-coded-decimal (BCD) form.

Instead of representing the value as a single binary number, the binary value of each digit is held in a nibble (half a byte).

The SYNCHRONIZED Clause

The SYNCHRONIZED clause is sometimes used with USAGE IS COMP or USAGE IS INDEX items. It is used to optimize the speed of processing but it does so at the expense of increased storage requirements.

The SYNCHRONIZED clause explicitly aligns COMP and INDEX items along their natural word boundaries. When there is no SYNCHRONIZED clause, data-items are aligned on byte boundaries. This can slow down computations as the CPU may need two fetch cycles to load a number from memory into its registers.

The word SYNC can be used instead of SYNCHRONIZED.

SYNCHRONIZED clause - boundary alignment

COMP SYNC (1 TO 4 Digits)	2 Byte boundary
COMP SYNC (5 TO 9 Digits)	4 Byte boundary
COMP SYNC (10 TO 18 Digits)	8 Byte boundary
INDEX	4 Byte boundary

General USAGE notes

The USAGE clause is one of the areas where many vendors have introduced extensions to the COBOL standard. It is not uncommon to see COMP-1, COMP-2, COMP-3, COMP-4, COMP-5, and POINTER usage items in programs written using these extensions.

Even though COMP-1 and COMP-2 are extensions to the COBOL standard, vendors seem to use identical representations for these usages. COMP-1 is usually defined as a single precision, floating point number, adhering to the IEEE specification for such numbers (Real or Float in typed languages). COMP-2 is usually defined as a double precision, floating point number (LongReal or Double in typed languages).

Declaring Records in COBOL

In COBOL, records are defined using an appropriate arrangement of level numbers. Level numbers are used to express data hierarchy: to decompose a record into its constituent parts.

In the data hierarchy, the higher the level number, the lower the item is in the hierarchy. At the lowest level the data is completely atomic.

In this hierarchical data description, what is important is the relationship of the level numbers to one another, not the actual level numbers used.

The level numbers 01 through 49 are general level numbers, but there are also special level numbers such as 66, 77, and 88.

Group and Elementary Items

In COBOL, the term *group item* is used to describe a data-item that has been further subdivided. A group item is declared using a level number and a data name only. It must not have a picture clause.

Where a group item is the highest item in a data hierarchy, it is referred to as a *record* and uses the level number 01.

The term *elementary item* is used to describe data-items that are atomic—that is, not further subdivided. The level number 77 can only be used to define elementary items.

Picture clauses are not specified for group items because the size of a group item is the sum of the sizes of its subordinate elementary items and its type is always assumed to be PIC X.

Group items example

```
WORKING-STORAGE SECTION.
01   StudentDetails.
     02 StudentName.
        03 Surname        PIC X(12).
        03 Initials       PIC XX.
     02 StudentId         PIC 9(7).
     02 CourseCode        PIC X(4).
     02 Gender            PIC X.
```

Student Details

C	O	U	G	H	L	A	N				M	S	9	7	3	0	1	6	5	L	M	5	1	M

Student Name		StudentID	CourseCode	Gender
Surname	Initials			

In the declarations above, the size of the StudentDetails record is 26 characters. In the memory schematic that follows the declarations, note the way the identifiers map onto the 26 characters of memory allocated to the record. All the identifiers in the record are current/active at the same time as the following COBOL statements demonstrate.

```
DISPLAY StudentDetails.
    displays the entire record "COUGHLAN     MS9730165LM51M"
DISPLAY StudentName.
    displays "COUGHLAN     MS"
DISPLAY Initials.
    displays "MS"
DISPLAY CourseCode.
    displays "LM51".
```

More data declarations

For more on data declarations see the following sections:

- For Level 88's (Condition Names), see "Selection Constructs"

- For file-oriented data descriptions, see "Sequential Files"

- For EDITED PICTURE clauses, see "Sequential Files"

- For the OCCURS and REDEFINES clauses, see "Tables/Arrays "

- For SORT file data descriptions, see "Sorting Files"

- For LINKAGE SECTION descriptions, see "COBOL sub-programs"

- For the REPORT SECTION descriptions, see "The COBOL Report Writer"

- For level 66s, refer to your vendor manual

PROCEDURE DIVISION Commands

The PROCEDURE DIVISION contains the code used to manipulate data described in the DATA DIVISION. This section examines the COBOL commands used in the PROCEDURE DIVISION.

Assignment in COBOL

In *strongly typed* languages, assignment is simple because it is only allowed between items with compatible types. The simplicity of assignment in these languages implies a large number of data types.

In COBOL, there are basically only three data types:

- Alphabetic (PIC A)
- Alphanumeric (PIC X)
- Numeric (PIC 9, Comp, Packed-Decimal)

However, this simplicity requires a complex assignment statement.

In COBOL, assignment is achieved using the MOVE verb (COBOL commands are known as *verbs*).

The MOVE verb

MOVE   Source$#il TO DestinationS#i...

The MOVE verb copies data from the source identifier or literal to one or more destination identifiers (note the ellipsis). The source and destination identifiers can be group or elementary data-items.

MOVE notes

- The source and destination identifiers can be group or elementary data-items.
- When data is moved into an item, the contents of the item are completely replaced. If the source data is too small to fill the destination item, the remaining area is filled with zeros or spaces, depending on whether the receiving item is numeric or alphabetic.
- When Destination$#i is alphanumeric or alphabetic (PIC X or A), data is copied into the destination area from left to right, with space filling or truncation on the right.
- When Destination$#i is numeric or edited numeric, then data is aligned along the decimal point, with zero filling or truncation as necessary.
- When the decimal point is not explicitly specified in either the source or destination items, the item is treated as if it had a decimal point immediately after its rightmost character.

Alphanumeric MOVE examples

In the first move, the text fills the item from left to right but is not long enough to fill the item, so the rest of the item is space-filled.

In the second move, the text is too long to fit into the item, and the letters "ick" are lost.

```
01   Surname   PIC X(8) VALUE ALL "-".
```

Before moves	-	-	-	-	-	-	-	-
After move 1	R	y	a	n				
After move 2	F	i	t	z	p	a	t	r

```
1.   MOVE   Ryan  TO Surname.
2.   MOVE   Fitzpatrick  TO Surname.
```

Numeric MOVE examples

In these examples, GrossPay is defined as a numeric data-item with four digits before the decimal point and two after. The position of the decimal point is indicated by the V in the picture clause and by a heavy black line in the memory schematic.

In the first move, GrossPay is filled with zeros.

In the second, 12.4 is inserted into GrossPay, aligned along the assumed decimal point. Since the value is not large enough to fill the whole item, it is zero-filled on both sides.

In the third move, 123.456 aligns along the decimal point, causing zero-filling on the left and truncating the 6 on the right.

In the fourth move, 12345.757 aligns along the decimal point, truncating the most significant digit on the left and the least significant on the right.

```
01 GrossPay     PIC 9(4)V99.
```

After move 1	0	0	0	0	0	0
After move 2	0	0	1	2	4	0
After move 3	0	1	2	3	4	5
After move 4	2	3	4	5	7	5

```
1.   MOVE ZERO TO GrossPay.
2.   MOVE 12.4 TO GrossPay.
3.   MOVE 123.456 TO GrossPay.
4.   MOVE 12345.757 TO GrossPay.
```

MOVE restrictions

Although COBOL is much less restrictive in this respect than many other languages, certain combinations of sending and receiving data types are not permitted.

- Alphanumeric items may be moved to any item.

- Alphanumeric Edited and Alphabetic items may only be moved to Alphanumeric, Alphanumeric Edited, and Alphabetic items.

- Numeric integers may be moved to any item, except alphabetic items.

- Numeric non-integers may be moved to any item, except Alphanumeric, Alphanumeric Edited, and Alphabetic items.

- Numeric Edited items may only be moved to Alphanumeric and Alphanumeric Edited items.

ACCEPT and DISPLAY

In COBOL, the ACCEPT and DISPLAY verbs are used to read from the keyboard and write to the screen.

The DISPLAY verb

The DISPLAY verb is used to send output to the computer screen or to a peripheral device.

> DISPLAY OutputItem1$#il [OutputItem2$#il]...
>
> [UPON Mnemonic - Name] [WITH NO ADVANCING]

A single DISPLAY can be used to display several data-items or literals or any combination of these.

After the items in the display list have been sent to the screen, the DISPLAY automatically moves the screen cursor to the next line unless a WITH NO ADVANCING clause is present.

The Mnemonic-Name is a user-defined name, connected to some peripheral device (such as a serial port) in the ENVIRONMENT DIVISION.

The ACCEPT verb

The ACCEPT verb is used to get data from the keyboard, a peripheral device, or certain system variables.

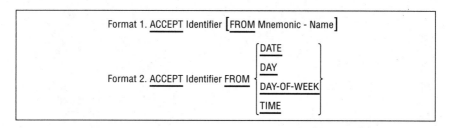

When the first format is used, the ACCEPT verb inserts the data typed at the keyboard (or coming from the peripheral device) into the Identifier.

When the second format is used, the ACCEPT verb moves the data from one of the system variables into the Identifier.

The declarations and comments here show the format required for each of the system variables.

```
01 CurrentDate        PIC 9(6).
* DATE is Current date in YYMMDD format

01 DayOfYear          PIC 9(5).
* DAY is current day in YYDDD format

01 DayOfWeek          PIC 9.
* DAY-OF-WEEK is a single digit where 1=Monday

01 CurrentTime        PIC 9(8).
```

```
* TIME is the current time in HHMMSSss format
* where ss represents hundredths of a second.
```

ACCEPT and DISPLAY examples

```
IDENTIFICATION DIVISION.
PROGRAM-ID. AcceptAndDisplay.
AUTHOR.  Michael Coughlan.

DATA DIVISION.
WORKING-STORAGE SECTION.
01  StudentName.
    02 Surname           PIC X(12).
    02 Initials          PIC XX.

01  CurrentDate.
    02  CurrentYear      PIC 99.
    02  CurrentMonth     PIC 99.
    02  CurrentDay       PIC 99.

01  DayOfYear.
    02  FILLER           PIC 99.
    02  YearDay          PIC 9(3).

01  CurrentTime.
    02  CurrentHour      PIC 99.
    02  CurrentMinute    PIC 99.
    02  FILLER           PIC 9(4).

PROCEDURE DIVISION.
Begin.
    DISPLAY "Enter Surname - " WITH NO ADVANCING.
    ACCEPT  Surname.
    MOVE "MS" TO Initials.
    ACCEPT  CurrentDate FROM DATE.
    ACCEPT  DayOfYear FROM DAY.
    ACCEPT  CurrentTime FROM TIME.

    DISPLAY "Name is ", Initials SPACE Surname.
    DISPLAY "Date is "  CurrentDay SPACE
            CurrentMonth SPACE CurrentYear.
    DISPLAY "Today is day " YearDay " of the year".
    DISPLAY "Time is " CurrentHour ":" CurrentMinute.
    STOP RUN.
```

When the program was run, it produced the following output:

```
Enter Surname - COUGHLAN
Name is MS COUGHLAN
Date is 24 01 97
Today is day 024 of the year
Time is 22:23
```

Arithmetic in COBOL

Most procedural programming languages perform computations by assigning the result of an arithmetic expression or a function to a variable. COBOL does provide a verb for evaluating arithmetic expressions, but it also provides specific commands for adding, subtracting, multiplying, and dividing.

In most procedural languages, data movement is from right to left. That is, the leftmost data-item receives the result of the calculation. In COBOL, all the arithmetic verbs except the COMPUTE verb assign the result of the calculation to the right-most data-items.

All COBOL arithmetic verbs move the result of a calculation into a receiving data-item according to the rules for a numeric move; that is, with alignment along the assumed decimal point and with zero-filling or truncation as necessary.

The ROUNDED Option

All the arithmetic verbs allow the ROUNDED phrase.

The ROUNDED phrase takes effect when, after decimal point alignment, the result calculated must be truncated on the right hand side. The option adds 1 to the receiving item when the leftmost truncated digit has an absolute value of 5 or greater.

ROUNDED examples

a	Actual Result	Truncated Result	Rounded Result
PIC 9(3)V9.	123.25	123.2	123.3
PIC 9(3).	123.25	123	123

The ON SIZE ERROR Phrase

It is possible for the result of a calculation to be too large to fit into the receiving data-item. When this occurs, there will be truncation of the result. The ON SIZE ERROR phrase allows the programmer to detect this condition.

All the arithmetic verbs allow the ON SIZE ERROR phrase.

A size error condition exists when, after decimal point alignment, the result is truncated on either the left- or the right-hand side.

If an arithmetic statement has a ROUNDED phrase then a size error only occurs if there is truncation on the left-hand side (most significant digits).

ON SIZE ERROR examples

Receiving Field	Actual Result	Size Error
PIC 9(3)V9.	245.96	YES
PIC 9(3)V9.	1245.9	YES
PIC 9(3).	124	NO
PIC 9(3).	1246	YES
PIC 9(3)V9 Not Rounded	124.45	YES

Receiving Field	Actual Result	Size Error
PIC 9(3)V9 Rounded	124.45	NO
PIC 9(3)V9 Rounded	3124.45	YES

The GIVING Phrase

Where the GIVING phrase is used, the item to the right of the word "giving" is the receiving field of the calculation but does not contribute to it. Where there is more than one item after the word "giving," each receives the result of the calculation.

The ADD Verb

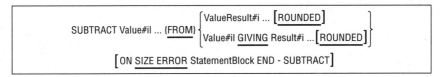

```
              ┌ TO ValueResult#i ... [ROUNDED]              ┐
ADD Value#i ...│                                            │
              └ [TO] Value#il GIVING Result#i ... [ROUNDED] ┘
         [ ON SIZE ERROR StatementBlock END - ADD ]
```

When the ADD verb is used, everything before the word "to" is added together and the combined result is then added to each of the items after the word "to" in turn.

ADD examples

ADD Takings TO CashTotal.

	Takings	CashTotal
Before	10	20
After	10	30

ADD Bonus, 10 TO CashTotal, FinalTotal.

	Bonus	CashTotal	FinalTotal
Before	55	20	100
After	55	85	165

ADD Males TO Females GIVING TotalStudents.

	Males	Females	TotalStudents
Before	25	15	325
After	25	15	040

The SUBTRACT Verb

```
                        ┌ ValueResult#i ... [ROUNDED]         ┐
SUBTRACT Value#il ... {FROM}│                                │
                        └ Value#il GIVING Result#i ... [ROUNDED] ┘
        [ ON SIZE ERROR StatementBlock END - SUBTRACT ]
```

When the SUBTRACT verb is used, everything before the word "from" is added together and the combined result is then subtracted from each of the items after the word "from" in turn.

SUBTRACT examples

```
SUBTRACT Tax, Surcharge FROM GrossPay.
```

	Tax	Surcharge	GrossPay
Before	120	30	275
After	120	30	125

```
SUBTRACT Tax FROM GrossPay GIVING NetPay.
```

	Tax	GrossPay	NetPay
Before	120	540	010
After	120	540	420

The MULTIPLY Verb

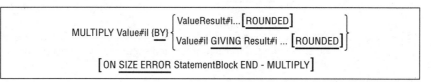

If the GIVING phrase is not used, then the item to the left of the word "by" is multiplied by each of the items after the word "by" in turn. The result of each calculation is placed in the item after the word "by."

MULTIPLY examples

```
MULTIPLY Subs BY Members GIVING TotalSubs
    ON SIZE ERROR DISPLAY "TotalSubs too small"
END-MULTIPLY.
```

	Subs	Members	TotalSubs
Before	15.50	100	0123.45
After	15.50	100	1550.00

```
MULTIPLY 10 BY Magnitude, Size.
```

	Magnitude	Size
Before	0355	0125
After	3550	1250

The DIVIDE Verb

```
                      ┌ BY ┐   ┌ ValueResult#i ... [ROUNDED] ┐
DIVIDE Value#il┤      ├      ┤                                ├
                      └ INTO ┘  └ Value#il GIVING Result#i... [ROUNDED] ┘

        [ ON SIZE ERROR StatementBlock END - DIVIDE ]


                      ┌ INTO ┐
DIVIDE Value#il┤      ├      ├ Value#il GIVING { Quotient#i [ROUNDED] } REMAINDER Remainder#i
                      └ BY ┘

        ┌ ┌ ON SIZE ERROR      ┐                                  ┐
        │ │                    ├ StatementBlock END - DIVIDE      │
        └ └ NOT ON SIZE ERROR  ┘                                  ┘
```

The DIVIDE verb conforms to one or the other of the syntax diagrams shown above.

If the GIVING phrase is not used, then the item to the left of the word "by" or "into" is divided by or into each of the items after the word in turn. The result of each calculation is placed in the item after the word "by" or "into."

When the REMAINDER phrase is used, the quotient is placed in the item after the word "giving" and the remainder is placed in the item after the word "remainder."

DIVIDE examples

```
DIVIDE Total BY Members GIVING MemberAverage.
```

	Total	Members	MemberAverage
Before	9234.55	100	1234.56
After	9234.55	100	0092.34

```
DIVIDE 201 BY 10 GIVING Quotient REMAINDER Remain.
```

	Quotient	Remain
Before	209	424
After	020	001

The COMPUTE Verb

```
COMPUTE { Result#i [ROUNDED] }... = Arithmetic Expression

┌ ┌ ON SIZE ERROR      ┐                                   ┐
│ │                    ├ StatementBlock END - COMPUTE      │
└ └ NOT ON SIZE ERROR  ┘                                   ┘
```

The COMPUTE verb assigns the result of an arithmetic expression to a data-item. The arithmetic expression is evaluated according to the normal arithmetic rules. That is, the expression is normally evaluated from left to right, but bracketing and the precedence rules shown here can change the order of evaluation.

Precedence	Symbol	Meaning
1.	**	Power NN
2.	*	multiply
	/	divide
3.	+	add
	-	subtract

COMPUTE example

```
COMPUTE SellingPrice = Price + Price * TaxRate
```

	SellingPrice	Price	TaxRate
Before	500.00	175	.21
After	211.75	175	.21

Iteration Constructs

In almost every programming job, there is some task that needs to be done over and over again.

For example:

- The job of processing a file of records is an iteration of the task: get and process record.

- The job of getting the sum of a stream of numbers is an iteration of the task: get and add number.

These jobs are accomplished using iteration constructs.

Other computer languages support a variety of looping constructs, including Repeat, While, and For loops.

Although COBOL has a set of looping constructs that are just as rich as other languages—richer in some cases—it only has one iteration verb. In COBOL, all iteration is handled by the PERFORM verb.

Iteration constructs and their COBOL equivalents

Repeat	PERFORM UNTIL ..WITH TEST BEFORE
While	PERFORM UNTIL ..WITH TEST AFTER
For	PERFORM ..VARYING

PERFORM..PROC

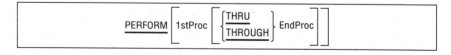

While the other formats of the PERFORM verb implement various types of iteration, this format is used to transfer control to a block of code. The block of code may be one or more paragraphs, or one or more sections.

This format of the PERFORM verb transfers control to an out-of-line block of code. When the end of the block is reached, control reverts to the statement (not the sentence) immediately following the PERFORM.

1stProc and EndProc are the names of paragraphs or sections.

When PERFORM..THRU is used, the paragraphs or sections from 1stProc to EndProc are treated as a single block of code.

COBOL programmers typically use this format of the PERFORM verb to divide a program into subroutines. These subroutines are not as powerful as the user-defined Procedures or Functions found in other languages, but when COBOL programmers require that kind of partitioning, they use sub-programs.

PERFORM..PROC notes

- PERFORMs can be nested. That is, a PERFORM verb may execute a paragraph that contains a PERFORM.

  In the following example, the paragraph TopLevel contains a PERFORM, which transfers control to OneLevelDown. In turn, this paragraph has a PERFORM, which transfers control to the paragraph TwoLevelsDown.

- The order of paragraph execution is independent of physical placement.

  For instance, although the paragraph OneLevelDown comes after TwoLevelsDown in the program text, it is executed before it.

- Although PERFORMs can be nested, neither direct nor indirect recursion is allowed.

  For example, it would not be valid for paragraph ThreeLevelsDown to contain the statement PERFORM ThreeLevelsDown. This would be direct recursion.

  Neither would it be valid for OneLevelDown to contain the statement PERFORM TopLevel. This would be indirect recursion since TopLevel contains the instruction PERFORM OneLevelDown.

PERFORM..PROC example

```
PROCEDURE DIVISION.
TopLevel.
    DISPLAY "In TopLevel. Starting to run program"
    PERFORM OneLevelDown
    DISPLAY "Back in TopLevel.".
    STOP RUN.

TwoLevelsDown.
    DISPLAY ">>>>>>>> Now in TwoLevelsDown."

OneLevelDown.
    DISPLAY ">>>> Now in OneLevelDown"
    PERFORM TwoLevelsDown
    DISPLAY ">>>> Back in OneLevelDown".
```

The output from this program fragment is:

```
In TopLevel. Starting to run program
>>>> Now in OneLevelDown
>>>>>>>> Now in TwoLevelsDown.
>>>> Back in OneLevelDown
Back in TopLevel.
```

PERFORM..TIMES

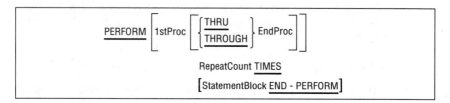

This version of PERFORM executes a block of code RepeatCount number of times before returning control to the statement following the PERFORM verb.

This and other formats of the PERFORM allow two types of execution. '

* Out-of-line execution of a block of code
* Inline execution of a block of code

In an inline PERFORM, the loop body is contained within the same paragraph as the PERFORM verb, and the scope of the loop is from the PERFORM verb to the END-PERFORM.

In an out-of-line PERFORM, the loop body is a separate paragraph or section.

PERFORM..TIMES example

```
IDENTIFICATION DIVISION.
PROGRAM-ID.   InLineVsOutOfLine.
AUTHOR.   Michael Coughlan.

DATA DIVISION.
WORKING-STORAGE SECTION.
01 NumOfTimes        PIC 9 VALUE 5.

PROCEDURE DIVISION.
Begin.
    DISPLAY "Starting to run program"
    PERFORM 3 TIMES
       DISPLAY ">>>>This is an in line Perform"
    END-PERFORM
    DISPLAY "Finished in line Perform"
    PERFORM OutOfLineEG NumOfTimes TIMES
    DISPLAY "Back in Begin. About to stop".
    STOP RUN.

OutOfLineEG.
    DISPLAY ">>>> This is an out of line Perform".
```

Program Output

```
Starting to run program
>>>>This is an in line Perform
>>>>This is an in line Perform
>>>>This is an in line Perform
Finished in line Perform
>>>> This is an out of line Perform
>>>> This is an out of line Perform
>>>> This is an out of line Perform
>>>> This is an out of line Perform
>>>> This is an out of line Perform
Back in Begin. About to stop
```

PERFORM..UNTIL

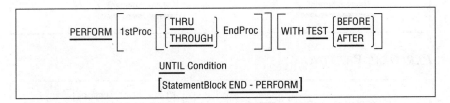

This format of the PERFORM verb is used like the While or Repeat constructs are used in other languages.

PERFORM..UNTIL notes

- If the WITH TEST BEFORE phrase is used, the PERFORM behaves like a While loop, and the condition is tested before the loop body is entered.

- If the WITH TEST AFTER phrase is used, the PERFORM behaves like a Repeat loop, and the condition is tested after the loop body is entered.

- The WITH TEST BEFORE phrase is the default, and so is rarely explicitly stated.

- The terminating condition is only checked at the beginning of each iteration (PERFORM WITH TEST BEFORE) or at the end of each iteration (PERFORM WITH TEST AFTER). If the terminating condition is reached in the middle of the iteration, the rest of the loop body will still be executed—although the terminating condition has been reached, it cannot be checked until the current iteration has finished.

- Although the PERFORM WITH TEST BEFORE is often said to be equivalent to a While loop, this is not entirely true. In a While loop, the condition is tested to see whether the iteration should continue (for example, While Count = 100 Do). In the equivalent PERFORM, the condition is tested to see if the iteration should stop (for example, PERFORM WITH TEST BEFORE UNTIL Count NOT = 100).

- The following flowcharts should help to explain how this format of the PERFORM verb works.

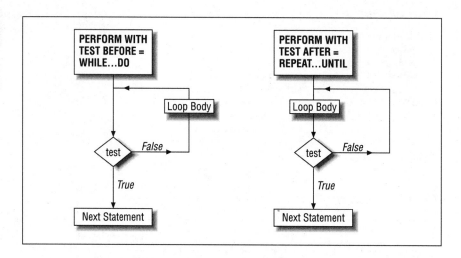

PERFORM..VARYING

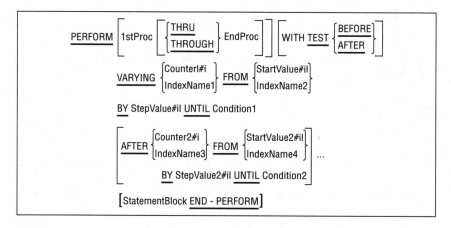

PERFORM..VARYING is used to implement counting iteration. It is similar to the For construct in languages like Modula-2, Pascal, and C.

However, these languages permit only one counting variable per loop instruction, while COBOL allows up to three.

Why three? Earlier versions of COBOL only allowed tables with a maximum of three dimensions, and PERFORM..VARYING was a mechanism for processing them.

PERFORM..VARYING notes

- Only one counter may be used with an inline PERFORM.

- The item after the VARYING phrase is the most significant counter, the counter following the first AFTER phrase is the next most significant, and the last counter is the least significant.

- The least significant counter must go through all of its values and reach its terminating condition before the next most significant counter can be incremented.

- The item after the FROM is the starting value of the counter.

- The item after the BY is the step value of the counter. This can be negative or positive. If a negative step value is used, the counter should be signed (PIC S99, etc.).

- As before, when no WITH TEST phrase is used, the WITH TEST BEFORE is assumed.

- Though the condition would normally involve some evaluation of the counter, it is not mandatory. For instance, the statement that follows is perfectly valid:

```
PERFORM CountRecords
     VARYING RecCount FROM 1 BY 1 UNTIL EndOfFile
```

- When the iteration ends, the counters retain their terminating values.

PERFORM.. VARYING example

In this example, the following table shows the number of times the loop body is processed, the values of the counters on each iteration, and the terminating values of the counters.

```
PERFORM IterationCount VARYING Idx1 FROM 1 BY 2
                       UNTIL   Idx1 EQUAL TO 5
                       AFTER   Idx2 FROM 6 BY −1
                       UNTIL   Idx2 LESS THAN 4
```

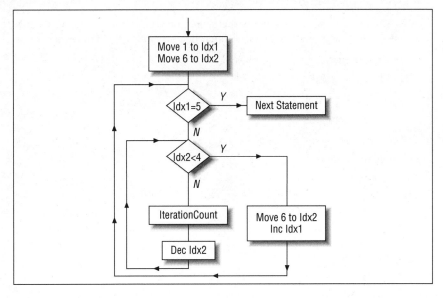

LoopCount	Indx1	Indx2
1	1	6
2	1	5
3	1	4
4	6	6
5	6	5
6	6	4
Exit loop	5	6

Selection Constructs

In most procedural languages, IF and CASE are the only selection constructs supported. COBOL supports advanced versions of both of these constructs, but it also introduces the concept of Condition Names—a kind of abstract condition.

The IF Statement

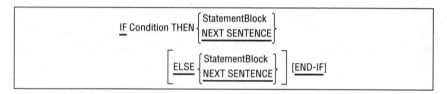

The scope of the IF statement may be delimited by a period (the old way) or by the END-IF (the new way).

The IF statement is not as simple as the syntax diagram above seems to suggest, because COBOL supports a number of different condition types. These include:

1. Simple Conditions

    – Relation Conditions

    – Class Conditions

    – Sign Conditions

2. Complex Conditions

3. Condition Names

Relation Conditions

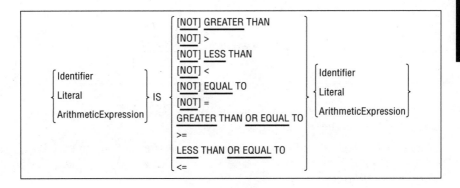

Class Conditions

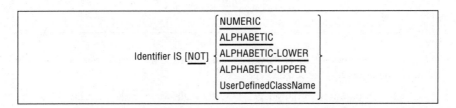

Although COBOL data-items are not *typed* they do fall into some broad categories, or classes, such as numeric or alphanumeric.

A Class Condition determines whether the value of a data-item is a member of one of these classes.

A Class Condition may be used to test a data-item to see if it contains values of a particular class. For instance, a NUMERIC Class Condition might be used on an alphanumeric (PIC X) or a numeric (PIC 9) data-item to see if it contains numeric data.

Class Condition rules

1. A data-item tested with a Class Condition must have an explicit or implicit usage of DISPLAY. In the case of NUMERIC tests, data-items with a usage of PACKED-DECIMAL may also be tested.

2. The NUMERIC test may not be used with data-items described as alphabetic (PIC A) or with group items when any of the elementary items specifies a sign.

3. The ALPHABETIC test may not be used with any data-items described as numeric (PIC 9).

4. A data-item conforms to the UserDefinedClassName if its contents consist entirely of the characters listed in the definition of the UserDefinedClassName.

5. The UserDefinedClassName may be defined in the SPECIAL-NAMES paragraph, of the CONFIGURATION SECTION, in the ENVIRONMENT DIVISION.

Sign Conditions

The Sign Condition determines whether or not the value of an arithmetic expression is less than, greater than, or equal to zero.

Sign Conditions are a shorter way of writing certain Relational Conditions.

Complex Conditions

Programs often require more Complex Conditions than simple tests of a single value or determination of a data class.

Like other programming languages, COBOL allows Simple Conditions to be combined using OR and AND to form Complex Conditions.

Like other conditions in COBOL, a Complex Condition evaluates to either True or False.

A Complex Condition is an expression. Like arithmetic expressions it is evaluated from left to right unless the order of evaluation is changed by the precedence rules or bracketing.

Complex Condition - Precedence Rules

Precedence	Condition Value	Arithmetic Equivalent
1.	NOT	**
2.	AND	* or /
3.	OR	+ or -

IF statement examples

```
IF Row > 0 AND Row < 26 THEN
    DISPLAY  On Screen
END-IF

IF VarA > VarC OR VarC = VarD OR VarA NOT = VarF
    DISPLAY  Done
END-IF
```

Implied Subjects

When a data-item in a Relation Condition is used with each of a number of other items, it can be tedious to have to repeat the data-item for each condition. For example:

```
IF TotalAmt > 10000 AND TotalAmt < 50000 THEN etc.

IF Grade = "A" OR Grade = "B+" OR GRADE = "B" THEN etc

IF VarA > VarB AND VarA > VarC AND VarA > VarD
   DISPLAY "VarA is the Greatest"
END-IF
```

COBOL provides an abbreviation mechanism, called Implied Subjects, for use in such situations.

Using the Implied Subjects "TotalAmt," "Grade =," and "VarA >," the statements above may be rewritten as:

```
IF TotalAmt > 10000 AND < 50000 THEN etc.

IF Grade="A" OR "B+" OR "B" THEN etc.

IF VarA > VarB AND VarC AND VarD
   DISPLAY "VarA is the Greatest"
END-IF
```

Nested IFs

COBOL allows nested IF statements. For example:

```
IF ( VarA < 10 ) AND ( VarB NOT > VarC ) THEN
    IF VarG = 14 THEN
        DISPLAY "First"
     ELSE
        DISPLAY "Second"
    END-IF
  ELSE
     DISPLAY "Third"
END-IF
```

Condition Names

Wherever a condition can occur, such as in an IF statement or an EVALUATE or a PERFORM..UNTIL, a Condition Name (Level 88) may be used. A Condition Name is essentially a Boolean, which returns a value of True or False.

Condition Names are defined in the DATA DIVISION using the special level number 88. They are always associated with a data-item and are defined immediately after the definition of the data-item.

Condition Name notes

- A Condition Name takes the value True or False, depending on the value of its associated data-item.

- A Condition Name may be associated with any data-item, whether it is a table element or a group or elementary item.

- The data values specified for a Condition Name must be consistent with the data type of the associated data-item.

- When used with Condition Names, the VALUE clause does not assign a value. It merely identifies the value(s) necessary to make the condition true.

- When identifying the values for the condition, a single value, a list of values, a range of values, or any combination of these may be specified.

- Listed values may be separated by commas or spaces but must terminate with a period.

- The keyword THRU, or THROUGH, is used to specify a range of values.

Condition Name examples

In the following example, the data-item InputChar is monitored by the Condition Names (Level 88s) shown. When InputChar contains the value mentioned in the VALUE clause of any of the Condition Names, that Condition Name is automatically set to True.

More than one Condition Name may be True at the same time. For instance, if the user enters the letter "U," the condition names Vowel and ValidChar are set to True.

```
01  InputChar    PIC X.
    88 Vowel     VALUE "A","E","I","O","U".
    88 Consonant VALUE "B" THRU "D", "F","G","H"
                       "J" THRU "N", "P" THRU "T"
                       "V" THRU "Z".
    88 Digit     VALUE "0" THRU "9".
    88 LowerCase VALUE "a" THRU "z".
    88 ValidChar VALUE "A" THRU "Z","0" THRU "9".


ACCEPT InputChar
IF ValidChar
   DISPLAY "Input OK."
END-IF
IF LowerCase
   DISPLAY "Lower case letter."
END-IF
IF Vowel
   DISPLAY "Vowel entered."
END-IF
```

The SET Verb

Condition names are usually set to true when their associated data-item contains the value mentioned in their VALUE clause. It is also possible to set a Condition Name to True using the SET verb.

When the SET verb is used to set a Condition Name, it moves the first value (specified after the VALUE clause in the definition) to the associated data-item. Thus, the value of the associated data-item is changed.

It is not possible to set a condition name to False.

The EVALUATE Verb

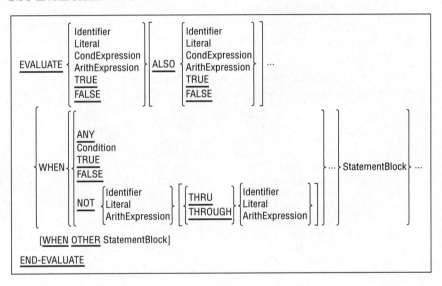

The EVALUATE verb is COBOL's version of the Case construct. The following notes briefly describe how the EVALUATE verb works, but you'll want to examine the syntax diagram in combination with the example given to gain a fuller understanding.

EVALUATE notes

- The items immediately after the word EVALUATE and before the first WHEN are called subjects.

- The items between the WHEN and its imperative statements are called objects.

- The number of subjects must equal the number of objects.

- Only one WHEN branch is chosen per execution of the EVALUATE, and the checking of the WHEN branches is done from top to bottom.

- If none of the WHEN branches can be chosen, and a WHEN OTHER phrase exists, the WHEN OTHER branch is executed.

- If none of the WHEN branches can be chosen, and there is no WHEN OTHER phrase, the EVALUATE simply terminates.

EVALUATE example

A company selling music CDs sells them at a discount when they are more than one month old. The following decision table is used to decide what discount to apply to a CD. Discounts depend on the CD's music category (type) and the number of days since its release (age).

Very broad music categories are used. The categories are:

* Modern (including pop, jazz, etc.)

* Classical

* Folk (including Country and Western)

The letters M, C, and F represent the music categories.

Type	ANY	M	M	M	C	C	C	F	F	F
Age	0–30	31–90	91–270	>270	31–90	91–270	>270	31–90	91–270	>270
% Dcount	0	5	15	50	0	0	10	0	5	10

In COBOL, this type of decision table is easily implemented using the EVALUATE verb. Note the use of Implied Subjects in the AND conditions.

```
EVALUATE Type  ALSO           TRUE
    WHEN   ANY  ALSO Age < 31                MOVE 0  TO Discount
    WHEN   "M"  ALSO Age > 30 AND < 91  MOVE 5  TO Discount
    WHEN   "M"  ALSO Age > 90 AND < 271 MOVE 15 TO Discount
    WHEN   "M"  ALSO Age > 270               MOVE 50 TO Discount
    WHEN   "C"  ALSO Age > 30 AND < 91  MOVE 0  TO Discount
    WHEN   "C"  ALSO Age > 90 AND < 271 MOVE 0  TO Discount
    WHEN   "C"  ALSO Age > 270               MOVE 10 TO Discount
    WHEN   "F"  ALSO Age > 30 AND < 91  MOVE 0  TO Discount
    WHEN   "F"  ALSO Age > 90 AND < 271 MOVE 5  TO Discount
    WHEN   "F"  ALSO Age > 270               MOVE 10 TO Discount
    WHEN OTHER DISPLAY "Error in Evaluate"
END-EVALUATE
```

Sequential Files

Files are repositories of data that reside on backing storage (hard disk or magnetic tape). A file may consist of hundreds of thousands, millions, or even tens of millions of records, and may require gigabytes of storage.

Files of this size cannot be processed by loading the whole file into the computer's memory at once. Instead, files are processed by reading one record into memory at a time. The computer uses the programmer's description of the record (the record template) to set aside sufficient memory to store one instance of the record. The memory allocated for storing a record is usually called a *record buffer*.

File Description

Before a file can be used in a COBOL program an alias must be defined for it, and the record buffer(s) for the file must be declared.

A file alias is defined in the SELECT and ASSIGN clause. The SELECT and ASSIGN clause is an entry in the FILE-CONTROL paragraph of the INPUT-OUTPUT SECTION, in the ENVIRONMENT DIVISION.

The record buffer(s) is described in an FD (File Description) entry, in the FILE SECTION of the DATA DIVISION. The FD entry consists of the letters FD and an internal file name, followed by a record(s) declaration.

If the file only contains one type of record, the record description and operation is the same as that described in the section, "Declaring Data-Items in COBOL."

Files Containing Multiple Record Types

If the file contains more than one type of record, there must be a record description for each record type in the file. Record descriptions always begin with level 01, so a 01 level for each record type in the file must be provided in the file's FD entry.

In the following example, the Transaction file contains three types of record—Insertion, Deletion, and Update—so there are three record descriptions in the file's FD entry. A *type code* is used to distinguish the records from one another.

Multiple record type file description example

```
DATA DIVISION.
FILE SECTION.
FD TransactionFile.
01 InsertionRec.
    02  TransCode          PIC X.
        88 Insertion       VALUE "I".
        88 Deletion        VALUE "D".
        88 Update          VALUE "U".
    02  StudentId          PIC 9(7).
    02  StudentName.
        03 Surname         PIC X(10).
        03 Initials        PIC XX.
    02  DateOfBirth.
        03 YOBirth         PIC 9(4).
        03 MOBirth         PIC 9(2).
        03 DOBirth         PIC 9(2).
        02  CourseCode     PIC X(4).
        02  Gender         PIC X.

01 DeleteRec.
    02  FILLER             PIC X(8).

01 UpdateRec.
    02  FILLER             PIC X(8).
    02  OldCourseCode      PIC X(4).
    02  NewCourseCode      PIC X(4).
```

Comment and buffer schematic

In the previous description of the transaction records, only a single *record buffer* is created for the file and this *record buffer* is only able to store a single record at a time. This means that all the TransactionFile record descriptions map to the same area of storage, and all the identifiers are current/active at the same time.

This explains why FILLER is used in the DeletionRec and UpdateRec. In general, FILLER is used when storage needs to be declared but does not need to be explicitly referenced. Since the TransCode and StudentId of the InsertionRec already identify the first eight characters of the buffer, there is no need for the DeletionRec or UpdateRec to name them explicitly.

The following schematic shows how the three record types map to the record buffer. Although an insertion record is currently in the buffer, it is possible to refer to any of the identifiers declared in any of the record descriptions. For example, the statement:

```
DISPLAY OldCourseCode
```

displays the text "HENN".

It is the programmer's responsibility to discover what type of record has been read into the buffer—that's the purpose of the TypeCode—and then to refer only to the appropriate identifiers. Although it's perfectly possible to refer to OldCourseCode or NewCourseCode when an insertion record is in the buffer, it does not make any sense to do so.

Writing to the Printer

In a business-programming environment, the ability to print reports is an important property for a programming language. COBOL allows programmers to write to the printer, either directly or through an intermediate print file. COBOL treats the printer as a serial file, but uses a special variant of the WRITE verb to control the placement of lines on the page.

In a printed report, there are a number of different types of print line. Some lines, such as headings, contain static information, while other lines are assigned the information at run time.

In a COBOL program, each different type of print line must be described as a record. However, these records cannot be declared in the FILE SECTION. Since all records declared for a particular file in the FILE SECTION share the same area of storage, any static print lines declared there would overwrite each other's data. To prevent just such an occurrence, a COBOL rule states that in the FILE SECTION, the VALUE clause can only be used with Condition Names (i.e., it cannot be used to give an initial value to an item).

To solve this problem the print-line records are declared in the WORKING-STORAGE SECTION, and a record the size of the largest print-line record is declared in the FILE SECTION. A line is printed by moving it from the WORKING-STORAGE SECTION to the record in the FILE SECTION, then writing that record to the printer.

Edited Picture Clauses

There would be little point in being able to write to the printer if the output could not be formatted properly. COBOL allows sophisticated formatting of output through its Edited Picture clauses.

Edited Pictures are PICTURE clauses that format data intended for output to the screen or a printer. To enable the data items to be formatted, COBOL provides additional picture symbols to supplement the basic 9, X, A, V, and S. The additional symbols are referred to as *Edit Symbols*, and PICTURE clauses that include edit symbols are called *Edited Pictures*.

Edited items cannot be used as operands in a computation, but they may be used as the result or destination of a computation. For example, they can be placed to the right of the word GIVING.

COBOL permits two basic types of editing:

1. Insertion Editing, which modifies a value by including additional items and has the following sub-categories:
   - Simple Insertion
   - Special Insertion
   - Fixed Insertion
   - Floating Insertion
2. Suppression and Replacement Editing, which suppresses and replaces leading zeros and has the following sub-categories:
   - Zero suppression and replacement with spaces
   - Zero suppression and replacement with asterisks

Editing symbols

The following editing symbols are used in Edited Pictures.

Edit Symbol	Editing Type
, B 0 /	Simple Insertion
.	Special Insertion
+ - CR DB $	Fixed Insertion
+ - S	Floating Insertion
Z *	Suppression and Replacement

Simple Insertion

Simple Insertion editing consists of specifying the relevant insertion character(s) in the PICTURE string. When a value is moved into the edited item, the insertion characters are inserted into the item at the position specified in the PICTURE.

The comma, the B, the 0, and the slash (/) are the Simple Insertion editing symbols.

Comma. The comma symbol (,) instructs the computer to insert a comma at the character position where the symbol occurs. The comma counts towards the size of the printed item. The comma symbol cannot be the first symbol in the PICTURE string.

If all characters to the left of the comma are zeros and zero-suppression is called for, the comma is replaced by the replacement symbol (asterisk or space).

The other Simple Insertion characters work in the same way.

Space or Blank. A space is inserted where the blank symbol (B) occurs.

Slash and Zero. A slash is inserted where the slash symbol (/) occurs, and a 0 is inserted where the zero symbol (0) occurs.

Simple Insertion examples

Sending Picture	Sending Data	Receiving Picture	Result
PIC 9(6)	123456	PIC 999,999	123,456
PIC 9(6)	000078	PIC 9(3),9(3)	000,078
PIC 9(6)	000078	PIC ZZZ,ZZZ	•••••78
PIC 9(6)	000178	PIC ***,***	****178
PIC 9(6)	002178	PIC ***,***	**2,178
PIC 9(6)	120183	PIC 99B99B99	12•01•83
PIC 9(6)	120183	PIC 99/99/99	12/01/83
PIC 9(6)	001245	PIC 990099	120045

Special Insertion editing

The period (.) is the only Special Insertion symbol. It represents the decimal point. A decimal point is inserted in the character position where the symbol occurs.

When a numeric data-item is moved into an edited data-item containing the decimal point symbol, alignment occurs along the position of the decimal point symbol, with zero-filling and truncation as necessary.

Special Insertion examples

Sending Picture	Sending Data	Receiving Picture	Result
PIC 999V99	12345	PIC 999.99	123.45
PIC 999V99	02345	PIC 999.9	023.4
PIC 999V99	51234	PIC 99.99	12.34
PIC 999	456	PIC 999.99	456.00

Fixed Insertion editing

Fixed Insertion editing inserts the symbol at the beginning or end of the edited item.

The Fixed Insertion editing symbols are the plus (+) and minus (-) signs, CR and DB, and the currency symbol. The default currency symbol is the dollar sign ($), but it may be changed to a different symbol by the CURRENCY SIGN IS clause in the SPECIAL-NAMES paragraph of the CONFIGURATION SECTION, in the ENVIRON-MENT DIVISION. All symbols count toward the size of the printed item.

Plus and minus symbols. The plus and minus symbols must appear in the left-most or right-most character positions of a PICTURE string.

> *Minus*
>> When the sending item is negative, a minus sign is printed, but when the sending item is positive, a space is printed instead.
>>
>> Use a minus sign only if you want to highlight negative values.
>
> *Plus*
>> When the sending item is negative, a minus sign is printed, and if the sending item is positive, a plus sign is printed.
>>
>> Use a plus sign if you always want the sign to be printed.

CR and DB. CR and DB may only appear in the right-most position. Both are **only** printed if the sending item is **negative**. Otherwise, two spaces are printed.

The currency symbol. The currency symbol must be the left-most character. It may be preceded by a plus or minus sign.

Fixed Insertion examples

Sending Picture	Sending Data	Receiving Picture	Result
PIC S999	-123	PIC -999	-123
PIC S999	+123	PIC -999	•123
PIC S9(5)	+12345	PIC +9(5)	+12345
PIC S9(3)	-123	PIC +9(3)	-123
PIC S9(4)	+1234	PIC 9(4)CR	1234••
PIC S9(4)	-1234	PIC 9(4)CR	1234CR
PIC S9(4)	+1234	PIC 9(4)DB	1223••
PIC S9(4)	-1234	PIC 9(4)DB	1234DB
PIC 9(4)	1234	PIC $99999	$01234
PIC 9(4)	0000	PIC $ZZZZZ	$•••••

Floating Insertion editing

Floating Insertion suppresses leading zeros, and *floats* the insertion symbol up against the first non-zero digit.

The plus and minus signs and the currency symbol are used in Floating Insertion. Every floating symbol counts toward the size of the printed item.

Except for the left-most one, each Floating Insertion symbol is a placeholder that may be occupied or replaced by a digit. Accordingly, there will always be *at least one* symbol printed, even though this may be at the cost of truncating the number (see the fourth row in the following example).

Sending Picture	Sending Data	Edited PICTURE	Result
PIC 9(4)	0000	PIC $$,$$9.99	$0.00
PIC 9(4)	0080	PIC $$,$$9.00	$80.00
PIC 9(4)	0128	PIC $$,$$9.99	$128.00
PIC 9(5)	57397	PIC $$,$$9	$7,397
PIC S9(4)	-0005	PIC ++++9	-5
PIC S9(4)	+0080	PIC ++++9	+80
PIC S9(4)	-0080	PIC ----9	-80
PIC S9(5)	+71234	PIC ----9	•1234

Zero Suppression editing

Suppression and Replacement editing is used to remove leading zeros from the value to be edited. The characters Z and * are the suppression symbols.

Using Z in an editing picture instructs the computer to suppress a leading zero in that character position by replacing it with a space.

Using an asterisk instructs the computer to suppress a leading zero in that character position by replacing it with an asterisk.

If all the character positions in a data-item are Z editing symbols and the sending item has a value of zero, then only spaces will be printed.

If a Z or * is used, the picture clause symbol 9 cannot appear to the left of it.

Sequential File Processing Verbs

COBOL sequential files are processed using the OPEN, CLOSE, READ, and WRITE verbs.

The OPEN Verb

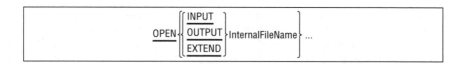

Before a program can access the data in an input file or place data in an output file, the file must be made available to the program by OPENing it.

OPEN notes

- When a file is opened for INPUT or EXTEND, the file must exist or the OPEN will fail.

- When a file is opened for INPUT, the Next Record Pointer is positioned at the beginning of the file.

- When the file is opened for EXTEND, the Next Record Pointer is positioned after the last record in the file. This allows records to be appended to the file.

- When a file is opened for OUTPUT, it is created if it does not exist and is over-written if it already exists.

The CLOSE Verb

```
CLOSE InternalFileName...
```

All open files must be closed before the program ends. Failure to do so may result in data not being written to the file or users being prevented from accessing the file.

The READ Verb

```
READ InternalFileName [NEXT] RECORD
     [INTO Identifier]
         AT END StatementBlock
     END-READ
```

The READ verb copies a record occurrence/instance from the file and places it in the record buffer.

READ notes

- When the READ verb attempts to read a record from the file and encounters the end of file marker, the AT END is triggered and the StatementBlock following the AT END is executed.

- Using the INTO Identifier clause causes the data to be read into the record buffer, then copied from there to the specified Identifier in one operation. When this option is used, there will be two copies of the data. It is the equivalent of a READ followed by a MOVE.

The WRITE Verb

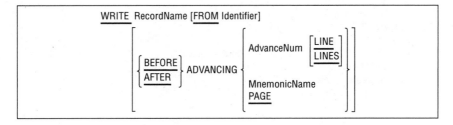

The WRITE verb copies the record it finds in the record buffer to the file.

The ADVANCING clause is used to position the lines on the page when writing to a print file or a printer. The PAGE option writes a form feed to the print file or printer.

WRITE notes

- The ADVANCING clause is used to position the lines on the page when writing to a print file or a printer.

- The PAGE option writes a form feed to the print file or printer.

- MnemonicName refers to a vendor-specific page control command. It is defined in the SPECIAL-NAMES paragraph.

Sequential file example program

```
IDENTIFICATION DIVISION.
PROGRAM-ID.  StudentNumbersReport.
AUTHOR. Michael Coughlan.

*INPUT
* The student record file STUDENTS.DAT. Records in
* this file are sequenced on ascending StudentId.
*OUTPUT
* Prints the number of student records in the file
* and the number of records for males and females.

ENVIRONMENT DIVISION.
INPUT-OUTPUT SECTION.
FILE-CONTROL.
     SELECT StudentFile ASSIGN TO "STUDENTS.DAT"
          ORGANIZATION IS LINE SEQUENTIAL.
     SELECT ReportFile ASSIGN TO "STUDENTS.RPT"
          ORGANIZATION IS LINE SEQUENTIAL.

DATA DIVISION.
FILE SECTION.
* Note: Since we are only interested in the Gender
* field, StudentDetails could be described as;
*01 StudentDetails.
*    88  EndOfStudentFile VALUE HIGH-VALUES.
*    02  FILLER             PIC X(32).
*    02  Gender             PIC X.
*        88 Male            VALUE "M", "m".
*        88 Female          VALUE "F", "f".

FD  StudentFile.
01  StudentDetails.
    88  EndOfStudentFile VALUE HIGH-VALUES.
    02  StudentId          PIC 9(7).
    02  StudentName.
        03 Surname         PIC X(10).
        03 Initials        PIC XX.
    02  DateOfBirth.
        03 YOBirth         PIC 9(4).
        03 MOBirth         PIC 9(2).
        03 DOBirth         PIC 9(2).
    02  CourseCode         PIC X(4).
```

```
      02  Gender            PIC X.
          88 Male           VALUE "M", "m".
          88 Female         VALUE "F", "f".


FD  ReportFile.
01  PrintLine             PIC X(40).


WORKING-STORAGE SECTION.
01  HeadingLine           PIC X(21)
        VALUE " Record Count Report".

01  StudentTotalLine.
    02  FILLER            PIC X(17)
          VALUE "Total Students = ".
    02  PrnStudentCount   PIC Z,ZZ9.

01  MaleTotalLine.
    02  FILLER            PIC X(17)
          VALUE "Total Males    = ".
    02  PrnMaleCount      PIC Z,ZZ9.

01  FemaleTotalLine.
    02  FILLER            PIC X(17)
          VALUE "Total Females  = ".
    02  PrnFemaleCount    PIC Z,ZZ9.

01  WorkTotals.
    02  StudentCount      PIC 9(4) VALUE ZERO.
    02  MaleCount         PIC 9(4) VALUE ZERO.
    02  FemaleCount       PIC 9(4) VALUE ZERO.

PROCEDURE DIVISION.
Begin.
    OPEN INPUT StudentFile
    OPEN OUTPUT ReportFile

    READ StudentFile
       AT END SET EndOfStudentFile TO TRUE
    END-READ
    PERFORM UNTIL EndOfStudentFile
       IF Male ADD 1 TO MaleCount,    StudentCount
        ELSE   ADD 1 TO FemaleCount, StudentCount
       END-IF
       READ StudentFile
          AT END SET EndOfStudentFile TO TRUE
       END-READ
    END-PERFORM

    PERFORM PrintReportLines

    CLOSE StudentFile, ReportFile
    STOP RUN.
```

```
PrintReportLines.
    MOVE StudentCount  TO PrnStudentCount
    MOVE MaleCount     TO PrnMaleCount
    MOVE FemaleCount   TO PrnFemaleCount

    WRITE PrintLine FROM HeadingLine
        AFTER ADVANCING PAGE
    WRITE PrintLine FROM StudentTotalLine
        AFTER ADVANCING 2 LINES
    WRITE PrintLine FROM MaleTotalLine
        AFTER ADVANCING 2 LINES
    WRITE PrintLine FROM FemaleTotalLine
        AFTER ADVANCING 2 LINES.
```

Sorting Files

The SORT verb is usually used to sort sequential files. Some programmers claim that the SORT verb is unnecessary, since a vendor-provided or *bought in* sort feature can be used. However, the SORT verb enhances the portability of COBOL programs. When programs that use the SORT verb have to be moved to a different computer system, they can make the transition without requiring any changes to the SORT. This is rarely the case when programs rely on a vendor-supplied or *bought in* sort feature.

How the SORT Works

As shown in the following diagram, the SORT takes records from the input file (SalesFile), sorts them in the temporary file (WorkFile) on the field(s) and sequence specified in the KEY phrase, and returns the sorted records in the output file (SortedSalesFile).

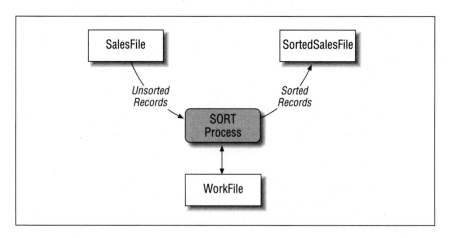

```
SORT WorkFile ON ASCENDING KEY WSalespsnNum
        USING SalesFile
        GIVING SortedSalesFile.
```

The Sort Syntax

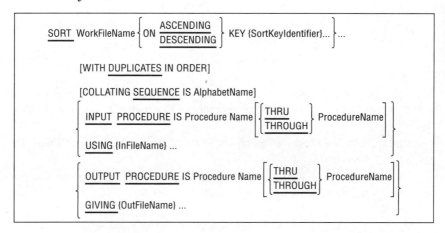

Example:

```
SORT WorkFile ON ASCENDING KEY WProvinceCode
              DESCENDING KEY WShopCode, WSalespsnCode
     USING UnsortedSales
     GIVING SortedSales.
```

SORT notes

- The WorkFileName identifies a temporary work file that the SORT process uses for sorting. It is defined in the FILE SECTION using an SD (Stream/Sort Description) entry. Even though WorkFileName is a temporary file, it must still have a SELECT and ASSIGN clause.

- Each SortKeyIdentifier identifies a field in the record of the WorkFile. This is the field or fields upon which the file will be sequenced.

- When more than one SortKeyIdentifier is specified, the keys decrease in significance from left to right (in other words, the left-most key is most significant, while the right-most is least significant).

- InFileName and OutFileName are the names of the input and output files, respectively. SORT automatically opens these files. When the SORT verb executes, they must *not* be open already.

- If the DUPLICATES clause is used, the final order of the duplicated keys is the same as that in which they were found.

- If no DUPLICATES clause is used, the return order is undefined.

- AlphabetName is an alphabet-name defined in the SPECIAL-NAMES paragraph of the ENVIRONMENT DIVISION. This clause is used to select the character set the SORT verb uses for collating the records in the file. The character set may be ASCII (8 or 7 bit), EBCDIC, or user-defined.

- The INPUT PROCEDURE is a block of code that supplies records to the sort process one at a time, by means of the RELEASE verb.

- The OUTPUT PROCEDURE is a block of code that gets records from the sort process one at a time, by means of the RETURN verb.

SORT rules

1. The SORT can be used anywhere in the PROCEDURE DIVISION except in an INPUT or OUTPUT PROCEDURE or another SORT or a MERGE or in the DECLARATIVES SECTION.

2. The records described for the Input file (USING) must be able to fit into the records described for the WorkFileName.

3. The records described for the WorkFileName must be able to fit into the records described for the output file (GIVING).

4. The SortKeyIdentifer description cannot contain an OCCURS clause (i.e., it can't be a table or array) nor can it be subordinate to an entry that does.

How the INPUT PROCEDURE Works

As the following diagram shows, the INPUT PROCEDURE sits between the SORT process and the input file. It uses the RELEASE verb to supply records to the SORT process, one at a time.

Note that since the SORT is disconnected from the input file, records the INPUT PROCEDURE sends to the SORT process can originate from anywhere (such as a table or the user console or an input file).

When an input file is used, the INPUT PROCEDURE can select which records to send to the SORT, and can even alter the structure of the records before they are sent.

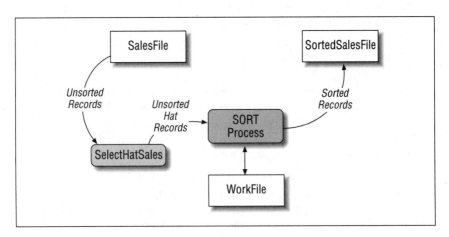

```
SORT WorkFile ON ASCENDING KEY WSalespsnNum
    INPUT PROCEDURE IS SelectHatSales
    GIVING SortedSalesFile.
```

INPUT PROCEDURE rules

1. The INPUT PROCEDURE must contain at least one RELEASE statement to transfer the records to the SORT File.

2. The old COBOL rules for the SORT verb stated that the INPUT and OUTPUT procedures had to be self-contained sections of code, and could not be entered from elsewhere in the program.

3. In COBOL '85, the procedures used in the INPUT and OUTPUT procedures can be any contiguous group of paragraphs or sections. The only restriction is that the range of paragraphs or sections used in the INPUT and OUTPUT procedures must not overlap.

4. If there is a USING phrase, there cannot be an INPUT PROCEDURE, and the input file must not be open when the SORT executes.

INPUT PROCEDURE example

The following program fragment prints a report showing the number of hats sold by each salesperson. The report is to be printed in ascending salesperson-number sequence, but the sales file, which contains the sales data, is currently unsorted. The SORT can be used to sort the file into salesperson-number sequence. However, since the report will only show hat sales, there is no point in sorting the whole sales file. An INPUT PROCEDURE is used to select only the hat-sales records.

```
IDENTIFICATION DIVISION.
PROGRAM-ID. InputProcExample.
AUTHOR. Michael Coughlan.
ENVIRONMENT DIVISION.
 INPUT-OUTPUT SECTION.
 FILE-CONTROL.
 SELECT WorkFile ASSIGN TO "WORK.TMP".
     SELECT SalesFile ASSIGN TO "SALES.DAT".
     SELECT SortedSalesFile ASSIGN TO "SORTED.DAT".

DATA DIVISION.
FILE SECTION.
FD  SalesFile.
01  SalesRec.
    88 EndOfSales          VALUE HIGH-VALUES.
    02 FILLER              PIC 9(5).
    02 FILLER              PIC X.
       88  HatRecord       VALUE "H".
    02 FILLER              PIC X(4).

SD  WorkFile.
01  WorkRec.
    02 WSalespsnNum         PIC 9(5).
    02 FILLER               PIC X(5).

FD  SortedSalesFile.
01  SortedSalesRec.
    02 SalespsnNum          PIC 9(5).
    02 ItemType             PIC X.
    02 QtySold              PIC 9(4).
```

```
PROCEDURE DIVISION.
Begin.
    SORT WorkFile ON ASCENDING KEY WSalespsnNum
          INPUT PROCEDURE IS SelectHatSales
          GIVING SortedSalesFile

    PERFORM PrintHatSalesReport

    STOP RUN.

SelectHatSales.
    OPEN INPUT SalesFile
    READ SalesFile
      AT END SET EndOfSales TO TRUE
    END-READ
    PERFORM UNTIL EndOfSales
      IF HatRecord
         RELEASE WorkRec FROM SalesRec
      END-IF
      READ SalesFile
         AT END SET EndOfSales TO TRUE
      END-READ
    END-PERFORM
    CLOSE SalesFile.

PrintHatSalesReport.
```

* The rest of program goes here.

How the OUTPUT PROCEDURE *Works*

As the following diagram shows, the OUTPUT PROCEDURE sits between the output file and the SORT. It uses the RETURN verb to retrieve records from the SORT process, one at a time.

Since the SORT process is disconnected from the output file, the OUTPUT PROCEDURE can do what it likes with the records it gets from SORT. For instance, it could put them into an array, display them on the screen, or send them to an output file.

When the OUTPUT PROCEDURE sends records to an output file, it can control which records and what type of records appear in the file.

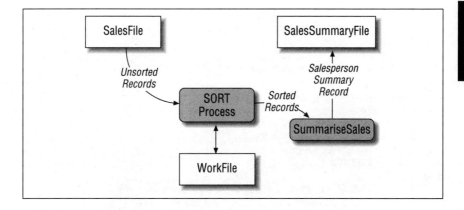

```
SORT WorkFile ON ASCENDING KEY WSalespsnNum
         USING SalesFile
         OUTPUT PROCEDURE IS SummarizeSales
```

OUTPUT PROCEDURE rules

1. The OUTPUT PROCEDURE must contain at least one RETURN statement to get the records from the SortFile.

2. If there is a GIVING phrase, there cannot be an OUTPUT PROCEDURE.

3. The output file must not be open when the SORT executes.

OUTPUT PROCEDURE example

The following example creates a sorted SalesSummaryFile from an unsorted Sales-File. The SalesSummaryFile is a sequential file, sorted on an ascending salesperson-number. Each record in the summary file is the sum of all the items sold by a particular salesperson. An OUTPUT PROCEDURE is used, because until the records have been sorted into salesperson-number order, the salesperson records cannot be summarized.

```
IDENTIFICATION DIVISION.
PROGRAM-ID. OutputProcExample.
AUTHOR. Michael Coughlan.
ENVIRONMENT DIVISION.
INPUT-OUTPUT SECTION.
FILE-CONTROL
    SELECT WorkFile ASSIGN TO "WORK.TMP".
    SELECT SalesFile ASSIGN TO "SALES.DAT".
    SELECT SortedSalesFile ASSIGN TO "SUMMARY.DAT".

DATA DIVISION.
FILE SECTION.

FD  SalesFile.
01  SalesRec          PIC X(10).
```

```
SD   WorkFile.
01   WorkRec.
     88 EndOfWorkFile      VALUE HIGH-VALUES.
     02 WSalespsnNum       PIC 9(5).
     02 FILLER             PIC X.
     02 WQtySold           PIC X(4).

FD   SalesSummaryFile.
01   SummaryRec.
     02 SalespsnNum        PIC 9(5).
     02 TotalQtySold       PIC 9(6).

PROCEDURE DIVISION.
Begin.
     SORT WorkFile ON ASCENDING KEY WSalespsnNum
          USING SalesFile
          OUTPUT PROCEDURE IS SummarizeSales
     STOP RUN.

SummariseSales.
     OPEN OUTPUT SalesSummaryFile
     RETURN WorkFile
        AT END SET EndOfWorkFile TO TRUE
     END-RETURN
     PERFORM UNTIL EndOfWorkFile
       MOVE WSalespsnNum TO SalespsnNum
       MOVE ZEROS TO TotalQtySold
       PERFORM UNTIL WSalespsnNum NOT = SalespsnNum
                   OR EndOfWorkFile
         ADD WQtySold TO TotalQtySold
         RETURN WorkFile
            AT END SET EndOfWorkFile TO TRUE
         END-RETURN
       END-PERFORM
       WRITE SummaryRec
     END-PERFORM
     CLOSE SalesSummaryFile.
```

Release and Return Syntax

The RELEASE is a special verb used in an INPUT PROCEDURE to send records to the SORT work file. It is the equivalent of a Write command.

RELEASE SDRecordName [FROM Identifier]

The RETURN verb is used in an OUTPUT PROCEDURE to get records from the SORT work file. It is the equivalent of a READ command, right down to the AT END clause.

```
        RETURN  SDFileName RECORD  [INTO Identifier]
                AT END StatementBlock
        END - RETURN
```

The MERGE Verb

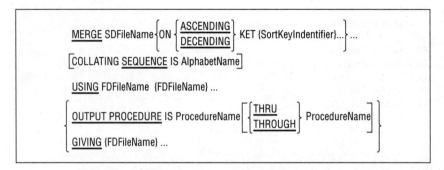

The MERGE verb takes two or more identically sequenced files and combines them according to the key values specified to produce a combined file. The combined file is then sent to an output file or OUTPUT PROCEDURE.

Example

```
MERGE WorkFile ON ASCENDING KEY StudentId
               USING InsertionsFile,  StudentFile
               GIVING NewStudentFile.
```

MERGE notes

* The results of the MERGE verb are predictable only when the records in the input files are ordered as described in the KEY clause associated with the MERGE statement.

* For instance, if the MERGE statement has an ON DESCENDING KEY StudentId clause, then the input files must be ordered on descending StudentId.

* As with the SORT, the WorkFileName is the name of a temporary file, with an SD entry in the FILE SECTION, and a SELECT and ASSIGN entry in the INPUT-OUTPUT SECTION.

MERGE example

```
IDENTIFICATION DIVISION.
PROGRAM-ID. MergeExample.
AUTHOR. Michael Coughlan.
ENVIRONMENT DIVISION.
INPUT-OUTPUT SECTION.
FILE-CONTROL.
    SELECT StudentFile    ASSIGN TO "STUDENTS.DAT".
    SELECT InsertionsFile ASSIGN TO "TRANSINS.DAT".
```

```
      SELECT NewStudentFile ASSIGN TO "STUDENTS.NEW".
      SELECT WorkFile      ASSIGN TO "WORK.TMP".

DATA DIVISION.
FILE SECTION.
FD   StudentFile.
01   StudentRec              PIC X(32).

FD   InsertionsFile.
01   InsertionRec            PIC X(32).

FD   NewStudentFile.
01   NewStudentRec           PIC X(32).

SD   WorkFile.
01   WorkRec.
     02 WStudentId           PIC 9(7).
     02 FILLER               PIC X(25).

PROCEDURE DIVISION.
Begin.
     MERGE WorkFile ON ASCENDING KEY WStudentId
         USING InsertionsFile,  StudentFile
         GIVING NewStudentFile
     STOP RUN.
```

Direct Access Files

Access to records in sequential files is serial. To reach a particular record, all the preceding records must be read. Direct access files, on the other hand, allow direct access to a particular record in the file via a key. COBOL supports two kinds of direct access file organizations: relative and indexed.

The type of file organization used is specified in an extension to the SELECT and ASSIGN clause. The ORGANIZATION phrase allows the file organization to be specified, but since it is possible to process direct access files sequentially, an entry specifying the mode of access is also required.

Direct Access SELECT and ASSIGN

The OPTIONAL phrase must be specified for files opened for INPUT, I-O, or EXTEND that need not be present when the program runs.

The ACCESS MODE of a direct access file refers to the way the file is to be used. If an ACCESS MODE of SEQUENTIAL is specified, it will only be possible to process the records sequentially. If RANDOM is specified, only direct access to the file will be allowed. If DYNAMIC is specified, the file may be processed both directly and sequentially.

The FILE STATUS clause identifies a two-character area of storage that holds the result of every I-O operation for the file. The FILE STATUS data item is declared as PIC X(2) in the WORKING-STORAGE SECTION. Whenever an I-O operation is performed, a value returned to FileStatus will indicate whether or not the operation was successful.

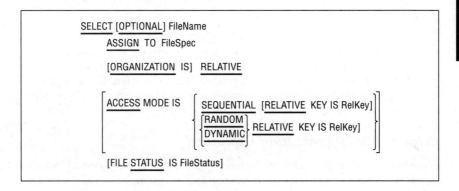
Relative Files – *SELECT and ASSIGN*

```
SELECT [OPTIONAL] FileName

    ASSIGN  TO FileSpec

    [ORGANIZATION  IS]  RELATIVE

    ┌                    ┌                                              ┐┐
    │  ACCESS MODE IS    │ SEQUENTIAL  [RELATIVE  KEY IS RelKey]        ││
    │                    │ ┌RANDOM ┐                                    ││
    │                    │ ┤       ├ RELATIVE  KEY IS RelKey]           ││
    │                    │ └DYNAMIC┘                                    ││
    │                    └                                              ┘│
    └                                                                    ┘

    [FILE STATUS  IS FileStatus]
```

Relative Files – *SELECT and ASSIGN notes*

There can be only one key in a Relative File. The RelKey must be a numeric data item and *must not be* part of the file's record description, although it may be part of another file's record description. It is normally described in the WORKING-STORAGE SECTION.

Indexed files – *SELECT and ASSIGN*

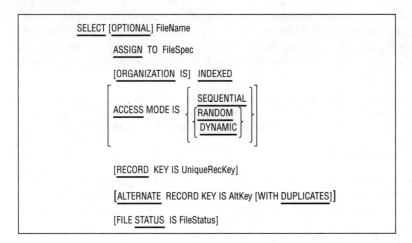

```
SELECT [OPTIONAL] FileName

    ASSIGN  TO  FileSpec

    [ORGANIZATION  IS]  INDEXED

    ┌                    ┌              ┐┐
    │                    │ SEQUENTIAL   ││
    │  ACCESS MODE IS    │ ┌RANDOM ┐    ││
    │                    │ ┤       ├    ││
    │                    │ └DYNAMIC┘    ││
    └                    └              ┘┘

    [RECORD  KEY IS UniqueRecKey]

    [ALTERNATE  RECORD KEY IS AltKey [WITH DUPLICATES]]

    [FILE STATUS  IS FileStatus]
```

Indexed files – *SELECT and ASSIGN notes*

- Every indexed file must have a primary key, and that key must be a field in the record description.

- The primary key must be unique for each record and must be a numeric or alphanumeric data-item.

- In addition to the primary key, up to 254 alternate keys may be defined for the file. Just as with the primary key, these alternate keys must be fields in the file's record description.

- Each alternate key may be unique or may have duplicate values.

- The indexed organization allows sequential access on any of the keys. For instance, if an indexed file had StudentId, StudentName, and CourseCode as its keys, it would be possible to process the file sequentially as if it were ordered in StudentId sequence, or StudentName sequence, or CourseCode sequence.

Relative File Organization Explained

Records in relative files are organized in ascending Relative Record Number sequence. A relative file may be visualized as a one-dimension table stored on disk. The Relative Record Number may be thought of as an index to the table.

Relative files support sequential access by allowing the active records to be read one after another.

Indexed File Organization Explained

Records in an indexed file are sequenced by ascending primary key. The file system builds an index for these data records. When direct access is required, the file system uses this index to find, read, insert, update, or delete the required record.

For each alternate key specified in an indexed file, an alternate index is built. However, entries in the alternate index do not point directly to the actual data records. Instead, they point to *base records*, which contain only the alternate key value and a pointer to the actual data record. These *base records* are organized in ascending alternate key order.

In addition to offering direct access to records on the primary key or on any of the 254 alternate keys, indexed files may be processed sequentially. When processed sequentially, the records may be read in ascending order on any of the keys.

The Key Of Reference

When an indexed file has an ACCESS MODE of SEQUENTIAL, the file is always processed in ascending primary key order. If an indexed file has an ACCESS MODE of DYNAMIC and is processed sequentially, the file system must be told which of the keys to use as the basis for the processing.

To tell the file system which key to use, the programmer must establish that key as the Key Of Reference. A key is established as the Key Of Reference by using it in a START or a direct READ.

Direct Access—File Processing Verbs

When any of these verbs are used for direct access, the INVALID KEY clause must be used unless declaratives have been specified.

When the INVALID KEY clause is specified, any I-O error, such as attempting to read a record that does not exist or to write a record that already exists, will activate the clause and cause the statement block following it to be executed.

The OPEN Verb

For direct access verbs, the OPEN syntax includes the I-O option.

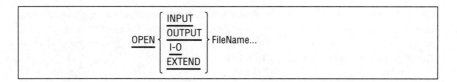

OPEN notes

- If the file is opened for input, then only READ and START will be allowed.

- If the file is opened for OUTPUT, then only WRITE will be allowed.

- If the file is opened for I-O, then READ, WRITE, START, REWRITE, and DELETE will be allowed.

The READ Verb

```
READ FileName RECORD [INTO DestItem]

     [KEY IS  KeyName]

     [ INVALID KEY IS  KEY StatementBlock]

[END - READ]
```

This format is used to access a file directly. The file must specify an ACCESS MODE of DYNAMIC or RANDOM and must be opened for I-O or INPUT.

After the READ, the next record pointer will point to the next record in the file.

READ - Relative specific notes

- When the READ is executed, the record with the Relative Record Number equal to the present value of the relative key will be read into the record buffer.

READ - Indexed specific notes

- When the READ is executed, the record with the key value equal to the present value of the key specified in KeyName will be read. The key may be the primary key or one of the alternate keys. If the KEY IS clause is omitted, the primary key will be used.

- When the READ is executed, the key mentioned in the KEY IS phrase will be established as the Key Of Reference. If there is no KEY IS phrase, the primary key will be established as the Key Of Reference.

- If duplicates are allowed, only the first in a group of duplicate records can be read directly. The rest of the duplicate records must be read sequentially using the READ NEXT.

- The KEY IS phrase can only be used with indexed files. It is used because an indexed file may have more than one key.

Reading a direct access file sequentially

When a direct-access file has an ACCESS MODE of SEQUENTIAL, only sequential access is allowed and the format specified for reading sequential files is used. When the ACCESS MODE is DYNAMIC, the READ NEXT format shown here is used. The file must be opened for INPUT or I-O.

```
READ FileName NEXT RECORD [INTO DestItem]

[ AT END StatementBlock]

[END - READ]
```

The READ NEXT reads the record pointed to by the next record pointer. This is the current record if positioned by the START, and the next record if positioned by a direct READ.

The AT END statement is activated when the end of the file has been reached.

When used with indexed files, this format is complicated by the presence of a number of keys and their associated indexes. When the file is read sequentially, it is read in ascending sequence on one of these keys. Whichever key has been established as the Key Of Reference is the key used as the basis for reading the file.

The WRITE Verb

```
WRITE RecName [FROM SourceItem]

[INVALID KEY StatementBlock]

[END -WRITE]
```

The ordinary WRITE format must be used for sequential access to indexed or relative files.

To write directly to a relative file, the record must be moved to the record buffer, the Relative Record Number must be moved to the key, and then the WRITE verb must be executed.

To write directly to an indexed file, the record must be moved to the record buffer, and then the WRITE must be executed.

The REWRITE Verb

REWRITE RecName [FROM SourceItem]

[INVALID KEY StatementBlock]

[END – REWRITE]

The REWRITE verb is used to update a record in situ. The record is updated by overwriting it with new values. To use REWRITE, the file must be opened for I-O.

The normal way to use the REWRITE verb is to READ the subject record into the record buffer, make the required changes to it, and then REWRITE the record to the file.

For indexed files, the REWRITE cannot change the value of the primary key, but it can change the value of any of the alternate keys.

The DELETE Verb

DELETE FileName RECORD

[INVALID KEY StatementBlock]

[END - DELETE]

To use the DELETE verb with relative files, the Relative Record Number of the record to be deleted is moved to the Relative Key data-item and then DELETE is executed.

To use the DELETE verb with indexed files, the key value of the record to be deleted is moved to the primary key data-item and then DELETE is executed.

The file must be opened for I-O in both cases.

When the ACCESS MODE is SEQUENTIAL, a READ statement must access the record to be deleted.

When the ACCESS MODE is RANDOM or DYNAMIC, the record to be deleted is identified by the file's relative key (relative files) or primary key (indexed files).

The START Verb

The START verb is used to position the next record pointer and, in the case of indexed files, to establish the Key Of Reference. It does not change the contents of the record buffer in any way.

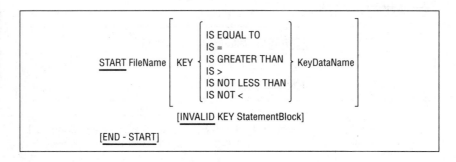

START verb notes

- The file must be opened for INPUT or I-O when START is executed.

- KeyDataName is the Relative Key in the case of relative files, and the primary key or any of the alternate keys in the case of indexed files. It is the key of comparison.

- Before the START is executed, some value must be moved to the KeyDataName. When the START executes, the filesystem compares the key values in the file against the value in the KeyDataName until the condition is satisfied or until it is established that the condition cannot be satisfied.

- If the condition is satisfied, the Next Record Pointer is set to the first record in the file whose key satisfied the condition. If the file is an indexed file, then the START also establishes the key used for comparison as the Key Of Reference.

- If no record satisfies the condition, the INVALID KEY clause is activated.

Writing to a Relative File—Example Program

```
IDENTIFICATION DIVISION.
PROGRAM-ID.  CreateRelativeFromSeq.
ENVIRONMENT DIVISION.
INPUT-OUTPUT SECTION.
FILE-CONTROL.
    SELECT SupplierFile ASSIGN TO "SUPP.DAT"
        ORGANIZATION IS RELATIVE
        ACCESS MODE IS RANDOM
        RELATIVE KEY IS SupplierKey
        FILE STATUS IS SupplierStatus.
    SELECT SupplierFileSeq ASSIGN TO "INSUPP.DAT".

DATA DIVISION.
FILE SECTION.
FD  SupplierFile.
01  SupplierRecord.
    02 SupplierCode            PIC 99.
    02 SupplierName            PIC X(20).
    02 SupplierAddress         PIC X(60).
```

```
FD   SupplierFileSeq.
01   SupplierRecordSeq.
     88 EndOfFile    VALUE HIGH-VALUES.
     02 SupplierCodeSeq        PIC 99.
     02 SupplierNameSeq        PIC X(20).
     02 SupplierAddressSeq     PIC X(60).

WORKING-STORAGE SECTION.
01   SupplierStatus           PIC X(2).
01   SupplierKey              PIC 99.

PROCEDURE DIVISION.
Begin.
     OPEN OUTPUT SupplierFile
     OPEN INPUT SupplierFileSeq
     READ SupplierFileSeq
       AT END SET EndOfFile TO TRUE
     END-READ
     PERFORM UNTIL EndOfFile
       MOVE SupplierCodeSeq TO SupplierKey
       MOVE SupplierRecordSeq TO SupplierRecord
       WRITE SupplierRecord
          INVALID KEY
          DISPLAY "SUPP STATUS :-", SupplierStatus
       END-WRITE
       READ SupplierFileSeq
          AT END SET EndOfFile TO TRUE
       END-READ
     END-PERFORM
     CLOSE  SupplierFile, SupplierFileSeg
     STOP RUN.
```

Reading a Relative File—Example Program

```
IDENTIFICATION DIVISION.
PROGRAM-ID.  ReadRelative.
* Reads a Relative file directly or in sequence
ENVIRONMENT DIVISION.
INPUT-OUTPUT SECTION.
FILE-CONTROL.
SELECT SupplierFile ASSIGN TO "SUPP.DAT"
       ORGANIZATION IS RELATIVE
       ACCESS MODE IS DYNAMIC
       RELATIVE KEY IS SupplierKey
       FILE STATUS IS SupplierStatus.

DATA DIVISION.
FILE SECTION.
FD SupplierFile.
01   SupplierRecord.
     88 EndOfFile  VALUE HIGH-VALUES.
     02 SupplierCode        PIC 99.
     02 SupplierName        PIC X(20).
     02 SupplierAddress     PIC X(60).
```

```
WORKING-STORAGE SECTION.
01  SupplierStatus          PIC X(2).
    88 RecordFound          VALUE "00".

01  SupplierKey             PIC 99.

01  PrnSupplierRecord.
    02 PrnSupplierCode      PIC BB99.
    02 PrnSupplierName      PIC BBX(20).
    02 PrnSupplierAddress   PIC BBX(50).

01  ReadType                PIC 9.
    88 DirectRead           VALUE 1.
    88 SequentialRead       VALUE 2.

PROCEDURE DIVISION.
BEGIN.
    OPEN INPUT SupplierFile.
    DISPLAY "Enter Read type (Direct=1, Seq=2)-> "
                              WITH NO ADVANCING.
    ACCEPT ReadType.
    IF DirectRead
       DISPLAY "Enter supplier key (2 digits)-> "
                              WITH NO ADVANCING
       ACCEPT SupplierKey
       READ SupplierFile
         INVALID KEY
             DISPLAY "SUPP STATUS :-", SupplierStatus
       END-READ
       PERFORM DisplayRecord
    END-IF
    IF SequentialRead
        READ SupplierFile NEXT RECORD
            AT END SET EndOfFile TO TRUE
        END-READ
        PERFORM UNTIL EndOfFile
            PERFORM DisplayRecord
            READ SupplierFile NEXT RECORD
                AT END SET EndOfFile TO TRUE
            END-READ
        END-PERFORM
    END-IF
    CLOSE  SupplierFile
    STOP RUN.

DisplayRecord.
    IF RecordFound
        MOVE SupplierCode TO PrnSupplierCode
        MOVE SupplierName TO PrnSupplierName
        MOVE SupplierAddress TO PrnSupplierAddress
        DISPLAY PrnSupplierRecord
    END-IF.
```

Sequential Read on an Indexed File—Example Program

```
IDENTIFICATION DIVISION.
PROGRAM-ID.  ReadingIndexedFile.
* Reads an indexed file sequentially
* on the primary key or the alternate key
ENVIRONMENT DIVISION.
INPUT-OUTPUT SECTION.
FILE-CONTROL.
    SELECT VideoFile ASSIGN TO "VIDEO.DAT"
           ORGANIZATION IS INDEXED
           ACCESS MODE IS DYNAMIC
           RECORD KEY IS VideoCode
           ALTERNATE RECORD KEY IS VideoTitle
               WITH DUPLICATES
           FILE STATUS IS VideoStatus.


DATA DIVISION.
FILE SECTION.
FD  VideoFile
01  VideoRecord.
    88 EndOfFile VALUE HIGH-VALUE.
    02 VideoCode            PIC 9(5).
    02 VideoTitle           PIC X(40).
    02 SupplierCode         PIC 99.

WORKING-STORAGE SECTION.
01  VideoStatus            PIC X(2).
01  RequiredSequence       PIC 9.
    88 VideoCodeSequence    VALUE 1.
    88 VideoTitleSequence   VALUE 2.
01  PrnVideoRecord.
    02 PrnVideoCode         PIC 9(5).
    02 PrnVideoTitle        PIC BBBBX(40).
    02 PrnSupplierCode      PIC BBBB99.

PROCEDURE DIVISION.
Begin.
    OPEN INPUT VideoFile.

    DISPLAY "Enter key : 1=VideoCode, 2=VideoTitle ->"
       WITH NO ADVANCING.
    ACCEPT RequiredSequence.

    IF VideoTitleSequence
      MOVE SPACES TO VideoTitle
      START VideoFile KEY IS GREATER THAN VideoTitle
         INVALID KEY
             DISPLAY "VIDEO STATUS :- ", VideoStatus
      END-START
    END-IF
```

```
    READ VideoFile NEXT RECORD
      AT END SET EndOfFile TO TRUE
    END-READ.
    PERFORM UNTIL EndOfFile
      MOVE VideoCode TO PrnVideoCode
      MOVE VideoTitle TO PrnVideoTitle
      MOVE SupplierCode TO PrnSupplierCode
      DISPLAY  PrnVideoRecord
      READ VideoFile NEXT RECORD
          AT END SET EndOfFile TO TRUE
      END-READ
    END-PERFORM.

    CLOSE VideoFile.
    STOP RUN.
```

Direct Read on an Indexed File—Example Program

```
IDENTIFICATION DIVISION.
PROGRAM-ID.   ReadingIndexedFile.
* Read the indexed file directly using any key
ENVIRONMENT DIVISION.
INPUT-OUTPUT SECTION.
FILE-CONTROL.
    SELECT VideoFile ASSIGN TO "VIDEO.DAT"
        ORGANIZATION IS INDEXED
        ACCESS MODE IS DYNAMIC
        RECORD KEY IS VideoCode
        ALTERNATE RECORD KEY IS VideoTitle
               WITH DUPLICATES
        FILE STATUS IS VideoStatus.

DATA DIVISION.
FILE SECTION.
FD   VideoFile.
01   VideoRecord.
     02 VideoCode          PIC 9(5).
     02 VideoTitle         PIC X(40).
     02 SupplierCode       PIC 99.

WORKING-STORAGE SECTION.
01   VideoStatus           PIC X(2).
     88  RecordFound       VALUE "00".
01   RequiredKey           PIC 9.
     88 VideoCodeKey       VALUE 1.
     88 VideoTitleKey      VALUE 2.
01   PrnVideoRecord.
     02 PrnVideoCode       PIC 9(5).
     02 PrnVideoTitle      PIC BBBBX(40).
     02 PrnSupplierCode    PIC BBBB99.

PROCEDURE DIVISION.
Begin.
    OPEN INPUT VideoFile.
```

```
DISPLAY "Chose key Code = 1, Title = 2 ->  "
                 WITH NO ADVANCING.
ACCEPT RequiredKey.
IF VideoCodeKey
  DISPLAY "Enter Video Code (5 digits) -> "
                         WITH NO ADVANCING
  ACCEPT VideoCode
  READ VideoFile
     KEY IS VideoCode
     INVALID KEY
        DISPLAY "VIDEO STATUS :- ", VideoStatus
  END-READ
END-IF
IF VideoTitleKey
  DISPLAY "Enter Video Title (40 chars) -> "
                         WITH NO ADVANCING
  ACCEPT VideoTitle
  READ VideoFile
     KEY IS VideoTitle
     INVALID KEY
        DISPLAY "VIDEO STATUS :- ", VideoStatus
  END-READ
END-IF
IF RecordFound
  MOVE VideoCode TO PrnVideoCode
  MOVE VideoTitle TO PrnVideoTitle
  MOVE SupplierCode TO PrnSupplierCode
  DISPLAY  PrnVideoRecord
END-IF.
CLOSE VideoFile.
STOP RUN.
```

Tables/Arrays

Most programming languages use the term *array* to describe repeated, or multiple-occurrence, data-items. COBOL uses the term *table*.

A table may be defined as a contiguous sequence of memory locations called elements, which all have the same name and which are uniquely identified by that name and by their position in the sequence. The position index is called a *subscript*, and the individual components of the table are referred to as *elements*.

COBOL tables have the following attributes:

- A single name is used to identify all the elements

- Individual elements can be identified using an index called a *subscript*

- All elements have the same structure

- In COBOL, table elements always start at 1 and go on to the maximum size of the table

- The required element is indicated by using the element name followed by the subscript in brackets

Examples

```
MOVE 2 TO StateNum
MOVE 10 TO StateTax(5)
MOVE 55 TO StateTax(StateNum)
MOVE 65 TO StateTax(StateNum + 2)
```

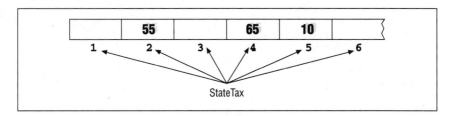

Rules for subscripts

1. Each subscript must be a positive integer, a data name whose value is a positive integer, or a simple expression that evaluates to a positive integer.

2. The value of the subscript must be between 1 and the number of elements in the table, inclusive.

3. When more than one subscript is used, they must be separated by commas.

4. One subscript must be specified for each dimension of the table.

5. Subscripts must be enclosed in parentheses/brackets.

Declaring Tables

Tables are declared by defining the structure of the element in terms of type and size, then noting how many times the element occurs. The number of times an element occurs is specified by using an extension to the PICTURE clause called the OCCURS clause.

In the following example, the element StateTax is defined as having ten digits before the decimal point and two after. The OCCURS clause indicates that there are 50 StateTax elements in the table.

```
01   TaxTotals.
      02   StateTax   PIC 9(10)V99 OCCURS 50 TIMES.
```

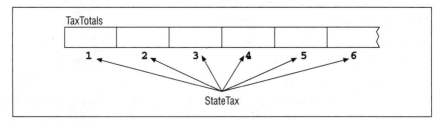

Group items as elements

Elements of a table do not have to be elementary items. An element can be a group item.

In the following example, TaxTotals is the name for the whole table and the element is called StateTaxDetails. The element is further subdivided into the elementary items StateTax and PayerCount.

To refer to an item that is subordinate to table element, the same number of subscripts must be used as when referring to the element itself. So, to refer to StateTaxDetails, StateTax, and PayerCount in the following table, the form StateTaxDetails(sub), StateTax(sub), and PayerCount(sub) must be used.

The effect of executing the statements:

```
MOVE 25 TO PayerCount(2).
MOVE 67 TO  CountyTax(5).
MOVE ZEROS TO CountyTaxDetails(3).
```

is shown in the following storage schematic.

Table example

```
01  TaxTotals.
    02  StateTaxDetails OCCURS 52 TIMES.
        03  StateTax     PIC 9(10)V99.
        03  PayerCount   PIC 9(7).
```

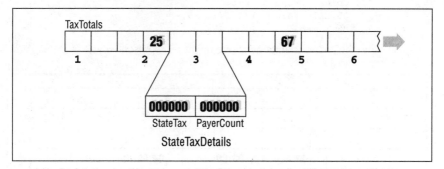

OCCURS clause syntax

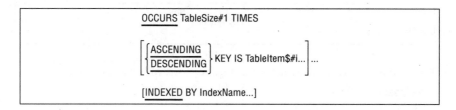

OCCURS clause notes

- When a table is searched using the SEARCH or SEARCH ALL, the INDEXED BY phrase must be used in the table declaration.

- When a table is searched using SEARCH ALL, the KEY phrase must also be used in the table declaration.

OCCURS clause rules

1. The OCCURS clause cannot appear in the description of a level 01 or a level 77 data name.

2. A subscript must be used to refer to any data name whose description includes an OCCURS clause.

3. A subscript must be used to refer to any data name that is subordinate to an item whose description contains an OCCURS clause.

4. When a data name requires more than one subscript, the first is associated with the first OCCURS clause, the second with the second, and so on.

Multi-Dimension Tables

Multi-dimension tables are declared by nesting OCCURS clauses. For example, a table designed to hold the number and value of jeans sold in each of three colors, to males and females, in each state, might be declared as:

```
01   JeansTable.
     02 State OCCURS 50 TIMES.
        03 Gender OCCURS 2 TIMES.
           04 Color OCCURS 3 TIMES.
              05 SalesValue  PIC 9(8)V99.
              05 NumSold     PIC 9(7).
```

Schematically, the data declarations above might be represented as:

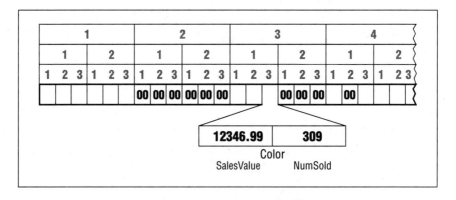

The various data items in the table might be accessed with statements like:

```
MOVE ZEROS TO State (2)
MOVE ZEROS TO Gender (3,2)
MOVE ZEROS TO Color (4,1,2)
MOVE 12346.99 TO SalesValue(3,1,3)
MOVE 309 TO NumSold(3,1,3)
```

Note that when a data item requires more than one subscript, the first subscript is associated with the first OCCURS clause in the table description, the second with the second, and so on.

Variable-Length Tables

Variable-length tables may be declared using the following syntax. The amount of storage allocated to these tables is defined by the value of LargestSize, and is assigned at compile time. Standard COBOL has no mechanism for dynamic memory allocation, although OO-COBOL addresses this problem.

```
OCCURS SmallestSize#1 TO LargestSize#1 TIMES DEPENDING ON DataItem#i

[[ASCENDING ]
 [DESCENDING] KEY IS TableItem$#i...]...

[INDEXED BY IndexName...]
```

Example

```
01 BooksReservedTable.
   02 BookId  PIC 9(7)
      OCCURS 1 TO 10 DEPENDING ON NumOfReservations.
```

The REDEFINES Clause

When a file contains more than one type of record, the different record descriptions defined for it all map to the same physical area of storage. In effect, they redefine the area of storage. However, this only happens to records defined in the FILE SECTION.

The REDEFINES clause lets programmers give different data descriptions to the same area of storage in other parts of the DATA DIVISION.

REDEFINES clause syntax

```
Level - No {Identifier1}  REDEFINES Identifier2
           {FILLER    }
```

REDEFINES clause rules

1. The REDEFINES clause must immediately follow Identifier1 (i.e., the REDEFINES must come before the PIC).

2. The level numbers of Identifier1 and Identifier2 must be the same and cannot be 66 or 88.

3. The data description of Identifier2 cannot contain an OCCURS clause (i.e., a table element cannot be redefined).

4. If there are multiple redefinitions of the same area of storage then they must all redefine the data-item that originally defined the area. (See the following rates example. Rate10 originally defined the area.)

5. The redefining entries cannot contain value clauses except in condition name entries.

6. No entry with a level number lower (i.e., higher in the hierarchy) than the level number of Identifier2 and Identifier 1 can occur between Identifier 2 and Identifier 1.

7. The entries redefining the area must immediately follow those that originally defined it.

8. There can be no intervening entries that define additional character positions.

REDEFINES clause example

The REDEFINES clause may be used to define different data descriptions for the same area of storage. For instance, in the following example the storage allocated to Rates is treated as if it had only 2 digits before the decimal point when Rate10 is referenced, but is treated as if it had 3 digits before the decimal point if Rate100 is used. Rate1000 treats it as if there were 4 digits before the decimal point.

If the value 123.456 were moved into Rate10, the leading 1 would be truncated. However, when moved to Rate100 the same value would truncate the 6, and when moved to Rate1000 it would cause zero-filling on the left and truncation of 5 and 6 on the right.

```
01 Rates.
   02 Rate10 PIC 99V999.
   02 Rate100 REDEFINES  Rate10 PIC 999V99.
   02 Rate1000 REDEFINES Rate10 PIC 9999V9.
```

Creating Pre-filled Tables

Although it can sometimes prove useful in other settings, the main use of the REDEFINES clause is to create pre-filled tables.

There are two steps to creating a pre-filled table.

1. Allocate an area of storage and fill it with the values required in the table. The allocated area is then simply a contiguous sequence of bytes filled with values.

2. Use the REDEFINES clause to impose a table structure on the area of storage containing the values (i.e., redefine the area as a table).

Pre-filled tables example

In this example, a table pre-filled with all the letters of the alphabet is created.

Step 1. Create an area of storage, 26 characters in size, containing the letters of the alphabet.

```
01  LetterTable.
    02 LetterValues.
       03 FILLER PIC X(13)
          VALUE "ABCDEFGHIJKLM".
       03 FILLER PIC X(13)
          VALUE "NOPQRSTUVWXYZ".
```

Step 2. Redefine the area of storage as a table.

```
01  LetterTable.
    02 LetterValues.
       03 FILLER PIC X(13)
          VALUE "ABCDEFGHIJKLM".
       03 FILLER PIC X(13)
          VALUE "NOPQRSTUVWXYZ".
    02 FILLER REDEFINES LetterValues.
       03 Letter PIC X OCCURS 26 TIMES.
```

Two-dimension, pre-filled table example

A video rental shop charges its customers a surcharge on late videos. The per-diem surcharge depends on how recently the video was released (Old, Recent, New) and the number of days the video is overdue (1–3, 4–7, >7). The actual surcharge is calculated as: the per-diem surcharge * number of days overdue.

A pre-filled, two-dimension table is required to hold the surcharge values.

Step 1. Create the SurchargeValues area of storage containing the required data.

```
01  SurchargeTable.
    02 SurchargeValues.
       03 FILLER PIC X(6) VALUE "050100150".
       03 FILLER PIC X(6) VALUE "075125200".
       03 FILLER PIC X(6) VALUE "100150300".
```

Step 2. Redefine the SurchageValues area as a two-dimension table.

```
01  SurchargeTable.
    02  SurchargeValues.
        03 FILLER PIC X(6) VALUE "050100150".
        03 FILLER PIC X(6) VALUE "075125200".
        03 FILLER PIC X(6) VALUE "100150300".
    02 FILLER REDEFINES SurchargeValues.
        03 Age OCCURS 3 TIMES.
            04 Overdue OCCURS 3 TIMES.
                05 PerDiemSurcharge  PIC 9V99.
```

Applying this table, a video that is 5 days overdue attracts a surcharge of $6.25 (1.25 * 5 days) if it is a recent video, and a surcharge of $7.50 (1.50 * 5) if it is a new video.

COBOL 85 Table Changes

COBOL 85 allows pre-filled tables to be created without using the REDEFINES clause as long as the number of values is small.

Example

```
01  DayTable VALUE "MonTueWedThrFriSatSun".
    02 Day OCCURS 7 TIMES PIC X(3).
```

COBOL 85 also allows tables to be initialized with the VALUE clause.

Example

```
01  TaxTable.
    02 State OCCURS 50 TIMES.
        03 StateTax  PIC 9(5)  VALUE ZEROS.
        03 StateName PIC X(12) VALUE SPACES.
```

Searching Tables

The task of searching a table to determine whether it contains a particular value is a common operation. However, search algorithms can be tricky to code. To alleviate the coding burden, COBOL provides the SEARCH verb for searching tables.

The method used to search a table depends heavily on how the values in the table are organized. For instance, if the values are not ordered, the table may only be searched sequentially. If the values are ordered, then either a sequential or a binary search may be used.

COBOL provides the SEARCH for sequential searches and the SEARCH ALL for binary searches.

The SEARCH Verb

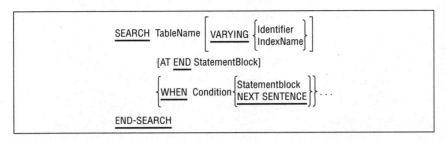

SEARCH notes

- This format of the SEARCH searches a table sequentially, starting at the element pointed to by the table index.

- Before SEARCH can be used to search a table, the table must have been defined as having a table index. The table index is the subscript the SEARCH uses to access the table.

- When SEARCH executes, the table index cannot have a value less than 1 or greater than the size of the table.

- Specifying the table index in an INDEXED BY clause is the only entry that needs to be made for it. The COBOL compiler automatically controls the item's declaration and chooses the most efficient representation possible.

- Because the computer handles the representation of the index, a special verb (SET) is used to manipulate index items.

- TableName must identify the lowest data-item in the table hierarchy with both OCCURS and INDEXED BY clauses.

- If there is a VARYING phrase and the associated identifier is not the controlling index, then the identifier is varied with the index.

- If the AT END is specified and the index is incremented beyond the highest legal occurrence for the table (i.e. the item has not been found), then the statement following the AT END will be executed and the SEARCH will terminate.

- The WHEN conditions attached to the SEARCH are evaluated one after another. As soon as one is true, the statements following the WHEN phrase are executed and the SEARCH ends.

SEARCH example

```
*Data Division declaration
01  LetterTable.
    02 LetterValues.
        03 FILLER PIC X(13)
           VALUE "ABCDEFGHIJKLM".
        03 FILLER PIC X(13)
           VALUE "NOPQRSTUVWXYZ".
```

```
02 FILLER REDEFINES LetterValues.
   03 Letter PIC X OCCURS 26 TIMES
                     INDEXED BY LetterIdx.

*Procedure Division code
   SET LetterIdx TO 1.
   SEARCH Letter
      AT END DISPLAY "Letter not found!"
      WHEN Letter(LetterIdx) = LetterIn
           DISPLAY LetterIn, "is in position ", Idx
   END-SEARCH.
```

Searching a multidimension table

The SEARCH can only search one dimension of a table at a time. If a multidimension table must be searched, the SEARCH must execute several times, and the programmer all must use the SET verb to control the values in the upper table indexes.

Searching a multidimension table example

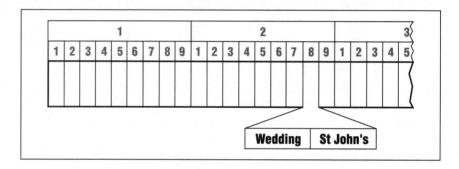

```
* Data Division entries
01  TimeTable.
    02 Day OCCURS 5 TIMES INDEXED BY DayIdx.
       03 Hour OCCURS 9 TIMES INDEXED BY HourIdx.
          04 Appointment   PIC X(12).
          04 Location      PIC X(12).

01  SearchItem            PIC X(12).

01  FILLER                PIC 9 VALUE ZERO.
    88 AppointmentFound   VALUE 1.

* Procedure Division entries
* Looking day, hour and location of Wedding
    MOVE "Wedding" TO SearchItem
    SET DayIdx TO 0.
    PERFORM UNTIL AppointmentFound OR DayIdx > 5
      SET DayIdx UP BY 1
      SET HourIdx TO 1
```

```
SEARCH Hour
    WHEN SearchItem = Appointment(DayIdx, HourIdx)
        SET MeetingFound TO TRUE
        DISPLAY SearchItem " is on day " DayIdx
                    " at " HourIdx + 8 ":00 hours"
                    " in " Location(DayIdx, HourIdx)
    END-SEARCH
    END-PERFORM.
```

Using the data shown in the storage schematic, the above code displays "Wedding is on day 2 at 16:00 hours in St John's"

The SEARCH ALL Verb

The SEARCH ALL is used when a binary search is required. For this reason, the SEARCH ALL will only work on an ordered table. The table must be ordered on some item in the element, either the element itself or one of its fields.

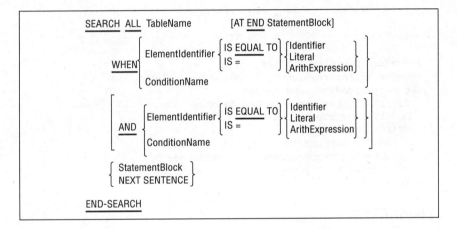

SEARCH ALL notes

- The OCCURS clause of the table to be searched must have a KEY IS clause in addition to an INDEXED BY clause. The KEY IS clause identifies the data-item upon which the table is ordered.

- When the SEARCH ALL is used, the programmer does not need to set the table index to a starting value because the SEARCH ALL controls it automatically.

SEARCH ALL rules

1. The ElementIdentifier must be the item referenced by the Key clause of the table.

2. The ConditionName must have only one value and it must be associated with a data-item referenced by the Key clause of the table.

SEARCH ALL example

```
*Data Division entries
01  InternetCountryCodesTable.
     02 CountryValues.
         03 FILLER PIC X(27) VALUE "ADAndorra".
         03 FILLER PIC X(27) VALUE "AEU. Arab Emirates".
```

!! 239 other codes and country names !!

```
         03 FILLER PIC X(27) VALUE "ZRZaire".
         03 FILLER PIC X(27) VALUE "ZWZimbabwe".

     02 FILLER REDEFINES CountryValues.
         03 Country OCCURS 243 TIMES
              ASCENDING KEY IS CountryCode
              INDEXED BY CIdx.
            04 CountryCode   PIC XX.
            04 CountryName   PIC X(25).

01  SearchCode              PIC XX.

* Procedure Division entries.
* Accepts an internet country code and displays
* the corresponding country name.
     DISPLAY "Enter the internet country code."
     ACCEPT SearchCode
     SEARCH ALL Country
        AT END DISPLAY "Country code not found"
        WHEN CountryCode(CIdx) =  SearchCode
           DISPLAY "Country is " CountryName(CIdx)
     END-SEARCH.
```

The SET Verb

```
┌─────────────────────────────────────────────────────────┐
│                                                         │
│         SET ⎧IndexName⎫ ...TO ⎧IndexName⎫               │
│             ⎩Identifier⎭       ⎨Identifier⎬              │
│                                ⎩Integer   ⎭              │
│                                                         │
│         SET {IndexName}... ⎡UP  ⎤ BY ⎧Identifier⎫        │
│                            ⎣DOWN⎦     ⎩Integer   ⎭       │
│                                                         │
│         SET {ConditionName}... TO TRUE                  │
│                                                         │
└─────────────────────────────────────────────────────────┘
```

An Index Name cannot be used in any type of arithmetic operation (ADD, SUBTRACT, etc.) or even in a MOVE statement. For Index Names, all these operations must be handled by the SET.

The SET is also used to set a Condition Name TO TRUE.

COBOL String Handling

Many programming languages rely on functions for string handling. In COBOL, Intrinsic Functions are also used for some of these tasks, but most string manipulation is done using Reference Modification and the three string-handling verbs: INSPECT, STRING, and UNSTRING.

The INSPECT Verb

The INSPECT verb has four formats: the counting INSPECT, the replacing INSPECT, the combined INSPECT, and the converting INSPECT.

How the INSPECT works

The INSPECT scans the source string from left to right, counting and/or replacing characters under the control of the TALLYING, REPLACING, or CONVERTING phrases.

The behavior of the INSPECT is modified by the LEADING, FIRST, BEFORE, and AFTER phrases.

An ALL, LEADING, CHARACTERS, FIRST, or CONVERTING phrase may only be followed by one BEFORE and one AFTER phrase.

The modifying phrases

- The LEADING phrase causes counting/replacement of all Compare$il characters, from the first valid one encountered to the first invalid one.

- The FIRST phrase causes only the first valid character to be replaced.

- The BEFORE phrase designates as valid those characters to the left of the delimiter associated with it.

- The AFTER phrase designates as valid those characters to the right of the delimiter associated with it.

- If the delimiter is not present in the SourceStr$i, then using the BEFORE phrase implies the whole string, and using the AFTER phrase implies no characters at all.

The counting INSPECT

The counting INSPECT is used to count characters in a string.

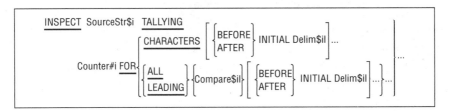

Counting INSPECT rules

If Compare$il or Delim$il is a Figurative Constant it is one character in size.

Examples. `INSPECT FullName TALLYING UnstrPtr`
`                FOR LEADING SPACES.`

```
INSPECT SourceLine TALLYING ECount
        FOR ALL "e" AFTER  INITIAL "start"
                 BEFORE INITIAL "end".
```

The replacing INSPECT

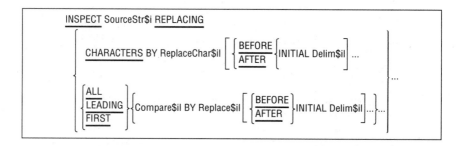

Replacing INSPECT rules

1. The sizes of Compare$il and Replace$il must be equal.

2. When Replace$il is a figurative constant, its size equals that of Compare$il.

3. When there is a CHARACTERS phrase, the size of ReplaceChar$il and the delimiter which may follow it (Delim$il) must be one character.

4. If Compare$il, Delim$il, or Replace$il is a figurative constant, it is 1 character in size.

Replacing INSPECT example 1

This example inspects TextLine, checking it for each of the four-letter swear words in the table. If one is found it is replaced by the text *#@!.

```
PERFORM VARYING idx FROM 1 BY 1 UNTIL EndOfSwearWords
  INSPECT TextLine
      REPLACING SwearWord(idx) BY "*#@!"
END-PERFORM.
```

Replacing INSPECT example 2

The following examples work on the data in StringData to produce the results shown in this storage schematic.

```
1. INSPECT StringData REPLACING ALL "R" BY "G"
        AFTER INITIAL "A" BEFORE INITIAL "Q".

2. INSPECT StringData REPLACING LEADING "R" BY "G"
        AFTER INITIAL "A" BEFORE INITIAL "Z".
```

```
3. INSPECT StringData REPLACING ALL "R" BY "G"
        AFTER INITIAL "A" BEFORE INITIAL "Z".

4. INSPECT StringData REPLACING FIRST "R" BY "G"
        AFTER INITIAL "A" BEFORE INITIAL "Q".

5. INSPECT StringData REPLACING
        ALL "RRRR" BY "FROG"
        AFTER INITIAL "A" BEFORE INITIAL "Q".

        01  StringData    PIC X(15).
```

Before	R	R	R	A	R	R	R	R	R	R	Q	R	R	R	Z
After 1	R	R	R	A	G	G	G	G	G	G	Q	R	R	R	Z
After 2	R	R	R	A	G	G	G	G	G	G	Q	R	R	R	Z
After 3	R	R	R	A	G	G	G	G	G	G	Q	G	G	G	Z
After 4	R	R	R	A	G	R	R	R	R	R	Q	R	R	R	Z
After 5	R	R	R	A	F	R	O	G	R	R	Q	R	R	R	Z

The combined INSPECT

The combined inspect is simply a combination of the two previous formats.

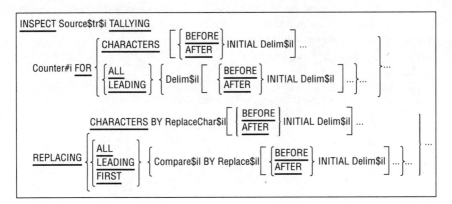

The converting INSPECT

```
             INSPECT SourceStr$i CONVERTING
                  Compare$il TO Convert$il
                     ⎡ ⎧BEFORE⎫               ⎤
                     ⎢ ⎨AFTER ⎬ INITIAL Delim$il ⎥ ...
                     ⎣ ⎩      ⎭               ⎦
```

The INSPECT..CONVERTING works on individual characters. Compare$il is a list of characters that will be replaced with the characters in Convert$il on a one-for-one basis. For instance, the statement

```
    INSPECT StringData CONVERTING "abc" TO "XYZ".
replaces "a" with "X," "b" with "Y," and "c" with "Z."
```

Converting INSPECT rules

1. Compare$il and Convert$il must be equal in size.

2. When Convert$il is a figurative constant, its size equals that of Compare$il.

3. The same character cannot appear more than once in the Compare$il, because each character in the Compare$il string is associated with a replacement character.

Converting INSPECT example 1

This example shows how the INSPECT..CONVERTING can be used to implement a simple encoding mechanism. It converts the character 0 to character 5, 1 to 2, 2 to 9, 3 to 8, and so on. Conversion starts when the word "codeon" is encountered in the string and stops when "codeoff" appears.

```
INSPECT TextLine CONVERTING
     "0123456789" TO "5298317046"
     AFTER  INITIAL "codeon"
     BEFORE INITIAL "codeoff".
```

Converting INSPECT example 2

This example shows how the INSPECT..CONVERTING can be used to convert upper-case letters to lowercase and visa-versa. You can also do this with the UPPER-CASE and LOWER-CASE Intrinsic Functions.

```
* Data Division entries
01 AlphaChars.
   02 AlphaLower PIC X(26) VALUE
          "abcdefghijklmnopqrstuvwxyz".
   02 AlphaUpper PIC X(26) VALUE
          "ABCDEFGHIJKLMNOPQRSTUVWXYZ".

* Procedure Division entries
INSPECT CustAddress
   CONVERTING AlphaLower TO AlphaUpper.

INSPECT CustAddress
   CONVERTING AlphaUpper TO AlphaLower.
```

The STRING Verb

```
STRING { Source$il ... DELIMITED BY { Delim$il } } ...
                                     { SIZE    }

       INTO Dest$i
       [WITH POINTER Pointer#i]
       [ON OVERFLOW StatementBlock]
       [NOT ON OVERFLOW StatementBlock]
       [END-STRING]
```

| Delim$il | = | Character or set of characters in a source string that terminates data transfer to the destination string. |
| Pointer#i | = | Points to the position in the destination string where the next character will go. |

STRING rules

1. Where a literal can be used, a Figurative Constant can be used except the ALL (literal).

2. When a Figurative Constant is used, its size is one character.

3. The destination item Dest$i must be an elementary data-item without editing symbols or the JUSTIFIED clause.

4. Pointer#i must be an integer item, and its description must allow it to contain a value one greater than the size of the destination string. For instance, a pointer declared as PIC 9 is too small if the destination string is 10 characters long.

STRING clauses

The statements following the ON OVERFLOW clause are executed if there are still characters left to pass across in the source field(s) but the destination field has been filled.

The WITH POINTER phrase allows an identifier/data-name to be defined that holds the next character's position in the destination string.

When the WITH POINTER phrase is used, the program must set the pointer to an initial value greater than 0 and less than the length of the destination string before the STRING statement executes.

If the WITH POINTER phrase is not used, operation on the destination field starts from the left-most position.

The DELIMITED BY SIZE clause causes the whole of the sending field to be added to the destination string.

How the STRING works

The STRING verb moves characters from the source string into the destination string from left to right, but no space filling occurs.

When there are a number of source strings, characters are moved from the left-most source string first.

When a WITH POINTER phrase is used, its value determines where the first character will be placed in the destination string.

The ON OVERFLOW clause executes if there are still valid characters left in the source strings but the destination string is full.

Data movement termination

Data movement from a particular source string ends when either:

* The end of the source string is reached
* The end of the destination string is reached
* The delimiter is detected

STRING termination

The STRING statement ends when either:

* All the source strings have been processed
* The destination string is full
* The pointer points outside the string

STRING examples

```
STRING Ident1, Ident2, "10" DELIMITED BY SIZE
     INTO DestString
END-STRING.


STRING Ident1 DELIMITED BY SIZE
     Ident2 DELIMITED BY SPACES
     Ident3 DELIMITED BY "Frogs"
   INTO Ident4 WITH POINTER StrPtr
END-STRING.
```

The UNSTRING Verb

```
UNSTRING SourceStr$i
     [ DELIMITED BY [ ALL ] Delim$il [ OR [ ALL ] Delim$il ] ... ]
     INTO { DestStr$i [ DELIMITER IN HoldDelim$i ]
               [ COUNT IN CharCounter#i ] } ...
     [ WITH POINTER Pointer#i ]
     [ TALLYING IN DestCounter#i ]
     [ ON OVERFLOW StatementBlock ]
     [ NOT ON OVERFLOW StatementBlock ]
     [ END-UNSTRING ]
```

Delim$il	=	Character or set of characters in the source string that terminate data transfer to a particular destination string.
HoldDelim$i	=	Holds the delimiter that caused data transfer to a particular destination string to terminate.
CharCounter#i	=	Is associated with a particular destination string and holds a count of the characters copied into it.
Pointer#i	=	Points to the position in the source string from which the next character will be taken.
DestCounter#i	=	Holds the count of the number of destination strings affected by the UNSTRING operation.

UNSTRING rules

1. Where a literal can be used, any figurative constant can be used except the ALL (literal).

2. When a figurative constant is used, then its length is one character.

3. Characters are moved from the source string to the destination strings according to the rules for the MOVE, with space-filling if required.

4. The delimiter is moved into HoldDelim$i according to the rules for the MOVE.

5. The DELIMITER IN and COUNT IN phrases may be specified only if the DELIMITED BY phrase is used.

How the UNSTRING works

The UNSTRING copies characters from the source string to the destination string, until a condition is encountered that terminates data movement.

When data movement ends for a particular destination string, the next destination string becomes the receiving area and characters are copied into it until once again a terminating condition is encountered.

Characters are copied from the source string to the destination strings according to the rules for alphanumeric moves with space-filling as needed.

Data movement termination

When the DELIMITED BY clause is used, data movement from the source string to the current destination string ends when either:

- A delimiter is encountered in the source string

- The end of the source string is reached

When the DELIMITED BY clause is not used, data movement from the source string to the current destination string ends when either:

- The destination string is full

- The end of the source string is reached

UNSTRING *termination*

The UNSTRING statement terminates when either:

- All the characters in the source string have been examined
- All the destination strings have been processed
- Some error condition is encountered

UNSTRING *clauses*

The ON OVERFLOW is activated if:

- The UNSTRING pointer (Pointer#i) is not pointing to a character position within the source string when the UNSTRING executes
- All the destination strings have been processed, but there are still valid un-examined characters in the source string

The statements following the NOT ON OVERFLOW are executed if the UNSTRING is about to terminate successfully.

The COUNT IN clause is associated with a particular destination string, and holds a count of the number of characters passed to the destination string.

The TALLYING IN clause holds a count of the number of destination strings affected by the UNSTRING operation. Only one TALLYING clause can be used with each UNSTRING.

When the WITH POINTER clause is used, the Pointer#i holds the position of the next non-delimiter character to be examined in the source string.

Pointer#i must be large enough to hold a value one greater than the size of the source string.

A DELIMITER IN clause is associated with a particular destination string. Hold-Delim$i holds the delimiter that was encountered in the Source String.

When the ALL phrase is used, contiguous delimiters are treated as if only one delimiter had been encountered.

If there is also a DELIMITER IN phrase then only one occurrence of the delimiter will be moved to HoldDelim$i.

If the ALL is not used, contiguous delimiters will result in spaces being sent to some of the destination strings.

When the DELIMITED BY phrase is used, characters will be examined in the source string and transferred to the current destination string until the specified delimiter is encountered or the end of the source string is reached.

If there is not enough room in the destination string to take all the characters sent to it from the source string, the remaining characters will be lost.

When the delimiter is encountered in the source string, the next destination string becomes current and characters are transferred into it from the source string.

Delimiters are not transferred or counted in CharCounter#i.

Comma-separated values (CSV) is a file format widely used in the computing industry. It allows data to be transferred between applications with incompatible file formats—Microsoft Excel, for example, can save spreadsheet data in this form, allowing the data to be easily imported by other programs.

The fields in a CSV file do not have a fixed length, and they are separated from one another by commas.

Before a record in a CSV format file can be processed, its comma-separated fields must be unpacked into individual data-items.

In this example, customer records are held in file with a CSV-like format. Each record contains a customer name, a customer address, and the customer balance. Commas separate the fields from one another. The individual parts of the customer address are separated by the slash (/) character. An example record is: Michael Ryan,3 Winchester Drive/Castletroy/Limerick/Ireland,0022456.

The following program reads the file, unpacks each record into separate fields, and writes the unpacked record to a new file.

```
IDENTIFICATION DIVISION.
PROGRAM-ID. CDFILE.
AUTHOR. Michael Coughlan.

ENVIRONMENT DIVISION.
INPUT-OUTPUT SECTION.
FILE-CONTROL.
     SELECT CommaDelimitedFile ASSIGN TO "CDFILE.DAT".
     SELECT CustomerFile ASSIGN TO "CustFile.DAT".

DATA DIVISION.
FILE SECTION.
FD  CommaDelimitedFile.
01  CommaDelimitedRec     PIC X(205).
     88 EndOfFile    VALUE HIGH-VALUES.

FD  CustomerFile.
01  CustomerRec.
     02 CustName    PIC X(40).
     02 AddrLinesUsed      PIC 9.
     02 CustAddress.
        03 AddrLine PIC X(25) OCCURS 1 TO 6
                 DEPENDING ON AddrLinesUsed.
     02 CustBalance PIC 9(5)V99.

WORKING-STORAGE SECTION.
01  TempAddress    PIC X(150).
01  TempBalance    PIC X(7).
01  AdjustedBalance REDEFINES TempBalance PIC 9(5)V99.

PROCEDURE DIVISION.
Begin.
     OPEN INPUT CommaDelimitedFile
     OPEN OUTPUT CustomerFile
```

```
READ CommaDelimitedFile
   AT END SET EndOfFile TO TRUE
END-READ

PERFORM UNTIL EndOfFile
   MOVE ZEROS TO AddrLinesUsed
   UNSTRING CommaDelimitedRec DELIMITED BY ","
      INTO CustName, TempAddress, TempBalance
   UNSTRING TempAddress DELIMITED BY "/"
         INTO AddrLine(1), AddrLine(2), AddrLine(3),
            AddrLine(4), AddrLine(5), AddrLine(6)
            TALLYING IN AddrLinesUsed
   MOVE AdjustedBalance TO CustBalance
   WRITE CustomerRec
   READ CommaDelimitedFile
      AT END SET EndOfFile TO TRUE
   END-READ
END-PERFORM
CLOSE CommaDelimitedFile, CustomerFile
STOP RUN.
```

UNSTRING example 2

This example takes a string containing a name with one or more first names followed by a surname, and converts it by reducing the first names to initials followed by a period. For example, "Michael John Timothy James Ryan" becomes "M.J.T.J. Ryan".

```
*Data Division entries
01 OldName  PIC X(80).

01 TempName.
   02 NameInitial  PIC X.
   02 FILLER       PIC X(15).

01 NewName        PIC X(30).

01 Pointers.
   02 StrPtr       PIC 99 VALUE 1.
   02 UnstrPtr     PIC 99 VALUE 1.
      88 NameProcessed VALUE 81.

*Procedure Division entries
PROCEDURE DIVISION.
ProcessName.
   ACCEPT OldName.
   UNSTRING OldName DELIMITED BY ALL SPACES
      INTO TempName WITH POINTER UnstrPtr
   END-UNSTRING
   PERFORM UNTIL NameProcessed
      STRING NameInitial "." DELIMITED BY SIZE
         INTO NewName WITH POINTER StrPtr
      END-STRING
      UNSTRING OldName DELIMITED BY ALL SPACES
         INTO TempName WITH POINTER UnstrPtr
      END-UNSTRING
```

```
END-PERFORM
STRING SPACE TempName DELIMITED BY SIZE
     INTO NewName WITH POINTER StrPtr
END-STRING
STOP RUN.
```

Reference Modification

Reference modification permits characters in any numeric (PIC 9) or alphanumeric (PIC X) data-item to be manipulated as if the data-item was an array. Sub-strings in the field are accessed using the form:

```
FieldName(StartPos:SubStrLength)
```

Reference modification may be used almost anywhere an alphanumeric data-item is permitted.

When no SubStrLength is given, the sub-string from StartPos to the end of the string is assumed.

Reference modification examples

The reference modification statements in the following examples produce the results shown.

```
WORKING-STORAGE SECTION.
01  xString         PIC X(40)
    VALUE "This is the alphanumeric string".
01  nString         PIC 9(5)V99 VALUE 34526.56.
01  SubStringSize   PIC 99 VALUE 12.
01  StartPos        PIC 99 VALUE 18.

PROCEDURE DIVISION.
Begin.
    DISPLAY xString(9:3)
    DISPLAY xString(13:SubStringSize)
    DISPLAY xString(StartPos:)
    DISPLAY xString(13:SubStringSize - 7)
    DISPLAY nString(3:3)
    DISPLAY nString(6:)
    MOVE "Fred was here" TO xString(18:4)
    DISPLAY xString
    STOP RUN.
```

Results

DISPLAY xString(9:3)	= the
DISPLAY xString(13:SubStringSize)	= alphanumeric
DISPLAY xString(StartPos:)	= numeric string
DISPLAY xString(13:SubStringSize - 7)	= alpha
DISPLAY nString(3:3)	= 526
DISPLAY nString(6:)	= 56
DISPLAY xString	= This is the alphaFredric string

Intrinsic Functions

Although COBOL does not permit user-defined functions or procedures, it does have a number of Intrinsic (built-in) Functions which programmers can use in their programs.

These functions fall into three broad categories: date functions, numeric functions, and string functions.

COBOL String Functions

CHAR(OrdPos)

Returns the character at ordinal position OrdPos of the collating sequence.

ORD(Char)

Returns the ordinal position of character Char.

LENGTH(DataItem)

Returns the number of characters in DataItem.

REVERSE(DataItem)

Returns a character string with the characters in DataItem reversed.

LOWER-CASE(DataItem)

Returns a character string with the characters in DataItem changed to their lower case equivalents.

UPPER-CASE(DateItem)

Returns a character string with the characters in DataItem changed to their upper case equivalents

String functions examples

The statements in the following examples produce the results shown.

```
WORKING-STORAGE SECTION.
01  xString         PIC X(40)
    VALUE "This is the alphanumeric string".
01  OrdPos          PIC 99.

PROCEDURE DIVISION.
Begin.
    DISPLAY "Char at pos 39 is = " FUNCTION CHAR(39)
    MOVE FUNCTION ORD("A") TO OrdPos
    DISPLAY "The ordinal position of A is = " OrdPos
    DISPLAY FUNCTION LENGTH(xString)
    DISPLAY FUNCTION REVERSE(xString(1:31))
    DISPLAY FUNCTION UPPER-CASE(xString)
    DISPLAY FUNCTION LOWER-CASE(xString)
    STOP RUN.
```

Results

Display 1 =   Char at pos 39 is = &
Display 2 =   The ordinal position of A is = 66
Display 3 =   40
Display 4 =   gnirts ciremunahpla eht si sihT
Display 5 =   THIS IS THE ALPHANUMERIC STRING
Display 6 =   this is the alphanumeric string

COBOL Date Functions

CURRENT-DATE

Returns a 21-character string representing the current date and time, and the difference between the local time and Greenwich Mean Time. The format of the string is yyyymmddhhmmsshhxhhmm, where xhhmm is the number of hours and minutes the local time is ahead or behind GMT (x = + or - or 0). If x = 0, the hardware cannot provide this information.

DATE-OF-INTEGER(IntD)

Returns the yyyymmdd (standard date) equivalent of the integer date - IntD. The integer date is the number of days that have passed since Dec 31st 1600 in the Gregorian Calendar.

DAY-OF-INTEGER(IntD)

Returns the yyyddd (Julian Date) equivalent of the integer date - IntD.

INTEGER-OF-DATE(Sdate)

Returns the integer date equivalent of standard date (yyyymmdd) - Sdate.

INTEGER-OF-DAY(Jdate)

Returns the integer date equivalent of Julian date (yyyyddd) - Jdate.

WHEN-COMPILED

Returns the date and time the program was compiled. Uses the same format as CURRENT-DATE.

Date functions examples

```
IDENTIFICATION DIVISION.
PROGRAM-ID.  DateFunctions.
AUTHOR.  Michael Coughlan.

DATA DIVISION.
WORKING-STORAGE SECTION.
01 DateAndTimeC.
    02 DateC.
        03 YearC             PIC 9(4).
        03 MonthC            PIC 99.
        03 DayC              PIC 99.
    02 TimeC.
        03 HourC             PIC 99.
        03 MinC              PIC 99.
        03 SecC              PIC 99.
        03 HundredC          PIC 99.
    02 GMT.
```

```cobol
    03 GMTDiff              PIC X.
       88 GMTNotSupported   VALUE "0".
    03 GMTHours             PIC 99.
    03 GMTMins              PIC 99.

01  BillDate                PIC 9(8).
01  DateNow                 PIC 9(8).
01  DaysOverdue             PIC S999.
01  NumOfDays               PIC 999.

01  IntFutureDate           PIC 9(8).
01  FutureDate              PIC 9(8).
01  DisplayDate REDEFINES FutureDate.
    02 YearD                PIC 9999.
    02 MonthD               PIC 99.
    02 DayD                 PIC 99.


PROCEDURE DIVISION.
Begin.
* This example gets the current date and displays
* its constituent parts.
    MOVE FUNCTION CURRENT-DATE TO DateAndTimeC
    DISPLAY "Current Date is " MonthC "/" DayC "/" YearC
    DISPLAY "Current Time is " HourC ":" MinC ":" SecC
    IF GMTNotSupported
        DISPLAY "This computer cannot supply the time"
        DISPLAY "difference between local and GMT."
      ELSE
        DISPLAY "The local time is - GMT "
                GMTDiff GMTHours ":" GMTMins
    END-IF.


* In this example bills fall due 30 days from
* the billing date.
    DISPLAY "Enter the date of the bill (yyyymmdd) "
        WITH NO ADVANCING
    ACCEPT BillDate
    MOVE DateC TO DateNow
    COMPUTE DaysOverDue =
            (FUNCTION INTEGER-OF-DATE(DateNow))
          - (FUNCTION INTEGER-OF-DATE(BillDate)+ 30)

    EVALUATE TRUE
       WHEN DaysOverDue > ZERO
           DISPLAY "This bill is over due"
       WHEN DaysOverDue = ZERO
           DISPLAY "This bill is due today"
       WHEN DaysOverDue < ZERO
           DISPLAY "This bill is not yet due"
    END-EVALUATE


* This example displays the date NumOfDays days
* from the current date
```

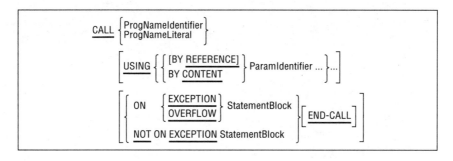
```
DISPLAY "Enter the number of days - "
        WITH NO ADVANCING
ACCEPT NumOfDays
COMPUTE IntFutureDate =
  FUNCTION INTEGER-OF-DATE(DateNow)+ NumOfDays + 1

MOVE FUNCTION DATE-OF-INTEGER(IntFutureDate)
     TO FutureDate

DISPLAY "The date in "
        NumOfDays " days time will be "
        MonthD "/" DayD "/" YearD

STOP RUN.
```

Results. Current Date is 01/26/1998
Current Time is 12:20:17
The local time is - GMT +00:00
Enter the date of the bill (yyyymmdd) 19971227
This bill is due today
Enter the number of days - 365
The date in 365 days time will be 01/27/1999

COBOL Sub-programs

A large software system is not usually written as a single monolithic program. Instead, it consists of many independently compiled sub-programs linked together to form one run unit. In such a system, there must be a mechanism that allows one program to invoke another and to pass data to it. In many programming languages, the procedure or function call serves this purpose. In COBOL, the CALL verb is used to invoke one program from another.

The CALL Verb

```
CALL { ProgNameIdentifier }
     { ProgNameLiteral    }

     [ USING { { [BY REFERENCE] } ParamIdentifier ... } ... ]
             { { BY CONTENT     }                       }

     [ [ { ON { EXCEPTION } StatementBlock } [ END-CALL ] ] ]
       [ {    { OVERFLOW  }                }             ]
       [ { NOT ON EXCEPTION StatementBlock }             ]
```

The CALL verb transfers control to another program. When the program has finished, control returns to the statement that follows the CALL. The called program may be independently compiled, or it may be contained within the text of the caller (see the following section on "Contained Sub-programs").

CALL notes

- If the CALL passes parameters, then the called program must have a USING phrase after the PROCEDURE DIVISION header and a LINKAGE SECTION to describe the parameters passed.

- Parameters passed from the calling program to the called program correspond by position, not by name. That is, the first parameter in the USING phrase of the CALL corresponds to the first in the USING phrase of the called program, and so on.

- The CALL statement has a USING phrase only if a USING phrase is used in the PROCEDURE DIVISION header of the called program.

- Both USING phrases must have the same number of parameters.

- Unlike languages like Modula-2, COBOL does not check the type of the parameters passed to a called program. It is the programmer's responsibility to make sure that only parameters of the correct type and size are passed.

- If the program being called has not been linked (does not exist in the executable image), the statement block following the ON EXCEPTION/OVERFLOW will execute. Otherwise, the program will terminate abnormally.

- BY REFERENCE is the default passing mechanism, and so is sometimes omitted.

- Note that vendors often extend the CALL by introducing BY VALUE parameter passing, and by including a GIVING phrase. These are non-standard extensions.

CALL example

Statement in calling program.

```
CALL "DateValidate"
     USING BY CONTENT TempDate
     USING BY REFERENCE DateCheckResult.
```

Outline of called program.

```
IDENTIFICATION DIVISION.
PROGRAM-ID DateValidate IS INITIAL.
DATA DIVISION.
WORKING-STORAGE SECTION.
         ? ? ? ? ? ? ? ? ? ? ? ?
LINKAGE SECTION.
01  DateParam            PIC X(8).
01  DateResult           PIC 9.
PROCEDURE DIVISION USING DateParam, DateResult.
Begin.
        ? ? ? ? ? ? ? ? ? ? ? ?
        ? ? ? ? ? ? ? ? ? ? ? ?
        EXIT PROGRAM.
??????.
        ? ? ? ? ? ? ? ? ? ? ? ?
```

Parameter Passing Mechanisms

In standard COBOL, the CALL has two parameter passing mechanisms: BY REFER-ENCE and BY CONTENT.

- BY REFERENCE is used when the called program needs to pass data back to the caller.

- BY CONTENT is used when data needs to be passed to, but not received from, the called program.

The following diagram shows how these two mechanisms work.

When data is passed BY REFERENCE, the address of the data-item is supplied to the called program, so any changes made to the data-item in the called program are also made to the data-item in the caller.

When data is passed BY CONTENT, a copy of the data-item is made and the address of the copy is supplied to the called program. Any changes made to the data-item affect only the copy.

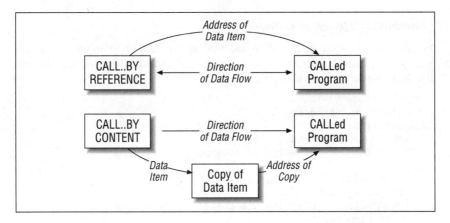

Contained Sub-Programs

COBOL sub-programs can be independently compiled or contained within the text of the main program.

Contained sub-programs are very similar to procedures, except that they are invoked with CALL and are better protected against accidental data corruption.

- In a procedure, all external data-items are visible within the procedure unless they are explicitly re-declared as local data-items.

- In a contained sub-program, no external data-items are visible within the contained sub-program, unless this has been explicitly permitted by using the IS GLOBAL clause in the data declaration.

Defining a contained sub-program

When contained sub-programs are used, the end of the main program, and each sub-program, is signaled by means of the END PROGRAM statement. This has the format:

> END PROGRAM ProgramIdName.

Contained sub-program restrictions

Contained sub-programs have the following restrictions:

1. Although contained sub-programs can be nested, a contained sub-program can only be called by the immediate containing program or by a sub-program at the same level.

2. Contained sub-programs can only call a sub-program at the same level if the called program uses the IS COMMON PROGRAM phrase in its PROGRAM-ID. For instance, DisplayData is called by the main program and by its sibling Insert-Data, but InsertData cannot call DisplayData.

Contained sub-program example

In this example, SharedItem can be accessed in the main program and in each of the sub-programs, because this has been explicitly specified in the data declaration by using the IS GLOBAL clause.

```
IDENTIFICATION DIVISION.
PROGRAM-ID. MainProgram.
DATA DIVISION.
WORKING-STORAGE SECTION.
01 SharedItem     PIC X(25) IS GLOBAL.

PROCEDURE DIVISION.
    CALL "InsertData"
    MOVE "Main can also use the share" TO SharedItem
    CALL "DisplayData"
    STOP RUN.

IDENTIFICATION DIVISION.
PROGRAM-ID. InsertData.
PROCEDURE DIVISION.
    MOVE "Shared area works" TO SharedItem
    CALL "DisplayData"
    EXIT PROGRAM.
END PROGRAM InsertData.

IDENTIFICATION DIVISION.
PROGRAM-ID. DisplayData IS COMMON PROGRAM.
PROCEDURE DIVISION.
    DISPLAY SharedItem.
    EXIT PROGRAM
END PROGRAM DisplayData.
END PROGRAM MainProgram.
```

Sub-program Clauses and Verbs

COBOL sub-programs are identical to standard COBOL programs with the following exceptions:

1. The Program-ID may take the IS INITIAL and IS COMMON PROGRAM clauses.

2. When there are parameters, the PROCEDURE DIVISION header may take the USING phrase.

3. When there are parameters, the DATA DIVISION may have a LINKAGE SECTION.

4. The EXIT PROGRAM statement is used where the STOP RUN would be used in a standard COBOL program.

5. Contained sub-programs must end with the END PROGRAM statement.

The IS INITIAL phrase

The first time a sub-program is called, it is in its initial state: all files are closed and the data-items are initialized to their VALUE clauses. The next time it is called, it remembers its state from the previous call. Any files that were opened are still open, and any data-items that were assigned values still contain those values.

Although it can be useful for a sub-program to remember its state from call to call, systems that contain sub-programs with *state memory* are often less reliable and more difficult to debug than those that do not.

A sub-program can be forced into its initial state each time it is called by including the IS INITIAL phrase in the PROGRAM-ID.

In the following examples, "Steadfast" produces the same result every time it is called with the same parameter value. But "Fickle," because it remembers its state from the previous call, will produce different results when called with the same value.

The CANCEL verb

Sometimes a program needs partial *state memory*. That is, it only needs to be reset to its initial state periodically. In COBOL this can be done with the CANCEL command. For example, the statements:

```
CALL "Fickle" USING BY CONTENT IncValue.
CANCEL "Fickle"
CALL "Fickle" USING BY CONTENT IncValue.
```

force "Fickle" to act like "Steadfast."

Using IS INITIAL and CANCEL example program

```
IDENTIFICATION DIVISION.
PROGRAM-ID. Steadfast IS INITIAL.

DATA DIVISION.
WORKING-STORAGE SECTION.
01 RunningTotal   PIC 9(7) VALUE 50.
```

```
LINKAGE SECTION.
01  Increment      PIC 99.


PROCEDURE DIVISION USING Increment.
Begin.
    ADD Increment TO RunningTotal.
    DISPLAY "Total = ", RunningTotal.
    EXIT PROGRAM.


IDENTIFICATION DIVISION.
PROGRAM-ID. Fickle.
DATA DIVISION.
WORKING-STORAGE SECTION.
01  RunningTotal    PIC 9(7) VALUE 50.


LINKAGE SECTION.
01  Increment      PIC 99.


PROCEDURE DIVISION USING Increment.
Begin.
    ADD Increment TO RunningTotal.
    DISPLAY "Total = ", RunningTotal.
    EXIT PROGRAM.
```

The IS EXTERNAL Phrase

The IS GLOBAL phrase allows a program and its contained sub-programs to share access to a data-item. The IS EXTERNAL phrase does the same for any sub-program in a run-unit (i.e. any linked sub-program). But while the data-item that uses the IS GLOBAL phrase only has to be declared in one place, each of the sub-programs that wish to gain access to an EXTERNAL shared item must declare the item in exactly the same way.

In the following example schematic, there are four programs in the run-unit. ProgramB and ProgramD wish to communicate using a shared data—which, by the way, is often very poor practice. To do this, both programs must contain the following declarations. These set up, and allow access to, the shared area.

Example

```
WORKING-STORAGE SECTION.
01  SharedRec IS EXTERNAL.
    02 PartA    PIC X(4).
    02 PartB    PIC 9(5).
```

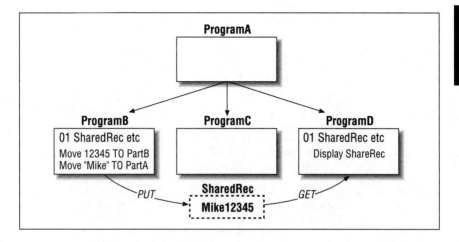

The COBOL Report Writer

Producing printed reports is an important aspect of business programming. Unfortunately, reports are often tedious to code. Report-writing programs are long, and they frequently consist of mere repetitions of the tasks and techniques used in other report-writing programs.

COBOL provides the Report Writer to make creating report programs simple.

The COBOL Report Writer is very large. It includes many new DATA DIVISION entries, including a REPORT SECTION and a number of new PROCEDURE DIVISION verbs.

It is beyond the scope of this section to explore all the syntactic elements of the Report Writer, but the following example program shows what the Report Writer can do.

An Example Report

The first page produced by the example Report Writer program is shown here. This is a report of the sales made by Bible salespersons in all of the cities of Ireland. The salespersons are paid a fixed salary plus a commission on their sales. The fixed salary is obtained from a two-dimension table indexed by the city code and salesperson number.

```
              An example COBOL Report Program
       Bible Salesperson - Sales and Salary Report

  City       Salesperson      Sale
  Name       Number           Value
  Dublin        1            $111.50
                             $222.50
                  Sales for salesperson 1      =      $334.00
                  Sales commission is          =       $16.70
                  Salesperson salary is        =      $139.70
```

```
                   Current  salesperson number = 2
                   Previous salesperson number = 1


Dublin             2            $1,111.50
                                $1,222.50
                                $1,333.50
                   Sales for salesperson 2    =    $3,667.50
                   Sales commission is        =      $183.38
                   Salesperson salary is      =      $504.38
                   Current  salesperson number = 3
                   Previous salesperson number = 2


Dublin             3             $777.70
                   Sales for salesperson 3    =      $777.70
                   Sales commission is        =       $38.89
                   Salesperson salary is      =      $473.89
                   Current  salesperson number = 1
                   Previous salesperson number = 3

                   Sales for Dublin           =    $4,779.20
                   Current City               = 2
                   Previous City              = 1


Belfast            1             $111.50
                                 $222.50
                   Sales for salesperson 1    =      $334.00
                   Sales commission is        =       $16.70
                   Salesperson salary is      =      $139.70
                   Current  salesperson number = 2
                   Previous salesperson number = 1
```

Programmer - Michael Coughlan   Page :   1

What Must the Program Do to Produce the Report

To produce the sales report just shown, the program must do the following tasks:

- Print the headers at the top of each page.

- Print a footer at the bottom of each page showing the programmer's name and a page number.

- Keep a line count, and change page when the count is greater than 42—unless the next thing to print is a salesperson total line, a city total line, or the final total.

- Accumulate all the sales values and print them as a final total at the end of the report.

- Accumulate the sales values for a particular city and print the city total when there is a change of city code.

- Print the name and code of the city for which the total has been accumulated, as well as the city code currently in the file buffer.

- Accumulate the sales values of a particular salesperson, and print the salesperson total when the salesperson code changes.

- Print the salesperson number for which the total has been accumulated, as well as the salesperson number currently in the file buffer.

- Calculate and print the commission on the accumulated sales.

- Get the fixed salary from the table, add it to the sales commission, and print it as the salesperson's salary.

- Print out the details of a particular salesperson's sales.

- Suppress the salesperson number after its first occurrence, unless there is a change of page in the middle of printing, in which case restore the salesperson number in the first line at the top of the page.

In a program that did not use the Report Writer, the PROCEDURE DIVISION required to implement these tasks would occupy a hundred lines or so of code. When the REPORT WRITER is used, only the PROCEDURE DIVISION code shown here is required.

```
PROCEDURE DIVISION.
DECLARATIVES.
Calc SECTION.
    USE BEFORE REPORTING Salespsn-Line.
Calculate-Salary.
    MULTIPLY SMS BY Percentage
        GIVING Commission ROUNDED.
    ADD Commission, Fixed-Rate(City-Code,Salespsn-Number)
        GIVING Salary.
END DECLARATIVES.

Main SECTION.
Begin.
    OPEN INPUT Sales-File.
    OPEN OUTPUT Print-File.
    READ Sales-File
        AT END SET EndOfFile TO TRUE
    END-READ.
    INITIATE Sales-Report.
    PERFORM Print-Salary-Report
        UNTIL EndOfFile.
    TERMINATE Sales-Report.
    CLOSE Sales-File, Print-File.
    STOP RUN.
```

```
Print-Salary-Report.
    MOVE City-Code TO Current-City.
    MOVE Salespsn-Number TO Current-Salespsn.
    GENERATE Detail-Line.
    READ Sales-File
        AT END SET EndOfFile TO TRUE
    END-READ.
```

So Much Work in so Little PROCEDURE DIVISION Code

To achieve so much in so little code, the Report Writer uses a declarative approach to programming rather than the procedural one familiar to most programmers. Most of the work in the Report Writer is actually done in the DATA DIVISION.

The Report Writer works by recognizing that many reports take the same shape. There are headers at the beginning of the report and footers at the end. There are headers at the top of each page and footers at the bottom. Footers and headers need to be printed whenever there is a control break (i.e., when the value in a specified field changes, such as when the salesperson number changes in the example). Detail lines need to be printed.

The Report Writer calls these different report items Report Groups. It recognizes seven types of report group.

- REPORT HEADING or RH group—printed at the beginning of the report

- PAGE HEADING of PH group—printed at the top of each page

- CONTROL HEADING or CH group—printed at the beginning of each control break

- DETAIL or DE group

- CONTROL FOOTING or CF group—printed at the end of each control break

- PAGE FOOTING or PF group—printed at the bottom of each page

- REPORT FOOTING or RF group—printed at the end of the report

Report Groups are defined as records in the REPORT SECTION. Most groups are defined once for each report, but control groups are defined for each control break item. For instance, in the example program, control footings are defined on the salesperson number, the city code, and FINAL. FINAL is a special control group that is invoked before the normal control groups (CONTROL HEADING FINAL) and after the normal control groups (CONTROL FOOTING FINAL).

Report Programs Made Easy

One of the difficulties of writing a report program is the vertical and horizontal placement of printed items. The Report Writer specifies these easily, using the LINE IS and COLUMN IS phrases.

The Report Writer also does the following, automatically:

- Generates report, page, and control headers and footers

- Counts pages and lines per page

- Moves data values to output items

- Recognizes control breaks, and generates the appropriate control headers and footers

- Accumulates totals, sub-totals, and final totals

Report Writer Exceptions: DECLARATIVES

Sometimes the structure of a required report is such that the standard Report Writer alone is an insufficient tool. In these cases, DECLARATIVES may be used to extend the functionality of the Report Writer. The code specified in the DECLARATIVES is executed just before a report group is printed. For instance, in the example report, the Report Writer cannot automatically calculate a salesperson's commission and salary. DECLARATIVES are used with the USE BEFORE REPORTING Salespsn-Line phrase to calculate these items when the Salespsn-Number control footer group is about to be printed.

The SUPPRESS PRINTING verb can be used in the DECLARATIVES to suppress the printing of a report group.

In addition to their Report Writer functions, DECLARATIVES can be used to set up standard error handling procedures for files. When this is done, the USE AFTER ERROR PROCEDURE ON phrase is used. Error-handling procedures can be defined for all errors on a specific file, or for all INPUT, OUTPUT, I-O, and EXTEND errors on all files.

Full Report Writer Example Program

```
IDENTIFICATION DIVISION.
PROGRAM-ID.  Full-Report-Example.
AUTHOR.  Michael Coughlan.

ENVIRONMENT DIVISION.
INPUT-OUTPUT SECTION.
FILE-CONTROL.
    SELECT Sales-File ASSIGN TO "GBPAY.DAT"
           ORGANIZATION IS LINE SEQUENTIAL.
    SELECT Print-File ASSIGN TO "REPORT1.LPT".


DATA DIVISION.
FILE SECTION.
FD  Sales-File.
01  Sales-Record.
    88 EndOfFile   VALUE HIGH-VALUES.
    02 City-Code        PIC 9.
    02 Salespsn-Number  PIC 9.
    02 Value-Of-Sale    PIC 9(4)V99.

FD  Print-File
    REPORT IS Sales-Report.

WORKING-STORAGE SECTION.
01  Name-Table.
```

```
   02 Table-Values.
      03 FILLER        PIC X(18)
         VALUE "Dublin    Belfast    ".
      03 FILLER        PIC X(18)
         VALUE "Cork      Galway     ".
      03 FILLER        PIC X(18)
         VALUE "Sligo     Waterford".
      03 FILLER        PIC X(9)
         VALUE "Limerick".
   02 FILLER REDEFINES Table-Values.
      03 City-Name     PIC X(9) OCCURS 7 TIMES.

01 Rate-Table.
   02 Table-Values.
      03 FILLER        PIC X(35)
         VALUE "12300321004350056700123002340034500".
      03 FILLER        PIC X(35)
         VALUE "12300543001230034200111001220013300".
      03 FILLER        PIC X(35)
         VALUE "12000321001760018700133001440015500".
      03 FILLER        PIC X(35)
         VALUE "32100123003210012000166001770018800".
      03 FILLER        PIC X(35)
         VALUE "34500345004560054300111001220013200".
      03 FILLER        PIC X(35)
         VALUE "19000180001780017900444003330022200".
      03 FILLER        PIC X(35)
         VALUE "16700156001450014600222001110021200".
      03 FILLER        PIC X(35)
         VALUE "12000132001230014300121003210043200".
      03 FILLER        PIC X(35)
         VALUE "15400165001640017600111007770033300".

   02 FILLER REDEFINES Table-Values.
      03 City OCCURS 7 TIMES.
         04 Fixed-Rate PIC 9(3)V99 OCCURS 9 TIMES.

01 Misc-Variables.
   02 Commission       PIC 9(4)V99.
   02 Percentage       PIC V99 VALUE .05.
   02 Salary           PIC 9(6)V99.
   02 Current-Salespsn PIC 9.
   02 Current-City     PIC 9.


REPORT SECTION.
RD  Sales-Report
    CONTROLS ARE FINAL
                City-Code
                Salespsn-Number
    PAGE LIMIT IS 66
    HEADING 1
```

```
        FIRST DETAIL 6
        LAST DETAIL 42
        FOOTING 52.

01   TYPE IS PAGE HEADING.
        02 LINE 1.
            03 COLUMN 12    PIC X(32)
               VALUE "An example COBOL Report Program".

        02 LINE 2.
            03 COLUMN 6     PIC X(17)
               VALUE "Bible Salesperson".
            03 COLUMN 23    PIC X(26)
               VALUE " - Sales and Salary Report".

        02 LINE 4.
            03 COLUMN 2     PIC X(4) VALUE "City".
            03 COLUMN 12    PIC X(11) VALUE "Salesperson".
            03 COLUMN 28    PIC X(4) VALUE "Sale".

        02 LINE 5.
            03 COLUMN 2     PIC X(4) VALUE "Name".
            03 COLUMN 13    PIC X(6) VALUE "Number".
            03 COLUMN 28    PIC X(5) VALUE "Value".


01   Detail-Line TYPE IS DETAIL.
        02 LINE IS PLUS 1.
            03 COLUMN 1     PIC X(9)
               SOURCE City-Name(City-Code) GROUP INDICATE.
            03 COLUMN 15    PIC 9
               SOURCE Salespsn-Number GROUP INDICATE.
            03 COLUMN 25    PIC $$,$$$.99 SOURCE Value-Of-Sale.


01   Salespsn-Line
        TYPE IS CONTROL FOOTING Salespsn-Number
                          NEXT GROUP PLUS 2.
        02 LINE IS PLUS 1.
            03 COLUMN 15    PIC X(21)
               VALUE "Sales for salesperson".
            03 COLUMN 37    PIC 9 SOURCE Salespsn-Number.
            03 COLUMN 43    PIC X VALUE "=".
            03 SMS COLUMN 45 PIC $$$$$,$$$.99 SUM Value-Of-Sale.

        02 LINE IS PLUS 1.
            03 COLUMN 15    PIC X(19)
               VALUE "Sales commission is".
            03 COLUMN 43    PIC X VALUE "=".
            03 COLUMN 45    PIC $$$$$,$$$.99 SOURCE Commission.

        02 LINE IS PLUS 1.
```

```
      03 COLUMN 15      PIC X(22)
         VALUE "Salesperson salary is".
      03 COLUMN 43      PIC X VALUE "=".
      03 COLUMN 45      PIC $$$$,$$$.99 SOURCE Salary.

   02 LINE IS PLUS 1.
      03 COLUMN 15      PIC X(30)
         VALUE "Current  salesperson number = ".
      03 COLUMN 45      PIC 9 SOURCE Current-Salespsn.

   02 LINE IS PLUS 1.
      03 COLUMN 15      PIC X(30)
         VALUE "Previous salesperson number = ".
      03 COLUMN 45      PIC 9 SOURCE Salespsn-Number.



   City-Line TYPE IS CONTROL FOOTING City-Code
                        NEXT GROUP PLUS 2.
   02 LINE IS PLUS 2.
      03 COLUMN 15      PIC X(9) VALUE "Sales for".
      03 COLUMN 25      PIC X(9)
         SOURCE City-Name(City-Code).
      03 COLUMN 43      PIC X VALUE "=".
      03 CS COLUMN 45   PIC $$$$,$$$.99 SUM SMS.

   02 LINE IS PLUS 1.
      03 COLUMN 15      PIC X(12)
                        VALUE "Current City".
      03 COLUMN 43      PIC X VALUE "=".
      03 COLUMN 45      PIC 9 SOURCE Current-City.

   02 LINE IS PLUS 1.
      03 COLUMN 15      PIC X(13)
                        VALUE "Previous City".
      03 COLUMN 43      PIC X VALUE "=".
      03 COLUMN 45      PIC 9   SOURCE City-Code.


01 Total-Sales TYPE IS CONTROL FOOTING FINAL.
   02 LINE IS PLUS 4.
      03 COLUMN 15      PIC X(11)
                        VALUE "Total sales".
      03 COLUMN 43      PIC X VALUE "=".
      03 COLUMN 45      PIC $$$$,$$$.99 SUM CS.


01 TYPE IS PAGE FOOTING.
   02 LINE IS 53.
      03 COLUMN 1       PIC X(29)
         VALUE "Programmer - Michael Coughlan".
      03 COLUMN 45      PIC X(6) VALUE "Page :".
      03 COLUMN 52      PIC Z9 SOURCE PAGE-COUNTER.
```

```
PROCEDURE DIVISION.
DECLARATIVES.
Calc SECTION.
    USE BEFORE REPORTING Salespsn-Line.
Calculate-Salary.
    MULTIPLY SMS BY Percentage
            GIVING Commission ROUNDED.
    ADD Commission, Fixed-Rate(City-Code,Salespsn-Number)
            GIVING Salary.
END DECLARATIVES.


Main SECTION.
Begin.
    OPEN INPUT Sales-File.
    OPEN OUTPUT Print-File.
    READ Sales-File
        AT END SET EndOfFile TO TRUE
    END-READ.
    INITIATE Sales-Report.
    PERFORM Print-Salary-Report
            UNTIL EndOfFile.
    TERMINATE Sales-Report.
    CLOSE Sales-File, Print-File.
    STOP RUN.


Print-Salary-Report.
    MOVE City-Code TO Current-City.
    MOVE Salespsn-Number TO Current-Salespsn.
    GENERATE Detail-Line.
    READ Sales-File
        AT END SET EndOfFile TO TRUE
    END-READ.
```

Further Reading

This chapter presents only a brief overview of COBOL. For more comprehensive explanations you may need to do some further reading.

Books

STRUCTURED COBOL PROGRAMMING 8th ed. by Nancy B. Stern and Robert A. Stern. Paperback, 816 pages. Published by John Wiley & Sons. Publication date: February 1997. ISBN: 047113886X.

TEACH YOURSELF COBOL IN 21 DAYS 2nd ed. by Mo Budlong. Paperback, 1056 pages. Published by Sams Publishing. Publication date: October 1997. ISBN: 0672311372.

STANDARD OBJECT-ORIENTED COBOL by Ned Chapin. Paperback, 394 pages. Published by John Wiley & Sons. Publication date: November 1996. ISBN: 0471129747.

Web sites

http://pw2.netcom.com/~wmklein/cobolfaq.htm contains the COBOL FAQ.

http://www.infogoal.com/cbd/cbdhome.htm contains a comprehensive set of COBOL related links.

http://www.csis.ul.ie/cobol/default.htm is a web site maintained by the author. It contains: COBOL lectures in the form of PowerPoint slides, COBOL exercises with sample solutions, and example COBOL programs.

PART IV

Date Function Reference

CHAPTER 11

Date Functions

Reference to Date Functions

This chapter provides a quick reference to date functions and how they are used in most popular programming languages. It will assist those whose COBOL or PL/1 date-manipulation skills are rusty, and those who are converting legacy systems to newer languages, such as C/C++ and Visual Basic.

Once one understands the theory of date manipulation, it can easily be applied to other languages. Accordingly, this chapter begins with a set of generic, or pseudo-code, date functions. These apply to any language, and are intended for use as a framework or template. For clarity, I have used the same names for these pseudo-code date functions as for home-made functions in other languages.

Whether you intend to solve your Year-2000 code problems by expanding date fields (adding century data to existing five- or six-digit fields) or by deriving the century on-the-fly within the code, the functions in the following chapters will be used time and time again. They will be valuable to programmers and code-scanning alike.

Content

Five types of date functions will be encountered when converting or checking existing code, as well as in new code:

1. Basic Date and Time functions, which retrieve the date and time from the system or a dating file. These are usually intrinsic to the language used, and well-defined in its documentation.

2. Functions that perform date arithmetic, such as DateAdd or DateSubtract. As their names indicate, these functions add or subtract days or other units to or from a date, respectively. Another function in this category, DateDiff, returns the difference between two dates.

215

3. Functions that support date-arithmetic functions with base dates, including DateToJulian and JulianToDate.

4. Functions that return parts of a date from a whole date, such as those that derive month and day from 11/9/98.

5. Functions that populate the missing century part (CC) of a date, which could be a year or a full six-digit date (YYMMDD,) including Window.

Dates and calendars do not conform to a completely uniform arithmetic progression: a year can be either 365 or 366 days, and a century doesn't always have the same number of leap years. (See the "Historical Dates and Leap-Year Theory" section in Chapter 5, *Technical Considerations.)*

To perform date-arithmetic, programs work from a base or reference date. This process is usually accomplished by:

- Converting a standard date to a Julian or Ordinal date (the number of days elapsed since 1600, 1582, or some other arbitrary year)

- Adding (or subtracting) the days

- Converting back to the standard date

Start-years used in conversion processes are sometimes chosen for mathematical convenience. For example, you might choose 1600 because it is the start of both the 400-year leap-year cycle and the four-year leap-year cycle.

The start-year concept and leap-year cycles are discussed in more detail in Chapter 5, but the important message here is that when performing date arithmetic, one should convert the date to a numerically simple and uniform format before attempting to add or subtract days.

Instead of duplicating functionality, the next six chapters present language-specific variations on tackling date arithmetic. In the case of Chapter 17, *C Date Functions*, the focus is on core library functions rather than on the higher-level renditions and intrinsic functions that exist in the many versions of this language.

Some basic language environments, such as MVS COBOL, do not have intrinsic functions for DateAdd and DateDiff. These languages only provide simple Date and Time functions. That's why I've provided some homemade ones that provide the same functionality and illustrate the underlying principles. Chapter 12, *Pseudo-Date Functions*, and Chapter 13, *COBOL Date Functions*, both include supporting functions, including DateToJulian and JulianToDate.

MVS-based environments, such as COBOL, C, and PL/1, have Language Environment (LE) extensions available. These extensions include supporting functions similar to DateToJulian, JulianToDate, and DayofWeek, so I've also included a brief overview of these in Chapter 15, *MVS LE Date Functions*.

The following table summarizes what can be found in each of the following chapters. Sometimes the function names differ slightly to comply with naming conventions. Some of the very low-level supporting functions are not listed, but they will still be useful when analyzing code. These supporting functions are listed at the end of each chapter that follows this one.

Table 11-1: Chapter Summary

Function	Pseudo	COBOL	PL/1	LE	VB	C
Date		Y	Y		Y	Y
Day	Y	Y	Y	Y	Y	Y
Month	Y	refer	Y		Y	Y
DateAdd	Y	Y	Y		Y	Y
DateDiff	Y	Y	Y		Y	Y
Window	Y	Y	Y	Y		
DateToJulian	Y	Y	Y	Y		
JulianToDate	Y	Y	Y	Y		

Logic or Data Solution?

It's unlikely that either the logic approach or the data approach will be sufficient to address your Year-2000 problems in and of itself, so even if you plan to rely on changing data you'll need to understand date functions. For example, there's no guarantee that your existing code will handle expanded data correctly. If existing code tests YY alone, the additional CC will not change the outcome—the code will have to be changed anyway.

If you change the database, the existing stored data will still contain six-digit dates. A batch process will have to be written to scan the data and decide (based on cusp dates) whether the century is 19 or 20, and then populate the field accordingly.

Whether screens or the database is changed, temporary storage and data structures must be redefined within code, interfaces, and copy-books.

In addition, if only the logic method is applied, output documents and screens will still need to display the century, to ensure that there's no confusion between empty fields and genuine Year-2000 data.

It's important to fully understand all the considerations and ripples discussed in Chapter 5 as well as those in the following chapters, before settling on a blanket solution. Sometimes it's useful to facilitate a workshop on all of the technical considerations, at which all concerned parties can explore the issues inherent in actual conversion and scanning at your site before commencing work. This helps to ensure that a uniform approach is applied.

CHAPTER 12

Pseudo-Date Functions

Pseudo-Code Date Functions

The pseudo-code date functions described in this chapter provide a foundation for learning how to manipulate dates within data files. They will help you understand the language-specific date functions that follow in subsequent chapters, and they can be used as models or templates for evaluating, converting, or designing new date-manipulation programs. These functions adhere to the same naming convention used in the following chapters, which facilitates easy conversion and lookup.

These pseudo-code functions are century and leap-year aware in the range 1601 to 3399. The year 1601 is the start of both a four-year leap cycle and a 400-year Gregorian century leap-year adjustment, which makes calculation coding easier. The functionality is limited to about 4,000 years, when an additional adjustment will be required. Your name will be mentioned when the witch-hunt begins again in 3390 or thereabouts, so pay attention!

The terms Long and Short apply to four- and two-digit years: any variables with either prefix are sub-parts of the main variable. For example, ShortInputMonth is the month part of ShortInputDate. All parts of variables are attained or derived from structures declared in the specific language in use at the time, and are not detailed in this chapter.

The operation Integer returns the integer part of a division. For instance, Integer (10/7) returns 1.

The operation MOD returns the remainder of an integer division: 10 MOD 7 returns 3, and so forth.

In most functions, the return data is assigned to the function name, and error status indicators are global. This technique is not common to all languages, and should only be used where applicable. Alternatively, you may use global indicators.

All global variables, tables, and data pertaining to pseudo-code functions can be found at the end of this chapter.

Figure 12-1 illustrates the hierarchical relationship between the pseudo-code functions and how they are called.

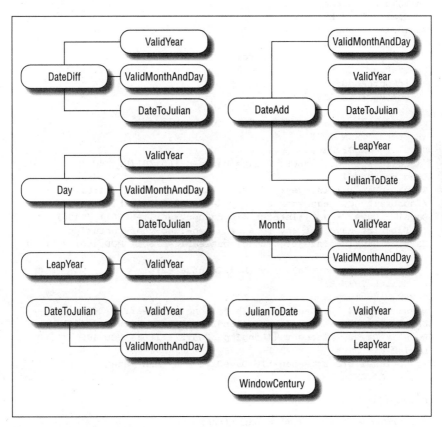

Figure 12-1: Pseudo-code function calls

DateDiff (LongInputDate1, LongInputDate2)

Arguments

LongInputDate1*, LongInputDate2*
    eight-digit input-dates formatted CCYYMMDD

    * and parts

Returns

Difference in days (DayDiff)

Local Variables

Days1, Days2 = days

Comment

DateDiff calculates the difference between LongInputDate1 and LongInputDate2.

```
FUNCTION DateDiff (LongInputDate1, LongInputDate2)
Status = 0
ValidYear (LongInputYear1)
IF Status THEN EXIT
ValidYear (LongInputYear2)
IF Status THEN EXIT
ValidMonthAndDay(LongInputDate1)
IF Status THEN EXIT
ValidMonthAndDay(LongInputDate2)
IF Status THEN EXIT

LongOrdDate  = DateToJulian (LongInputDate1)
IF Status THEN EXIT
Days1 = LongOrdDays
// Calculate the number of days between 1601/01/01 and
LongInputDate1
Days1 = Days1 + Integer( 365.25 * (LongInputYear1 - 1601) )
//subtract non-leap-year-century days (not divisible by 400)
Days1 = Days1 - 3 * (Integer ((LongInputYear1 - 1601) / 400) )
// Subtract days for any remaining non-leap-year-centuries
Days1 = Days1 - Integer( (LongInputYear1 - 1601) MOD 400) / 100 )

LongOrdDate  = DateToJulian (LongInputDate2)
IF Status THEN EXIT
Days2 = LongOrdDays
Days2 = Days2 + Integer( 365.25 * (LongInputYear2 - 1601) )
Days2 = Days2 -  3 * (Integer(LongInputYear2 - 1601) / 400)
Days2 = Days2 - Integer ((LongInputYear2 - 1601) MOD 400) / 100 )
DateDiff = ( Days1 - Days2 )
// Optional error message IF DaysDiff < 0 THEN  Status = 03
END FUNCTION
```

Example call

AccountAge = DateDiff(Date*, PurchaseDate)

* Date is returned from the system-date, and should be pre-formatted correctly.

DateAdd (LongInputDate1, Days)

Arguments

LongInputDate1*
    eight-digit input-dates formatted CCYYMMDD

Days
    number of days to add

    * and parts

Returns

New Long Date (formatted CCYYMMDD)

Comment

DateAdd adds *Days to LongInputDate1*

Local Variables

RemainingDays
days

DaysInThisYear
days

Balance
days

```
FUNCTION DateAdd(LongInputDate1, Days)
Status = 0
ValidYear (LongInputYear1)
IF Status THEN EXIT
ValidMonthAndDay(LongInputDate1)
IF Status THEN EXIT
IF Days IS NOT NUMERIC THEN Status = 51: EXIT
LongOrdDate  = DateToJulian (LongInputDate1)
IF Status THEN EXIT
LeapYear(LongOrdYear)
IF Leap
    DaysInThisYear = 366
ELSE
    DaysInThisYear = 365
RemainingDays = DaysInThisYear - LongOrdDays
Balance = Days
// subtract all full years from days to add
IF Balance > RemainingDays
    WHILE Balance > RemainingDays
        Balance = Balance - RemainingDays
        LongOrdYear = LongOrdYear + 1
        LeapYear(LongOrdYear)
        IF Leap
            DaysInThisYear = 366
        ELSE
            DaysInThisYear = 365
            RemainingDays = DaysInThisYear
    END WHILE
    LongOrdDays = Balance
ELSE
    LongOrdDays = LongOrdDays + Balance
DateAdd = JulianToDate(LongOrdDate)
END FUNCTION
```

Example call

DueDate = DateAdd(PurchaseDate + 90)

Day (LongInputDate1)

Arguments

LongInputDate1*
eight-digit input-date formatted CCYYMMDD

* and parts

Returns

Day of the Week

Comment

Calculates the days since 1601/01/01, and divides the result by seven. The remainder, which will be less than seven, is used to index the lookup table. A name is allocated to each of these remainder values from the table tDays.

```
FUNCTION Day(LongInputDate1)
Status = 0
ValidYear (LongInputYear1)
IF Status THEN EXIT
ValidMonthAndDay(LongInputDate1)
IF Status THEN EXIT
LongOrdDate  = DateToJulian (LongInputDate1)
IF Status THEN EXIT
Temp = LongOrdDays
Temp = Temp + Integer( 365.25 * (LongInputYear1 - 1601) )
Temp = Temp -  3 * (Integer (LongInputYear1 - 1601) / 400) )
Temp = Temp - Integer( (LongInputYear1 - 1601)MOD 400) / 100 )
Day = tDays(Temp MOD 7)
END FUNCTION
```

Example call

ChristmasDay = Day(19981225)

Month (LongInputDate1)

Arguments

LongInputDate1*
  eight-digit input-date formatted CCYYMMDD

  * and parts

Returns

Month from table

Comment

This very simple function uses the pre-loaded structure LongInputDate1 to get the month number, then applies it as an index to the table tMonths.

```
FUNCTION Month(LongInputDate1)
Status = 0
ValidYear (LongInputYear1)
IF Status THEN EXIT
ValidMonthAndDay(LongInputDate1)
IF Status THEN EXIT
Month = tMonths(LongInputMonth1-1)
END FUNCTION
```

Example call

BirthMonth = Month(19470505)

Window (ShortInputDate, Base)

Arguments

ShortInputDate*
   six-digit date formatted YYMMDD

   *and parts

Base
   two-digit year

Returns

Long Date—eight-digit date formatted CCYYMMDD

Comment

Converts ShortInputDate to LongDate. Century is attached to ShortInputYear, which will be either 19 or 20. The term *CONC means concatenate (strings)*.

```
FUNCTION Window (ShortInputDate, Base)
Status = 0
IF Base < 1 OR Base  > 99
   Status = 31
   EXIT
IF ShortInputDate IS NOT NUMERIC THEN Status = 32: EXIT
Window = '20' CONC ShortInputDate                //default
IF ShortInputYear >= Base
   Window = '19' CONC ShortInputDate
END FUNCTION
```

Example Call

8Digitdate = Window (961207, 50)

Returns

19961207

Pseudo-Code Supporting Functions

Like pseudo-code functions, supporting functions include arguments, returns, and example calls. Global indicators, variables, and messages are also used.

LeapYear (year)

Arguments

year - formatted CCYY

Returns

0 = not a leap year, 1 = leap year

```
FUNCTION LeapYear(year)
Status = 0
```

```
ValidYear (year)
IF Status THEN EXIT
Leap = 0
IF year MOD 4 <> 0 THENEXIT
IF year MOD 100 <> 0      //wholly divisible by 4 and not a century
    Leap = 1              //normal leap year
    EXIT
IF year MOD 400 <> 0      // wholly divisible by 4, is a century
                         // but not a 4th century
    EXIT
Leap = 1                 // is a 4th century leap year
END FUNCTION
```

Example call

This function is used by most of the others, so there is no example required.

DateToJulian (LongInputDate1)

Arguments

LongInputDate1*
  eight-digit input-date formatted CCYYMMDD

  * and parts

Returns

Long Julian Date formatted CCYYDDD

Comment

Convert an eight-digit date (CCYYMMDD) to Julian day (YYDDD) and extended Julian day (CCYYDDD) format. The Julian (or ordinal) day is simply the number of days since January 1st of any year. The table tJulian contains the number of days in a year, up to the beginning of each month for both leap and non-leap years.

Local Variables

TempOrd
  Julian (ordinal) date

Century
  part of LongInputDate1, i.e., CC

Year
  part of LongInputDate1, i.e., YY

```
FUNCTION  DateToJulian(LongInputDate1)
Status = 0
ValidYear(LongInputYear1)
IF Status > 0 THEN EXIT//with Status from ValidYear
LeapYear(LongInputYear1)
IF Status > 0 THEN EXIT//with Status from LeapYear
ValidMonthsAndDays(LongInputYear1)
IF Status > 0 THEN EXIT//with Status from ValidMonthsAndDays
TempOrd = (Year * 1 000)
```

```
TempOrd = TempOrd + (Century  * 100 000)
TempOrd = TempOrd + tJulian(LongInputMonth,LeapYear)
TempOrd = TempOrd + LongInputDay
DateToJulian = TempOrd
END FUNCTION
```

JulianToDate (LongOrdDate)

Arguments

LongOrdDate*

seven-digit input-date (CCYYDDD)

* and parts

Returns

*Date**

eight-digit (CCYYMMDD)

* and parts

Comments

Converts an extended ordinal (CCYYDDD) day to an eight-digit date value. **LongOrdDate** is validated, and if no errors occur it is converted to eight-digit format.

Local Variables

RowIndex

Table subscript counter, starts at the second entry

MonthCount

Month counter

Month

Output month

```
FUNCTION JulianToDate (LongOrdDate)
Status = 0
ValidYear(LongOrdYear)
IF Status > 0 THEN EXIT          //with Status from ValidYear
LeapYear(LongOrdYear)
IF Status > 0 THEN EXIT          //with Status from LeapYear
IF LongOrdDays  < 1 OR LongOrdDays > (365 + Leap)
    Status = 41
    EXIT
MonthCount = 0
RowIndex = 0
DO:
    RowIndex = RowIndex + 1
    MonthCount = MonthCount + 1
WHILE LongOrdDays  > tJulian (RowIndex,Leap)
Month = MonthCount * 100
// Step to previous month in table
RowIndex = RowIndex - 1
```

```
// Add the day
Month = Month + (LongOrdDays - tJulian   (RowIndex,Leap))
// Add the year
Month = Month + (LongOrdYear * 10 000)
END FUNCTION
```

ValidYear (LongInputYear)

Arguments

LongInputDate1*
    eight-digit input-date (CCYYMMDD)

Returns

a Status indicator

```
FUNCTION ValidYear (LongInputYear)
Status = 0
IF LongInputYear IS NOT NUMERIC
    Status = 11
    EXIT
Temp = LongInputCentury
IF Temp < 1601 OR Temp > 3399
    Status = 12
    EXIT
END FUNCTION
```

ValidMonthAndDay (LongInputYear1)

Arguments

LongInputDate1*
    eight-digit input-date (CCYYMMDD)

    * and parts

Returns

a Status indicator

```
FUNCTION ValidMonthAndDay (LongInputYear1)
Status = 0
IF LongInputMonth1 <  1 or LongInputMonth1 > 12
    Status = 21
    EXIT
    Temp = LongInputMonth1
IF Temp < 1 OR Temp > tDaysInMonth(Temp, Leap)
    Status = 22
    EXIT
END FUNCTION
```

Global Indicators, Variables, and Messages

Indicators and Variables

Status: set by all the functions (Error Status = True = non-zero)

Table 12-1: Status of Functions

Leap:	set to 0 or 1
LongOrdDate:	Julian date CCYYDDD
LongOrdYear:	CCYY part of LongOrdDate
LongOrdDays:	DDD part of LongOrdDate
LongInputDate1:	Eight-digit date
LongInputYear1:	Year part of LongInputDate1
LongInputMonth1:	Month part of LongInputDate1
LongInputDay1:	Day part of LongInputDate1
LongInputDate2:	Eight-digit date
LongInputYear2:	Year part of LongInputDate2
LongInputMonth2:	Month part of LongInputDate2
LongInputDay2:	Day part of LongInputDate2
ShortInputDate:	Six-digit date
ShortInputYear1:	Year part of ShortInputDate1
ShortInputMonth1:	Month part of ShortInputDate1
ShortInputDay1:	Day part of ShortInputDate1

Error Messages

A non-zero (True) status indicates an error.

ValidYear
>   11 - non-numeric year
>
>   12 - year out of scope

ValidMonthAndDay
>   21 - invalid month
>
>   22 - invalid day

WindowCentury
>   31 - base year is invalid
>
>   32 - input year is invalid

JulianToDate
>   41 - DDD of LongOrd is out of range

DateAdd
>   51 - non-numeric days

Tables

Table 12-2: tMonths

January
February
March
April
May
June
July
August
September
October
November
December

Table 12-3: tDays

Sunday
Monday
Tuesday
Wednesday
Thursday
Friday
Saturday

Special care must be observed when dealing with table indices and default index bases.

Table 12-4: tJulian

Ordinary year	Leap year
000	000
031	031
059	060
090	091
120	121
151	152
181	182
212	213
243	244
273	274
304	305
334	335

Table 12-5: tDaysInMonth

Ordinary year	Leap year
31	31
28	29
31	31
30	30
31	31
30	30
31	31
31	31
30	30
31	31
30	30
31	31

CHAPTER 13

COBOL Date Functions

Intrinsic (Built-In) Functions

In COBOL, two primary functions are used for getting the date and time from the system. Appropriately enough, these are called Date and Time. The following code illustrates their use. First, define a working storage area, then use "Accept" to move the system date into this area.

Date and Time

```
. WB-SYSTEM-DATE.
        WB-SYSTEM-YY                    PIC 99.
        WB-SYSTEM-MM                    PIC 99.
        WB-SYSTEM-DD                    PIC 99.

    WB-Yr2K-DATE.
        WB-Yr2K-CC                      PIC 99.
        WB-Yr2K-YY                      PIC 99.
        WB-Yr2K-MM                      PIC 99.
        WB-Yr2K-DD                      PIC 99.

    WB-SYSTEM-TIME.
        WB-SYSTEM-H                     PIC 99.
        WB-SYSTEM-M                     PIC 99.
        WB-SYSTEM-S                     PIC 99.
        WB-SYSTEM-SS                    PIC 99.

    9900-ACCEPT-DATE-TIME.
        ACCEPT WB-SYSTEM-DATE FROM DATE
        ACCEPT WB-SYSTEM-TIME FROM TIME
        *CONVERTS DATE TO Yr2K FORMAT
        MOVE WB-SYSTEM-DD               TO WB-Yr2K-DD
        MOVE WB-SYSTEM-MM               TO WB-Yr2K-MM
```

```
    MOVE WB-SYSTEM-YY              TO WB-Yr2K-YY
    * IMPROVE THE FUNCTIONALITY HERE BY USING
    * ANOTHER CONTROL VARIABLE (CUSP YEAR)
    IF WB-Yr2K-YY > 80
        MOVE 19                    TO WB-Yr2K-CC
    ELSE
        MOVE 20                    TO WB-Yr2K-CC
    END-IF
9900-ACCEPT-DATE-TIME-EXIT.
EXIT.
```

Practices like ACCEPT FROM DATE, which returns the system date in six-digit format, should be avoided if possible. A variety of functions are available for various platforms that return the century or some form of century indicator. Functions, standard date files, or standard date tables should be used instead, if you want to ensure that century-aware dates are passed to programs. When dates are accepted from the system, you'll need to put logic windows in place.

COBOL compilers of more-recent vintage offer a variety of built-in intrinsic functions, many of which can assist programmers with date-conversion routines. The IBM versions COBOL/370 and LE/370, for example, offer DATE-OF-INTEGER, DAY-OF-INTEGER, INTEGER-OF-DATE, and INTEGER-OF-DAY functions, which serialize Gregorian dates using a Julian date calculation. The LE/370 callable services offer similar functionality, but the initial date for functions and services is different. COBOL/370 uses an initial date of January 1, 1601, while LE/370 starts on October 15, 1582. The two versions will return different values for the same input date.

LE functions are demonstrated in their own chapter (Chapter 15, *MVS LE Date Functions*). Although PL/1 is used for the examples, they are also available for COBOL and C.

Primary User-Developed Date Functions

The following reference section details the input, output, and comments of each date function, and also provides an example.

WINDOW

Input

six-digit system date

Output

eight-digit date

Comment

This procedure extends the previous date and time examples, and uses their data definitions. It determines the relationship of the input year (in this case, system) and derives a century. To enhance functionality, input the *comparison* year.

```
9900-ACCEPT-DATE-TIME.
    ACCEPT WB-SYSTEM-DATE FROM DATE
    *CONVERTS DATE TO Year2000 FORMAT
    MOVE WB-SYSTEM-DD            TO WB-Yr2K-DD
    MOVE WB-SYSTEM-MM            TO WB-Yr2K-MM
    MOVE WB-SYSTEM-YY            TO WB-Yr2K-YY
    * IMPROVE THE FUNCTIONALITY HERE BY USING
    * ANOTHER CONTROL VARIABLE (CUSP YEAR)
    IF WB-Yr2K-YY > 80
        MOVE 19                 TO WB-Yr2K-CC
    ELSE
        MOVE 20                 TO WB-Yr2K-CC
    END-IF
9900-ACCEPT-DATE-TIME-EXIT.
EXIT.
```

DATE-ADD

Input

GREGORIAN-DATE, DAYS-INTERVAL

Output

GREGORIAN-DATE

Comment

Adds a number of days to a Gregorian date and returns a new Gregorian date.

```
9900-DATE-ADD.
    PERFORM 9900-GREGORIAN-TO-SERIAL
        THRU 9900-GREGORIAN-TO-SERIAL-EXIT.
    MOVE ZERO TO GREGORIAN-DATE.
    IF DATE-IS-VALID
        ADD DAYS-INTERVAL TO SERIAL-DATE;
        PERFORM 9900-SERIAL-TO-GREGORIAN
            THRU 9900-SERIAL-TO-GREGORIAN-EXIT.
9900-DATE-ADD-EXIT.
    EXIT.
```

DATE-SUBTRACT

Input

GREGORIAN-DATE, DAYS-INTERVAL

Output

GREGORIAN-DATE

Comment

Subtracts a number of days from a Gregorian day. The result is a new Gregorian date.

```
9900-DATE-SUBTRACT.
    PERFORM 9900-GREGORIAN-TO-SERIAL
        THRU 9900-GREGORIAN-TO-SERIAL-EXIT.
    MOVE ZERO TO GREGORIAN-DATE.
    IF DATE-IS-VALID
        SUBTRACT DAYS-INTERVAL FROM SERIAL-DATE;
        PERFORM 9900-SERIAL-TO-GREGORIAN
            THRU 9900-SERIAL-TO-GREGORIAN-EXIT.
9900-DATE-SUBTRACT-EXIT.
    EXIT.
```

DATE-DIFF

Input

GREGORIAN-DATE-1ST (must be before GREGORIAN-DATE-2ND)

GREGORIAN-DATE-2ND

Output

DAYS-INTERVAL

Comment

Calculates the difference (in days) between two Gregorian dates. The order of the input dates is important, as the routine does not validate the order itself.

```
9900-DATE-DIFF.
    MOVE GREGORIAN-DATE-1ST TO GREGORIAN-DATE.
    PERFORM 9900-GREGORIAN-TO-SERIAL
        THRU 9900-GREGORIAN-TO-SERIAL-EXIT.
    MOVE ZERO TO DAYS-INTERVAL.
    IF DATE-IS-VALID
        MOVE SERIAL-DATE TO DATE-WORK-1-I;
        MOVE GREGORIAN-DATE-2ND TO GREGORIAN-DATE;
        PERFORM 9900-GREGORIAN-TO-SERIAL
            THRU 9900-GREGORIAN-TO-SERIAL-EXIT;
        IF DATE-IS-VALID
            MOVE SERIAL-DATE TO DATE-WORK-2-I;
            COMPUTE DAYS-INTERVAL =
                DATE-WORK-2-I - DATE-WORK-1-I.
9900-DATE-DIFF-EXIT.
    EXIT.
```

DAY-OF-WEEK

Input

GREGORIAN-DATE

Output

WEEK-DAY

Comment

Determines the day of the week of a particular date.

```
    9900-DAY-OF-WEEK.
PERFORM 9900-GREGORIAN-TO-SERIAL
THRU 9900-GREGORIAN-TO-SERIAL-EXIT.
MOVE ZERO TO WEEK-DAY.
IF DATE-IS-VALID
            PERFORM 9900-SERIAL-TO-DOW
                THRU 9900-SERIAL-TO-DOW-EXIT.
  9900-DAY-OF-WEEK-EXIT.
    EXIT.
```

COBOL Supporting Functions

The following reference section details the input, output, and comments of each date function, and also provides an example.

GREGORIAN-TO-SERIAL

Input

GREGORIAN-DATE

Output

SERIAL-DATE

Comment

Converts a Gregorian date to a serial date. The serial date is really the number of days that have passed since January 1, 1900. If the Gregorian date is not valid, zeros will be returned in the serial date.

```
    9900-GREGORIAN-TO-SERIAL.
        PERFORM 9900-GREGORIAN-VALIDATE
            THRU 9900-GREGORIAN-VALIDATE-EXIT.
        MOVE ZERO TO SERIAL-DATE.
        IF DATE-IS-INVALID
            GO TO 9900-GREGORIAN-TO-SERIAL-EXIT.
        MOVE GREGORIAN-DATE TO GREGORIAN-WHOLE-DATE.
        IF GREGORIAN-CENTURY = ZERO
            PERFORM 9900-SELECT-CENTURY
                THRU 9900-SELECT-CENTURY-EXIT;
            ADD DEFAULT-CENTURY TO GREGORIAN-CENTURY.
        COMPUTE SERIAL-WORK =
            ((GREGORIAN-YEAR - BASE-DATE-YEAR) * SERIAL-FACTOR)
            + DAYS-MONTH-PAST (GREGORIAN-MONTH) + GREGORIAN-DAY.
        IF ((SERIAL-FRACTION = ZERO)AND (GREGORIAN-MONTH NOT >
FEBRUARY-MONTH))
            SUBTRACT 1 FROM SERIAL-INTEGER.
        MOVE SERIAL-INTEGER TO SERIAL-DATE.
    9900-GREGORIAN-TO-SERIAL-EXIT.
        EXIT.
```

SERIAL-TO-GREGORIAN

Input

SERIAL-DATE

Output

GREGORIAN-DATE

Comment

Converts a serial date into a Gregorian date, with the proper century added.

```
9900-SERIAL-TO-GREGORIAN.
    MOVE ZERO TO GREGORIAN-DATE.
    DIVIDE SERIAL-DATE BY SERIAL-FACTOR GIVING GREGORIAN-YEAR.
    MULTIPLY GREGORIAN-YEAR BY SERIAL-FACTOR
        GIVING DATE-WORK-1.
    ADD BASE-DATE-YEAR TO GREGORIAN-YEAR.
    SUBTRACT DATE-WORK-1-I FROM SERIAL-DATE
        GIVING DATE-WORK-2.
    IF DATE-WORK-1-F = ZERO
        IF DATE-WORK-2-I > 58
            IF DATE-WORK-2-I = 59
                MOVE FEBRUARY-MONTH TO GREGORIAN-MONTH;
                COMPUTE GREGORIAN-DAY =
                    DAYS-IN-MONTH (FEBRUARY-MONTH) + 1;
                MOVE GREGORIAN-WHOLE-DATE TO GREGORIAN-DATE;
                GO TO 9900-SERIAL-TO-GREGORIAN-EXIT
            ELSE
                NEXT SENTENCE
        ELSE
            ADD 1 TO DATE-WORK-2-I.
    PERFORM 9900-SERIAL-LOOP
        VARYING GREGORIAN-MONTH FROM 1 BY 1
        UNTIL DATE-WORK-2-I NOT > DAYS-MONTH-PAST (GREGORIAN-MONTH).
    SUBTRACT 1 FROM GREGORIAN-MONTH.
    SUBTRACT DAYS-MONTH-PAST (GREGORIAN-MONTH)
        FROM DATE-WORK-2-I GIVING GREGORIAN-DAY.
        MOVE GREGORIAN-WHOLE-DATE TO GREGORIAN-DATE.
9900-SERIAL-TO-GREGORIAN-EXIT.
    EXIT.
*
9900-SERIAL-LOOP.
*    ******************************
*    * No code, Merely for looping *
*    ******************************
```

SERIAL-TO-DOW

Input

SERIAL-DATE

Output

WEEK-DAY

Comment

Calculates the day of the week (1 = Sunday, 2= Monday, etc.)

```
9900-SERIAL-TO-DOW.
    DIVIDE SERIAL-DATE BY DAYS-IN-WEEK
    GIVING DATE-WORK-1-I REMAINDER WEEK-DAY.
    ADD 1 TO WEEK-DAY.
9900-SERIAL-TO-DOW-EXIT.
EXIT.
```

SELECT-CENTURY

Comment

This routine selects the default century for those dates that do not include a century. In some cases, these assumptions may be dangerous, so be sure that this defaulting process is what you want. The default can be easily changed in this routine, or you can change the defined constants. This routine is used internally.

```
9900-SELECT-CENTURY.
    MOVE ZERO TO DEFAULT-CENTURY.
    IF GREGORIAN-YEAR > DEFAULT-CENTURY-BREAK
        MOVE DEFAULT-CENTURY-1900 TO DEFAULT-CENTURY
    ELSE
        MOVE DEFAULT-CENTURY-2000 TO DEFAULT-CENTURY.
9900-SELECT-CENTURY-EXIT.
    EXIT.
```

GREGORIAN-VALIDATE

Input

GREGORIAN-DATE

Output

DATE-VALID-FLAG

Comment

This routine validates a Gregorian date, and sets a flag indicating validity.

```
9900-GREGORIAN-VALIDATE.
    MOVE ZERO TO DATE-VALID-FLAG.
    MOVE GREGORIAN-DATE TO GREGORIAN-WHOLE-DATE.
```

```
        IF ((GREGORIAN-YEAR IS NUMERIC)AND (GREGORIAN-MONTH IS NUMERIC)
            AND (GREGORIAN-DAY IS NUMERIC))
            NEXT SENTENCE
        ELSE
            GO TO 9900-GREGORIAN-VALIDATE-EXIT.
        IF GREGORIAN-CENTURY = ZERO
            PERFORM 9900-SELECT-CENTURY
                THRU 9900-SELECT-CENTURY-EXIT;
            ADD DEFAULT-CENTURY TO GREGORIAN-YEAR.
        IF ((GREGORIAN-YEAR < BASE-DATE-YEAR)
            OR
            (GREGORIAN-YEAR > MAXIMUM-YEARS)
            OR
            (GREGORIAN-MONTH < MINIMUM-MONTHS)
            OR
            (GREGORIAN-MONTH > MAXIMUM-MONTHS)
            OR
            (GREGORIAN-DAY < MINIMUM-DAYS)
            )
            GO TO 9900-GREGORIAN-VALIDATE-EXIT.
        IF GREGORIAN-MONTH = FEBRUARY-MONTH
            DIVIDE GREGORIAN-YEAR BY LEAP-YEAR-MODULUS
            GIVING DATE-WORK-LEAP-1 REMAINDER DATE-WORK-LEAP-2;
            IF DATE-WORK-LEAP-2 = ZERO
                COMPUTE DATE-WORK-LEAP-1 = DAYS-IN-MONTH (FEBRUARY-
MONTH) + 1
            ELSE
                MOVE DAYS-IN-MONTH (FEBRUARY-MONTH)
                    TO DATE-WORK-LEAP-1
        ELSE
            MOVE DAYS-IN-MONTH
                (GREGORIAN-MONTH)TO DATE-WORK-LEAP-1.
        IF GREGORIAN-DAY > DATE-WORK-LEAP-1
            GO TO 9900-GREGORIAN-VALIDATE-EXIT.
        MOVE 1 TO DATE-VALID-FLAG.
    9900-GREGORIAN-VALIDATE-EXIT.
        EXIT.
```

COBOL Program Variables

DATE INTERFACE VARIABLES

These variables are the interface to the date routines. The input variables should be loaded with relevant data prior to calling the function. Results are returned in the variable appropriate for the function called.

```
01  DATE-INTERFACE-VARIABLES.
    03  SERIAL-DATE                      PIC 9(05) VALUE ZERO.
    03  SERIAL-TIME                      PIC 9(06) VALUE ZERO.
    03  GREGORIAN-DATE                PIC 9(08) VALUE ZERO.
    03  GREGORIAN-TIME                PIC 9(06) VALUE ZERO.
    03  GREGORIAN-DATE-1ST        PIC 9(08) VALUE ZERO.
```

```
03  GREGORIAN-DATE-2ND     PIC 9(08) VALUE ZERO.
03  JULIAN-DATE                  PIC 9(07) VALUE ZERO.
03  DAYS-INTERVAL            PIC 9(05) VALUE ZERO.
03  WEEK-DAY                      PIC 9(01) VALUE ZERO.
03  DATE-VALID-FLAG          PIC 9(01) VALUE ZERO.
    88  DATE-IS-INVALID             VALUE ZERO.
    88  DATE-IS-VALID               VALUE 1.
03  DATE-STRING-DINGY       PIC X(08) VALUE SPACES.
03  DATE-STRING-SHORT       PIC X(10) VALUE SPACES.
03  DATE-STRING-MEDIUM      PIC X(11) VALUE SPACES.
03  DATE-STRING-LONG        PIC X(18) VALUE SPACES.
03  DATE-STRING-SUPER       PIC X(30) VALUE SPACES.
```

DATE ROUTINE VARIABLES

These variables are used by the date-manipulation routines, and ideally should not be used externally.

```
01  DATE-ROUTINE-VARIABLES.
```

The following list is used to provide the long and short name of the month for text purposes.

```
03  MONTH-NAMES-DEFINED.
    05  FILLER              PIC X(09) VALUE "January  ".
    05  FILLER              PIC X(09) VALUE "February ".
    05  FILLER                  PIC X(09) VALUE "March    ".
    05  FILLER                  PIC X(09) VALUE "April    ".
    05  FILLER                  PIC X(09) VALUE "May      ".
    05  FILLER                  PIC X(09) VALUE "June     ".
    05  FILLER                  PIC X(09) VALUE "July     ".
    05  FILLER                  PIC X(09) VALUE "August   ".
    05  FILLER                  PIC X(09) VALUE "September".
    05  FILLER                  PIC X(09) VALUE "October  ".
    05  FILLER                  PIC X(09) VALUE "November ".
    05  FILLER                  PIC X(09) VALUE "December ".
03  MONTH-NAMES-SINGLE REDEFINES MONTH-NAMES-DEFINED
    OCCURS 12 TIMES INDEXED BY MONTH-NAME-INDX.
    05  MONTH-NAME.
        07  MONTH-NAME-SHORT        PIC X(03).
        07  FILLER                  PIC X(06).
```

The following list is used to extract the long and short name of the date of the week.

```
                            03  DAY-NAMES-DEFINED.
    05  FILLER              PIC X(09) VALUE "Sunday   ".
    05  FILLER              PIC X(09) VALUE "Monday   ".
    05  FILLER              PIC X(09) VALUE "Tuesday  ".
    05  FILLER                  PIC X(09) VALUE "Wednesday".
    05  FILLER                  PIC X(09) VALUE "Thursday ".
    05  FILLER                  PIC X(09) VALUE "Friday   ".
    05  FILLER                  PIC X(09) VALUE "Saturday ".
03  DAY-NAMES REDEFINES DAY-NAMES-DEFINED
    OCCURS 7 TIMES INDEXED BY DAY-NAME-INDX.
```

```
05  DAY-NAME.
    07  DAY-NAME-SHORT              PIC X(03).
    07  FILLER                      PIC X(06).
```

The following list provides the days in each month. The entry for February will be modified dynamically for those years that are leap years. Note that this table could have been used to eliminate the next table, but repeated calculations were too slow.

```
03  DAYS-IN-MONTHS-DEFINED.
    05  FILLER                      PIC 9(02) VALUE 31.
    05  FILLER                      PIC 9(02) VALUE 28.
    05  FILLER                      PIC 9(02) VALUE 31.
    05  FILLER                      PIC 9(02) VALUE 30.
    05  FILLER                      PIC 9(02) VALUE 31.
    05  FILLER                      PIC 9(02) VALUE 30.
    05  FILLER                      PIC 9(02) VALUE 31.
    05  FILLER                      PIC 9(02) VALUE 31.
    05  FILLER                      PIC 9(02) VALUE 30.
    05  FILLER                      PIC 9(02) VALUE 31.
    05  FILLER                      PIC 9(02) VALUE 30.
    05  FILLER                      PIC 9(02) VALUE 31.
03  DAYS-IN-MONTHS REDEFINES DAYS-IN-MONTHS-DEFINED
    OCCURS 12 TIMES INDEXED BY DAY-IN-MNTH-INDX.
    05  DAYS-IN-MONTH               PIC 9(02).
```

The following list contains the days that elapsed by month. This provides a quick method for calculating and converting serial dates. Using a table is quicker than calculating each time, especially since the data does not change. Entries for February are modified dynamically for leap years.

```
03  DAYS-MONTHS-PAST-DEFINED.
    05  FILLER                      PIC 9(03) VALUE 000.
    05  FILLER                      PIC 9(03) VALUE 031.
    05  FILLER                      PIC 9(03) VALUE 059.
    05  FILLER                      PIC 9(03) VALUE 090.
    05  FILLER                      PIC 9(03) VALUE 120.
    05  FILLER                      PIC 9(03) VALUE 151.
    05  FILLER                      PIC 9(03) VALUE 181.
    05  FILLER                      PIC 9(03) VALUE 212.
    05  FILLER                      PIC 9(03) VALUE 243.
    05  FILLER                      PIC 9(03) VALUE 273.
    05  FILLER                      PIC 9(03) VALUE 304.
    05  FILLER                      PIC 9(03) VALUE 334.
    05  FILLER                      PIC 9(03) VALUE 365.
03  DAYS-MONTHS-PAST REDEFINES DAYS-MONTHS-PAST-
    DEFINED OCCURS 13 TIMES INDEXED BY DAYS-PAST-INDX.
    05  DAYS-MONTH-PAST             PIC 9(03).
```

The serial-date work area allows the date to be split and results from calculations to be stored.

```
03  SERIAL-WORK-AREA.
05  SERIAL-WORK                     PIC 9(05)V9(02) VALUE ZERO.
05  SERIAL-WORK-SPLIT REDEFINES SERIAL-WORK.
    07  SERIAL-INTEGER      PIC 9(05).
    07  SERIAL-FRACTION     PIC 9(02).
```

The following list contains the Gregorian-date work areas that contain redefinitions and date-split sections. They make it easy to add century and build dates.

```
03  GREGORIAN-WORK-AREA.
    05  GREGORIAN-WHOLE-DATE     PIC 9(08) VALUE ZERO.
  05 GREGORIAN-DATE-SPLIT REDEFINES GREGORIAN-WHOLE-DATE.
07  GREGORIAN-YEAR               PIC 9(04).
07  GREGORIAN-YEAR-SPLIT REDEFINES GREGORIAN-YEAR.
            09  GREGORIAN-CENTURY      PIC 9(02).
            09  GREGORIAN-YEAR-2       PIC 9(02).
        07  GREGORIAN-MONTH            PIC 9(02).
        07  GREGORIAN-DAY              PIC 9(02).
    05  GREGORIAN-TIME-WORK            PIC 9(06) VALUE ZERO.
    05  GREGORIAN-TIME-SPLIT REDEFINES GREGORIAN-TIME-WORK.
07 GREGORIAN-TIME-YY      PIC 9(02).07 GREGORIAN-TIME-MM
PIC 9(02).07  GREGORIAN-TIME-DD        PIC 9(02).
    05  GREGORIAN-WHOLE-DATE-N         PIC 9(08).
    05  GREGORIAN-DATE-SPLIT-N REDEFINES GREGORIAN-
WHOLE-DATE-N.
07  GREGORIAN-YEAR-N               PIC 9(04).
07  GREGORIAN-MONTH-N              PIC 9(02).
        07  GREGORIAN-DAY-N                PIC 9(02).
```

The following list shows the Julian-date work area that allows the date to be split.

```
03  JULIAN-WORK-AREA.
    05 JULIAN-DATE-WHOLE            PIC 9(07) VALUE ZERO.
    05  JULIAN-DATE-SPLIT REDEFINES JULIAN-DATE-WHOLE.
        07  JULIAN-YEAR               PIC 9(04).
        07  JULIAN-YEAR-SPLIT REDEFINES JULIAN-YEAR.
        09  JULIAN-CENTURY            PIC 9(02).
        09  JULIAN-YEAR-2             PIC 9(02).
        07  JULIAN-DAY                PIC 9(03).
```

The following list shows the date work areas for manipulating dates and doing some math.

```
03  DATE-WORK-AREAS.
    05  DATE-WORK-LEAP-1             PIC 9(02) VALUE ZERO.
    05  DATE-WORK-LEAP-2             PIC 9(04) VALUE ZERO.
    05  DATE-WORK-1                  PIC 9(05)V9(02) VALUE ZERO.
    05  DATE-WORK-1-AGN REDEFINES DATE-WORK-1.
        07  DATE-WORK-1-I             PIC 9(05).
        07  DATE-WORK-1-F                        PIC 9(02).
    05  DATE-WORK-2                             PIC 9(05)V9(02)
VALUE ZERO.
        05  DATE-WORK-2-AGN REDEFINES DATE-WORK-2.
        07  DATE-WORK-2-I             PIC 9(05).
        07  DATE-WORK-2-F             PIC 9(02).
```

This is the divisor for calculating the year.

```
        03  DATE-ROUTINE-CONSTANTS.
```

This is the base year that all serial dates relate to. This can be changed by modifying the starting point. The month and day are always January 1. If you change this, be sure to also change the day-of-week calculation routine, as it will surely be affected.

```
05  SERIAL-FACTOR                PIC 9(03)V9(02) VALUE 365.25.
```

The century constants are used in calculations, and might be modified by the program. The 1900 and 2000 century are used to modify the default century, based on the defined split. Note that the century break determines which century to use for years that do not have a century associated with them.

```
05  BASE-DATE-YEAR               PIC 9(04) VALUE 1900.
05  DEFAULT-CENTURY              PIC 9(04) VALUE 1900.
05  DEFAULT-CENTURY-AGN REDEFINES DEFAULT-CENTURY.
    07  DEFAULT-CENTURY-H        PIC 9(02).
    07  FILLER                   PIC 9(02).
05  DEFAULT-CENTURY-BREAK        PIC 9(02) VALUE 10.
05  DEFAULT-CENTURY-1900         PIC 9(04) VALUE 1900.
05  DEFAULT-CENTURY-2000         PIC 9(04) VALUE 2000.
```

The following constants do not get modified. They are used to avoid inline literals that sometimes cause trouble.

```
05  FEBRUARY-MONTH               PIC 9(01) VALUE 2.
05  LEAP-YEAR-MODULUS            PIC 9(01) VALUE 4.
05  MAXIMUM-YEARS                PIC 9(04) VALUE 2099.
05  MINIMUM-MONTHS               PIC 9(01) VALUE 1.
05  MAXIMUM-MONTHS               PIC 9(02) VALUE 12.
05  MINIMUM-DAYS                 PIC 9(01) VALUE 1.
05  DAYS-IN-WEEK                 PIC 9(01) VALUE 7.
05  LEAP-YEAR-DAYS               PIC 9(03) VALUE 366.
05  NORMAL-YEAR-DAYS             PIC 9(03) VALUE 365.
05  DAYS-IN-360-YEAR             PIC 9(03) VALUE 360.
05  DAYS-IN-360-MONTH            PIC 9(02) VALUE 30.
05  DATE-SEPARATOR               PIC X(01) VALUE "/".
```

CHAPTER 14

PL/1 Date Functions

Intrinsic Functions

PL/1 has only two date-specific intrinsic functions. These provide date and time information derived from the system clock.

Accordingly, time zone and accuracy are system-dependent. The date is obtained from the system clock, unless the PL/1 internal function has been modified through an installation-written exit. Such an exit might return the date as specified in an external file, rather than using the system clock. Both application developers and code-testers use this type of modified *dating file* to test code under different date scenarios.

In the section that follows, optional choices are enclosed in square brackets ([ ]).

DATE [( )];

Returns

character string, length six, in the format of YYMMDD.

The returned character string represents:

YY
    Last two digits of current year

MM
    Current month

DD
    Current day

Example

```
DCL 01 DATE_STRUC,
    03 YY CHAR(2),
```

```
    03 MM CHAR(2),
    03 DD CHAR(2);
DCL (DATE, STRING) BUILTIN;

STRING(DATE_STRUC) = DATE();
```

DATETIME [( )];

Returns

character string, length 17, in the format YYYYMMDDHHMMSSTT.

The returned character string represents:

yyyy
> Current year

mm
> Current month

dd
> Current day

hh
> Current hour

mm
> Current minute

ss
> Current second

ttt
> Current millisecond

Example

```
DCL 01 DATETIME_STRUC,
    03 DATE_STRUC,
        05 YYYY CHAR(4),
        05 MM   CHAR(2),
        05 DD   CHAR(2),
    03 TIME_STRUC,
        05 MM   CHAR(2),
        05 SS   CHAR(2),
        05 TTT  CHAR(3);
DCL (DATETIME, STRING) BUILTIN;

STRING(DATETIME_STRUC) = DATETIME();
```

Primary User-Developed Date Functions

Generally speaking, computers convert a character date to a serial date when they do date arithmetic. A serial date is an integer-day number that is relative to a base date. When serial days are used, it's easy for programs to determine the number of days between two dates—all they have to do is subtract one serial date from another.

PL/1 Date Functions

Base date choices are quite arbitrary—see Chapter 5, *Technical Considerations*, for an explanation of common base-date systems.

The Lilian serial-number system described in that chapter has been adopted by IBM as the basis for date-calculation routines in the IBM Language Environment for VM and MVS.

A PL/1 routine for calculating the difference between two dates could be written as follows, with no error checking.

DTDIFF (YYYYMMDD1, YYYYMMDD2)

Input

Two character (8) dates in the format YYYYMMDD.

Returns

A fixed binary (31) number corresponding to the difference between two dates.

Example

```
DTDIFF: Proc(YYYYMMDD1, YYYYMMDD2) RETURNS(FIXED BIN(31));
  DCL YYYYMMDD1 CHAR(8);
  DCL YYYYMMDD2 CHAR(8);
  DCL ABS       BUILTIN; /* ABSOLUTE BUILTIN FUNCTION */
  RETURN( ABS( DT2LIL0(YYYYMMDD1) - DT2LIL0(YYYYMMDD2) ) );
END DTDIFF;
```

DTADD (OR SUBTRACT) (YYYYMMDD, DAYS)

Input

An eight-byte character string in the format YYYYMMDD.

A positive (or negative) number of days to be added (or subtracted) from the date.

Returns

Normal
 An eight-byte character string containing a date in the format YYYYMMDD.

Invalid date
 A null string.

Example

```
DTADD: PROC(YYYYMMDD, DAYS) RETURNS (CHAR(8));

  DCL YYYYMMDD  CHAR(8);
  DCL DAYS      FIXED BIN(31);
  DCL LILIAN    FIXED BIN(31);
  DCL MOD       BUILTIN;

  Lilian = DT2LIL(YYYYMMDD);
  If Lilian <= 0 Then
    YYYYMMDD = '';
```

```
   Else
      YYYYMMDD = LIL2DT((LILIAN+DAYS));
   Return(YYYYMMDD);
End DTADD;
```

DT2DAY (YYYYMMDD) RETURNS (CHAR(10) VARYING)

Input

An eight-byte character string in the format YYYYMMDD.

Returns

Normal

   A character string containing the day of the week.

Invalid date

A null string.

Comment

Calculating the day of the week is simplified by use of a Lilian day, since Lilian 1 is a Friday by definition.

Example

```
DT2DAY: PROC(YYYYMMDD) RETURNS (CHAR(10) VARYING);

   DCL YYYYMMDD  CHAR(8);
   DCL DAYOFWEEK CHAR(10) VARYING;
   DCL LILIAN    FIXED BIN(31);
   DCL MOD       BUILTIN;

   LILIAN = DT2LIL(YYYYMMDD);
   If LILIAN <= 0 Then
      Dayofweek = '';
   Else
      Select(Mod(Lilian,7));
         When(1) DAYOFWEEK = 'Friday';
         When(2) DAYOFWEEK = 'Saturday';
         When(3) DAYOFWEEK = 'Sunday';
         When(4) DAYOFWEEK = 'Monday';
         When(5) DAYOFWEEK = 'Tuesday';
         When(6) DAYOFWEEK = 'Wednesday';
         When(0) DAYOFWEEK = 'Thursday';
         Otherwise DAYOFWEEK = '';
      End;
   Return(DAYOFWEEK);
End DT2DAY;
```

DT2MNTH (YYYYMMDD) RETURNS (CHAR(10) VARYING)

Input

An eight-byte character string in the format YYYYMMDD.

Returns

Normal

  A character string containing the month.

Invalid date

A null string.

Example

```
DT2MNTH: PROC(YYYYMMDD) RETURNS (CHAR(10) VARYING);

  DCL YYYYMMDD  CHAR(8);
  DCL MONTH     CHAR(10) VARYING;
  DCL SUBSTR    BUILTIN;

If DT2LIL(YYYYMMDD) Then  /* check for a valid date */
  MONTH = '';
Else
  Select(Substr(YYYYMMDD,5,2));
    When('01') MONTH = 'January';
    When('02') MONTH = 'February';
    When('03') MONTH = 'March';
    When('04') MONTH = 'April';
    When('05') MONTH = 'May';
    When('06') MONTH = 'June';
    When('07') MONTH = 'July';
    When('08') MONTH = 'August';
    When('09') MONTH = 'September';
    When('10') MONTH = 'October';
    When('11') MONTH = 'November';
    When('12') MONTH = 'December';
    Otherwise MONTH = '';
  End;
  Return(MONTH);
End DT2MNTH;
```

WINDOW (YYMMDD, BASE)

Input

A six-byte character string in the format YYMMDD, and a two-byte binary number between 0 and 99, representing the number of years prior to the current year where the 100-year century window is to begin.

For example, if 1998 is the current year, then a base of 0 implies a window of 1998 to 2097, a base of 50 implies a window of 1948 to 2047, and a base of 99 implies a window of 1899 to 1998.

Returns

An eight-byte character string in the format YYYYMMDD.

Example

```
WINDOW: PROC(YYMMDD, BASE) RETURNS (CHAR(8));
   DCL BASE          FIXED BIN(15);  /* Only 0 to 99 is valid */
   DCL BASE_YEAR     FIXED BIN(15);
   DCL BASE_CEN      FIXED BIN(15);
   DCL DATETIME      BUILTIN;
   DCL NEW_YYYY      PIC'9999';
   DCL THIS_YEAR     PIC'9999';
   DCL YYMMDD        CHAR(6);
   DCL 1 YYMMDD_DEF  DEFINED YYMMDD,
         3 YY        PIC'99',
         3 MMDD      CHAR(4);
    DCL YYYYMMDD     CHAR(8);

   IF BASE >= 0 & BASE <= 99 THEN
      DO;
         THIS_YEAR = SUBSTR(DATETIME,1,4);   /* Get current year */
         BASE_YEAR = THIS_YEAR - BASE;       /* Set base year */
         BASE_CEN  = MOD(BASE_YEAR,100);     /* Extract the century */
         NEW_YYYY  = BASE_CEN*100 + YY;      /* Put century in front */
         IF NEW_YYYY < BASE_YEAR THEN        /* If before base year */
            NEW_YYYY = NEW_YYYY + 100;       /* Add 100 years */
         YYYYMMDD = NEW_YYYY||MMDD;
      END;
   ELSE
      YYYYMMDD = '';
   RETURN (YYYYMMDD);
END WINDOW;
```

Supporting Functions

The PL/1 subroutines shown previously are very basic. They do not perform any error-checking, and they require support from the supporting functions below. Furthermore, these PL/1 subroutines don't accommodate blank date fields or erroneous dates. Consequently, we make the following definitions and assumptions:

1. Although Lilian Day 0 corresponds to 14 October 1582, define 0 (zero) as the numeric equivalent of a blank date.

2. Define negative Lilian dates to be invalid, and let –1 (minus one) signify an invalid date.

3. The highest Lilian date corresponds to 31 December 3267.

DT2LIL (YYYYMMDD) RETURNS(FIXED BIN(31))

Input

An eight-byte character string, usually a date in the format YYYYMMDD.

Returns

Normal

Lilian date.

0

Input is blank

1

Input date is invalid

-1

Input date is outside the year range

Example

```
DT2LIL: PROC(YYYYMMDD) RETURNS(FIXED BIN(31));
  DCL YYYYMMDD    CHAR(8);
  DCL 01 YYYYMMDD_STRUC DEFINED YYYYMMDD,
      03 YYYY    PIC'9999',
      03 MM    PIC'99',
      03 DD    PIC'99';
  DCL LILIAN      FIXED BIN(31);
  DCL VERIFY      BUILTIN;
  Select;
    When (YYYYMMDD=' ') Then Lilian = 0;
    When (Verify(YYYYMMDD,'1234567890')>0) Then Lilian = -1;
    When (YYYY < 1582 | YYYY > 3268)        Then Lilian = -1;
    When (MM < 1 | MM > 12 )                Then Lilian = -1;
    When (MM = 1 & (DD < 1 | DD > 31 )      Then Lilian = -1;
    When (MM = 2 & (DD<1 | DD>29 )          Then Lilian = -1;
    When (MM = 2 & (YYYY/4>0 | (YYYY/100=0 & YYYY/400>0)) & (DD=29)
Then
      Lilian = -1;
    When (DD < 1 | DD > 31) Then Lilian = -1;
    When ((MM = 4 | MM = 6 | MM = 9 | MM = 11) & (DD = 31)) Then
      Lilian = -1;
    When (YYYY = 1582 & MM < 10) Then Lilian = -1;
    When (YYYY = 1582 & MM = 10 & (DD>=1 & DD <=14)) Then Lilian =
-1;
    Otherwise Lilian = DT2LIL0(YYYYMMDD);
  End;
Return (Lilian);
End DT2LIL;
```

LIL2DT (LILIAN) RETURNS (CHAR(8))

Input

A fixed binary integer, usually corresponding to a Lilian date.

Returns

Normal

An eight-byte character string denoting the Gregorian date (YYYYMMDD).

Blank or **ERROR** is returned in certain circumstances.

Example

```
LIL2DT: PROC(LILIAN) RETURNS (CHAR(8));
  DCL YYYYMMDD CHAR(8);
  DCL YYYY     PIC'9999';
  DCL MM       PIC'99';
  DCL DD       PIC'99';
  DCL LILIAN   FIXED BIN(31);

  Select;
    When (Lilian = 0) Then YYYYMMDD = ' ';
    When (Lilian < 0 | Lilian > DT2LIL0('32671231')) Then
      YYYYMMDD='ERROR' ;
    Otherwise YYYYMMDD = DT2LIL0(Lilian);
  End;
  Return(YYYYMMDD);
End LIL2DT;
```

DT2LIL0 (YYYYMMDD) RETURNS(FIXED BIN(31))

Input

An eight-byte string representing YYYYMMDD.

Returns

A fixed binary(31) number representing a Lilian date.

Example

```
DT2LIL0: PROC(YYYYMMDD) RETURNS(FIXED BIN(31));
  DCL YYYYMMDD CHAR(8);
  DCL 01 YYYYMMDD_STRUC DEFINED YYYYMMDD,
      03 YYYY   PIC'9999',
      03 MM   PIC'99',
      03 DD   PIC'99';
  DCL LILIAN FIXED BIN(31);

  LILIAN = ( 1461 * ( YYYY + 4800 + ( MM - 14 ) / 12 ) ) / 4 +
( 367 * ( MM - 2 - 12 * ( ( MM - 14 ) / 12 ) ) ) / 12 -
( 3 * ( ( YYYY + 4900 + ( MM - 14 ) / 12 ) / 100 ) ) / 4 +
DD - 32075 - 2299160;
  RETURN(LILIAN);
END DT2LIL0;
```

The inverse function can be achieved as follows:

LIL2DT0 (LILIAN) RETURNS (CHAR(8))

Input

A fixed binary(31) number representing a Lilian date.

Returns

An eight-byte string representing YYYYMMDD.

Example

```
LIL2DT0: PROC(LILIAN) RETURNS (CHAR(8));
  DCL YYYYMMDD CHAR(8);
  DCL YYYY      PIC'9999';
  DCL MM        PIC'99';
  DCL DD        PIC'99';
  DCL (LILIAN, T1, T2, T3, T4) FIXED BIN(31);

  T1 = 68569 + 2299160 + LILIAN;
  T2 = ( 4 * T1 ) / 146097;
  T1 = T1 - ( 146097 * T2 + 3 ) / 4;
  T3 = ( 4000 * ( T1 + 1 ) ) / 1461001;
  T1 = T1 - (1461 * T3 ) / 4 + 31;
  T4 = ( 80 * T1 ) / 2447;
  DD = T1 - ( 2447 * T4 ) / 80;
  T1 = T4 / 11;
  MM = T4 + 2 - ( 12 * T1 );
  YYYY = 100 * ( T2 - 49 ) + T3 + T1;
  YYYYMMDD = YYYY || MM || DD;
  RETURN(YYYYMMDD);
END LIL2DT0;
```

CHAPTER 15

MVS LE Date Functions

IBM Language Environment/370 contains code solutions for working with time and dates in PL/1, COBOL and C++, amongst others. The IBM documentation is a lot more detailed and descriptive so this chapter should only be used as a starting point.

The date functions are based on the concept of Lilian Days, a serial date starting on Friday, 15 October 1582 and extending to 3,074,324, (December 31, 9999).

All calls to these functions are in a standard format that makes cross-language investigation and coding easier. The last parameter is an optional 12-byte return code used to supply the status of the call. For example:

```
DCL CEEDATE ENTRY(*,*,*,* OPTIONAL) OPTIONS(ASM);
DCL 1 FBT,  /* Feedback Token */
        3 Severity   FIXED BINARY (15),
        3 MsgNo      FIXED BINARY (15),
        3 Flags,
          5 Case     BIT (2),
          5 Severity BIT (3),
          5 Control  BIT (3),
        3 FacID      CHAR (3),
        3 Detail     FIXED BINARY (31);

CALL CEEDATE(a,b,c,*);    /* valid   */
  or
CALL CEEDATE(a,b,c,FBT);   /* valid   */
```

Calls that omit the feedback parameter are illegal. For example:

```
DCL CEEDATE ENTRY OPTIONS(ASM);
CALL CEEDATE(a,b,c);      /* invalid as there are only 3
params.*/
```

Any return-value greater than zero corresponds to an error number and a descriptive message.

251

CEEDYWK
(Lilian_day, Day_of_week, FBT)

Input

Lilian_day
A fixed binary (31) integer representing the Lilian Day.

Returns

Day_of_week
A 32-bit binary integer representing the day of the week that corresponds with the Lilian_day integer: 1 equals Sunday, 2 equals Monday, and so on through 7 for Saturday.

If Lilian_day is invalid, Day_of_week is set to 0 and CEEDYWK terminates with FBT.Msgno <> 0.

FBT

Comment
CEEDYWK calculates the day of the week on which a Lilian Day falls. The number returned by CEEDYWK is useful for setting up end-of-week calculations.

Usage
CALL CEEDYWK (Lilian_day, Day_of_week, FBT)

CEEDATE
(Lilian_day, picture_spec, char_date, FBT)

Input

Lilian_day (input)
A 32-bit integer denoting the Lilian day.

Picture_spec (input)
A variable-length character string illustrating the required format of char_date. For example, MM/DD/YY. Each character in picture_spec represents a digit in char_date.

Returns

char_date
A fixed-length 80-character string, which results from converting Lilian_day to the format specified by picture_spec. If Lilian_day is invalid, out_char_date is set to all blanks. CEEDATE terminates with FBT.Msgno <> 0.

FBT

Comment
CEEDATE converts a Lilian day to a date in character format such as 1993/03/13. The inverse of CEEDATE is CEEDAYS, which converts character dates to a Lilian number.

If picture_spec is null or blank, CEEDATE bases picture_spec on the setting of the COUNTRY run-time option. For example, if the the COUNTRY run-time option was ZIM (Zimbabwe), the date format might be YY/MM/DD.

Usage:

CALL CEEDATE (Lilian_day, picture_spec, char_date, FBT)

Examples for Lilian_day = 148138:

picture_spec	char_date
YYYY-MM-DD	1988-05-16
YYDDD	88139
WWW., MMM DD, YYYY	MON., MAY 16, 1988
Wwwwwwwwz, Mmmmmmmmmmz DD,YYY	Monday, May 16,1988

CEEDAYS   (char_date, picture_spec, Lilian_day, FBT)

Input

char_date

A variable-length string denoting a date or time in the format specified by picture_spec. The character string is limited to a minimum of 5 and a maximum of 255 characters and can contain leading or trailing blanks.

Parsing the string (for a date) begins with the first non-blank character, unless the picture string itself is defined with leading blanks. In such a case, CEEDAYS starts parsing after skipping this "mask."

After finding the date described in the picture_spec, CEEDAYS ignores remaining characters. Acceptable char_dates are between 15 October 1582 and 31 December 9999.

picture_spec

A variable-length character string describing the format of char_date.

Each valid character in the picture_spec matches a character in char_date. If delimiters (e.g. '/' or ':') occur in picture_spec, leading zeros are optional. These delimiters are used as a mask and ignored.

For example:

```
CALL CEEDAYS('5/12/99' , 'MM/DD/YY', lilian_day, FBT);
```

would return 152151 to lilian_day.

and

```
CALL CEEDAYS('5/14/99' , 'MM/DD/YY', lilian_day, FBT);
```

would return 152153 to lilian_day.

NOTE

See Table 15-1 for a list of valid picture characters, and Table 15-2 for examples of valid picture strings.

MVS LE Date
Functions

Returns

Lilian_day (output)

A 32-bit binary integer denoting the Lilian day.

If char_date does not contain a valid date, Lilian_day is set to 0 and CEEDAYS terminates with FBT.Msgno <> 0.

Date calculations are performed easily on the Lilian_day integer. Leap year and end-of-year anomalies do not affect the calculations.

FBT

Comment

CEEDAYS converts a date string into a Lilian number.

CEEDAYS can also perform date-arithmetic, (e.g. the difference between two dates.)

Any two-digit years that fall in the 100-year range (from 80 less than current system date to 19 greater than the system date) are assigned default centuries. which can be over-ridden using CEESCEN (see later in this chapter).

Usage

CALL CEEDAYS (char_date, picture_spec, Lilian_day, FBT)

CEEQCEN   (first_year, FBT)

Returns

first_year

An integer between 0 and 100 depicting the first year of the default century.

If CEEQCEN returns '80' the Language Environment default is active and in 1999 all years between 29 and 99 will default to CC=19 and those in the range 00 - 18 will be assigned CC=20.)

FBT

Comment

CEEQCEN queries the two-digit year value "century" stored in the Language Environment. Use CEESCEN to change the current setting.

Usage

CALL CEEQCEN (first_year, FBT)

CEESCEN   (first_year, FBT)

Input

first_year

An integer between 0 and 100, which sets the start-year of a century defaulting range.

For example, a setting of "30" in 1999 sets the window to 1969-2068

FBT

Comment

CEESCEN configures the start year of a century that Language Environment uses to determine the CC component. Use CEEQCEN and CEESCEN to process 6 digit dates when the default LE range (-80/+19) does not apply to your program.

NOTE

These settings are at thread-level and do not affect the interval in another thread.

Usage

CALL CEESCEN(first_year, FBT)

Example using LE functions

```
DCL LILIAN FIXED BINARY(31);
DCL 01 FBT, /* Feedback token */
        03 Urgency FIXED BINARY(15,0),
        03 Number  FIXED BINARY(15,0),
        03 Indicators,
           05 Instance BIT(2),
           05 level    BIT(3),
           05 Cont     BIT(3),
        03 Loc         CHAR(3),
        03 ISI         FIXED BINARY(31,0);

DCL DATETIME BUILTIN;
DCL SUBSTR   BUILTIN;
TODAY = SUBSTR(DATETIME(),1,8);
PUT SKIP LIST('The system clock says that today is', TODAY);
CALL PRINTIT('850516');      /* assumes a window of +19/-80 */
CALL CEESCEN(10, FBT); /* Change default window to +89/-10 */
CALL PRINTIT('850516');

PRINTIT: PROC(DATE6);
  DCL DATE6    CHAR(6);
  DCL DATELONG CHAR(30);

  CALL CEEQCEN(FIRST_YEAR, FBT);
  PUT SKIP LIST('The 100 year window starts', FIRST_YEAR,
               'years ago');
  CALL CEEDAYS('850516', 'YYMMDD', LILIAN, FBT);
  CALL CEEDATE(LILIAN, 'Www, DD Mmm YYYY', DATELONG, FBT);
  PUT SKIP LIST(DATE6, 'corresponds to', DATELONG);
END PRINTIT;
```

The sample output will be:

```
The system clock says that today is 19980118
The 100 year window starts 80 years ago
600516 corresponds to Mon, 16 May 1960
The 100 year window starts 10 years ago
600516 corresponds to Sun, 16 May 2060
```

Table A

NOTE

This table is a subset of the full range of settings and should not be used in place of the IBM documentation.

Picture Terms	Description	Valid Values	Notes
Y	One-digit year	0 through 9	1
YY	Two-digit year	00 through 99	1
YYYY	Four-digit year	1582 through 9999	1
MM	Two-digit month	01 through 12	2
ZM	One- or two-digit month	1 through 12	2
RRRR	Roman-numeral month	I through XII, left-justified	3
RRRZ	Roman-numeral month	Left-justified, Trailing blanks suppressed	3
MMM	Three-character month, uppercase	JAN to DEC	4
Mmm	Three-character month, mixed case	Jan to Dec	4
MMMM...M	Three- to 20-character month, uppercase	JANUARY to DECEMBER	4
Mmmm...m	Three- to 20-character month, mixed case	January to December	4
MMMMMMMMZ	Trailing blanks suppressed	JANUARY to DECEMBER	4
Mmmmmmmmmz	Trailing blanks suppressed	January to December	4
DD	Two-digit day of month	01-31	5
ZD	One- or two-digit day of month	1-31	5
DDD	Day of year (Julian)	001 through 366	5

Picture Terms	Description	Valid Values	Notes
W	One-character day-of-week	S, M, T, W, T, F, S	9
WWW	Three-character day-of-week, uppercase	SUN to SAT	9
Www	Three-character day-of-week, mixed case	Sun to Sat	9
WWW...W	Three to 20-character day-of-week, uppercase	SUNDAY to SATURDAY	9
Www...w	Three- to 20-character day-of-week, mixed	Sunday to Saturday	9
WWWWWWW-WWWZ	One-char day-of-week	SUNDAY to SATURDAY	9
Wwwwwwwwwz	One-char day-of-week	Sunday to Saturday	9

Notes

1. A single "Y" is only valid for output. "YY" assumes the century window set by CEESCEN.

2. The leading zero is suppressed when used for output. For input, "ZM" treated the same as "MM."

3. The source string is converted to uppercase on input. Output is in uppercase only. III=Mar, XI=Nov.

4. The input source-string is always converted to uppercase. Output corresponds to the picture case. Output is padded with blanks or truncated unless "Z" is used.

5. The leading zero is always suppressed on output while "ZD" equates to "DD" on input.

6. The leading zero is removed for output. "ZH" treated as "HH" on inut. If "AP" is used the values 01-12 are valid.

7. No rounding takes place.

8. The input source-string is always converted to uppercase while a setting of "AP" outputs uppercase and "ap." lowercase.

9. "W" is ignored on input but "W" outputs uppercase and "w," lowercase. Unless "Z" is used, the output is padded with blanks or truncated to match the "W"'s mask, to a limit of 20.

MVS LE Date Functions

Table B

Date and Time Services Picture Strings	Examples	Notes
YYMMDD	990819	
YYYYMMDD	19990819	
YYYY-MM-DD	1999-08-19	1
MMDDYY	081999	
MM/DD/YY	08/19/99	
ZM/ZD/YY	8/19/99	
MM/DD/YYYY	08/19/1999	
MM/DD/Y	08/19/9	2
DD.MM.YY	19.08.99	
DD-RRRR-YY	19-V111-99	
DD MMM YY	19 AUG 99	
DD Mmmmmmmmmm YY	19 August 99	
ZD Mmmmmmmmmz YY	7 August 99	3
Mmmmmmmmmmz ZD, YYYY	August 7 1999	
ZDMMMMMMMMzYY	7AUGUST99	
YY.DDD	99.137	4
YYDDD	99137	
YYYY/DDD	1999/137	
YYMMDDHHMISS	990817130248	
YYYYMMDDHHMISS	19990817130248	
YYYY-MM-DD HH:MI:SS.999	1999-08-17 13:02:48.162	
WWW, ZM/ZD/YY HH:MI: AP	WED, 7/8/99 11:14 PM	
WwwwwwwwwwZ, DD Mmm YYYY, ZH:MI: AP	Wednesday, 12 July 1999, 11:14 PM	

Notes

1. 999-8-19 is also acceptable.

2. The one-digit year (Y) applies to output only.

3. Z causes zeros and blanks to be removed.

4. A Julian date.

Source: IBM Language Environment for MVS & VM: Programming Reference (SC26-3312-02)

CHAPTER 16

Visual Basic Date Functions

Although Visual Basic is a relatively new language, I have included this chapter for those who are converting their frontend system from programs written in older languages to this platform—in many cases, a smart Year-2000 option.

Visual Basic provides all of the functions used for normal date manipulation. To specifically derive logic windows that create Year-2000 compliant dates, you can use the same logical operations discussed in Chapter 12, *Pseudo-Date Functions,* Chapter 13, *COBOL Date Functions,* and Chapter 14, *PL/1 Date Functions.* Visual Basic does use a cusp system to automatically Window where applicable.

Due to backward compatibility issues, Visual Basic assumes that any year designated by two digits is in the 20th or 21st century. If a two-digit year is 30 or greater, 1900 is added; if the year is 29 or less, 2000 is added. In Visual Basic, "Date" is both a data type used to store and derive dates, and a function for getting the system date. Each Date is stored as an IEEE eight-byte floating point, and is capable of caching any authentic date prior to January 1st, 10,000.

Visual Basic also provides Now, an expanded instance of the Date type that includes the time. Now is always assigned the current system date. If you wish to store the current date, you must create a new Date variable and set it to Now (or part of Now). You may also use Now in place of any request for a Date type (see the example under "DateDiff," in the following section).

The Date format is set by the International Date and Time settings of the system. Accordingly, outputting or inputting a Date in a file could give different results on different platforms. Date's constructor is quite forgiving, and will accept a variety of input formats when setting a Date. These formats include a three-digit string separated by spaces, commas, or forward slashes or formats in which the month's number is replaced by the first three or more letters of its name. For extra stability, use the written month to avoid accidentally swapping month and day. A Date may also be set with a Literal Date, or set indirectly with a String value.

Only a String data-type may set a date at run-time, and this is the method that most applications require. Although documentation usually suggests using a conversion function (CDate()) to set a Date with a String, new type-casting tends to take care of the conversion. However, there is one advantage to the old policy: you may use a pre-conversion checking function (IsDate()) as a precautionary measure to avoid run-time errors.

Literal Dates are run through the Visual Basic's syntax checker just after they have been input, so any incorrect dates (for example, February 31, 1998) will be brought to your attention immediately. A Literal Date must be braced at each end by an octothorpe character (#).

Example

This code shows the three methods of setting a Date:

```
Dim dateA As Date
Dim stringA As String
dateA = #Dec 31 1999#          'setting a Date with a Literal
Date;
dateA = #12/31/99#             'all three of these Literal Dates
dateA = #December, 31, 1999#   'suggest December 31st, 1999;
dateA = "Dec 31 1999"          'setting a Date directly with a
String (not endorsed);
stringA = "Dec 31 1999"
if (IsDate(stringA)) then      'will stringA make a good Date?
    dateA=CDate(stringA)       'setting a Date with a converted
String
else
    MsgBox("Bad Date Encountered")
endif
```

Year

Returns

Four-digit rendition (0100 to 9999, or Null) for the year of a set Date type.

Usage

Day(dateA)

Arguments

PART	TYPE	DESCRIPTION
date	Date	the date from which to withdraw the year

If the Date in question has not been set, Null is returned.

Example

Output the four-digit year of a pre-set date, and send the result to a dialog box.

```
Dim dateA As Date
dateA = #Dec/31/99#
MsgBox Year(dateA)    'this will always return "1999" as opposed
to "99"
```

Month

Returns

An integer with range of 1 to 12, or Null.

Usage

Month(dateA)

Arguments

The only argument is mandatory.

PART	TYPE	DESCRIPTION
date	Date	the date from which to withdraw the month

If the Date in question has not been set, Null is returned.

Example

Output the three-letter month name of a pre-set date, and send the result to a dialog box.

```
Dim dateA As Date
Dim ShortMonth(1 To 12) As String
ShortMonth(1) = "Jan":ShortMonth(2) = "Feb"
ShortMonth(3) = "Mar":ShortMonth(4) = "Apr"
ShortMonth(5) = "May":ShortMonth(6) = "Jun"
ShortMonth(7) = "Jul":ShortMonth(8) = "Aug"
ShortMonth(9) = "Sep":ShortMonth(10) = "Oct"
ShortMonth(11) = "Nov":ShortMonth(12) = "Dec"
dateA = #Dec/31/99#
MsgBox ShortMonth(Month(dateA))
```

Day

Usage

Day(dateA)

Returns

An integer with range of 1 to 31, or Null.

Arguments

The only argument is mandatory.

If the Date in question has not been set, Null is returned.

PART	TYPE	DESCRIPTION
dateA	Date	the date from which to withdraw the MonthDay

Example

Output an eight-digit date from a six-digit date, and send the result to a dialog box.

```
Dim dateA As Date
Dim stringA As String
Dim stringB As String
stringA = "Jan/01/99"
if (IsDate(stringA)) then
    dateA=CDate(stringA)
    stringB = Format(Month(dateA), "00") & "/" &
Format(Day(dateA), "00") & "/" & Format(Year(dateA), "0000")
    MsgBox stringB    'displays "01/01/1999"
else
    MsgBox("Bad Date Encountered")
endif
```

WeekDay

Usage

(dateA[, TheFirstDayofTheWeek])

Returns

An integer within the range of 1 to 7, representing the day of the week.

Arguments

The first argument is mandatory.

PART	TYPE	DESCRIPTION
date	Date	the date from which to withdraw the WeekDay
TheFirstDayofTheWeek	Integer/Constant	allows you to offset the WeekDay from which the system starts counting (this is usually used for porting)

The value of "TheFirstDayofTheWeek" must be within the range 1 to 7. Predefined Visual Basic constants can be used for clarity.

Return Value

In the range 1 to 7, based on setting of "TheFirstDayofTheWeek."

If the Date in question has not been set, Null is returned.

Example

Output the three-letter WeekDay of a pre-set date, and send the result to a dialog box.

```
Dim dateA As Date
Dim ShortWeekDay(1 To 7) As String
ShortWeekDay(1) = "Sun":ShortWeekDay(2) = "Mon"
ShortWeekDay(3) = "Tue":ShortWeekDay(4) = "Wed"
ShortWeekDay(5) = "Thu":ShortWeekDay(6) = "Fri"
ShortWeekDay(7) = "Sat"
dateA = #Dec/31/99#
MsgBox ShortWeekDay(WeekDay(NewDate))
```

DateDiff

Usage

interval=DateDiff(unit,dateA,dateB[,TheFirstDayofTheWeek[,
TheFirstWeekofTheYear]])

Returns

The number of units between the two dates specified.

Arguments

The first three arguments are mandatory.

PART	TYPE	DESCRIPTION
unit	String	Describes the method of counting used between the two dates
dateA	Date	Reference date
dateB	Date	Comparison date
TheFirstDayofTheWeek	Integer/Constant	Allows you to offset the WeekDay from which the system starts counting
TheFirstWeekofTheYear	Integer/Constant	Allows you to specify what constitutes the first week in a year

The value of "unit" must be one of the following pre-defined formats:

VALUE	COUNTS NUMBER OF
s	Seconds
n	Minutes
h	Hours
w	Weeks
ww	Calendar Weeks (counts the number of Sundays between the dates; dateA is not included in the calculation)
d	Days
m	Months
q	Quarters
yyyy	Years

With "w" and "ww," "TheFirstDayofTheWeek" must be within the range 0 to 7 (0 indicates *use system defaults*). Pre-defined Visual Basic constants can be used for clarity.

The value of "TheFirstWeekofTheYear" must be within the range 0 to 4 (0 indicates *use system defaults*). Pre-defined Visual Basic constants can be used for clarity.

If dateB is greater than dateA, DateDiff will return a negative number.

Example

Displays the number of days before January 1, 2000.

```
Dim dateA As Date
Dim stringA As String
dateA = #Jan 1 2000#
stringA = "The number of days before old applications will
crash: "
stringA = stringA & DateDiff("d", Now, dateA)
MsgBox stringA
```

DateAdd

Adds or subtracts a specified amount of time to a Date.

Usage

DateAdd(unit, number, dateA)

Returns

The modified Date

Arguments

All three of these arguments are mandatory.

PART	TYPE	DESCRIPTION
unit	String	describes the method of counting used between the two dates
number	Integer	number or units to add/subtract
dateA	Date	reference Date

The value of "unit" must be one of the following pre-defined formats:

VALUE	NUMBER SPECIFIES
s	Seconds
n	Minutes
h	Hours
w	Weeks
ww	Calendar Weeks (counts the number of Sundays between the dates; dateA is not included)

VALUE	NUMBER SPECIFIES
d	Days
m	Months
q	Quarters
yyyy	Years

If the number is negative, subtraction takes place.

Unlike other programming languages, Visual Basic's DateAdd takes care of both exact units, such as days or weeks, and variable-length units, such as months or years. No illegal dates can be returned with this function, as it accommodates month-lengths and leap years.

Example

Sets a record-expiration date for 10 months from now.

```
Dim dateA As Date
dateA = DateAdd("m", 10, Now)
MsgBox "Record expires at " & dateA
```

CHAPTER 17

C Date Functions

There are many versions of C and C++, most with their own suites of high-level intrinsic date functions. For that reason, this chapter concentrates on the core functionality of date arithmetic in the C language family. Remember that LE functions are available for C++ on MVS.

time_t Type (TIME.H)

The time_t declaration is a type used in conjunction with a function. It returns the current time, defined as the number of seconds since 00:00:00 GMT, January 1, 1970. It can handle any date after 1970, and due to the size of the variable of type time_t, it is virtually limitless. Usually, time_t is a signed long integer, but this may vary from system to system.

TIME.H provides a useful function to return the current time (i.e., time(NULL)). After you have declared a variable as type time_t, place the return value of time(NULL) into your time_t variable (see the following example). The value of your variable will be the number of seconds passed since 00:00:00 GMT, January 1, 1970.

Because the time_t value is one big number, it is often of very little use in this form. It is more useful when converted to the structure tm (discussed later in the chapter). Time_t should only be used to get the current time and for precise time modifications. The time_t type is best suited for simple, measured time changes. For example, if you want to add exactly one day to the time, you can simply add (60*60*24) seconds. Greater than and less than comparisons are also easy with time_t, as are difference calculations.

Conversely, time_t is limited. It cannot handle subjective time modifications, such as adding one month or one year to the current time. It has no way to make allowances for leap years and other unusual circumstances. For these operations, use time_t's counterpart, the structure tm, instead.

Example

Output the number of seconds since January 1, 1970, then add 10 days.

```
#include <time.h>
#include <stdio.h>

void main(void)
    {
    time_t  t;
    t = time(NULL);         //Set variable t to current time
    printf( 'Number of seconds since January 1, 1970: %ld\n', t
);
    t += (60*60*24*10);//Add 10 days (in seconds)
    printf('Number of seconds since January 1,1970,in 10
days:%ld',t );
    }
```

struct tm (TIME.H)

The structure tm (struct tm) is a format for storing distinct components of dates independently. It is merely a collection of integers, not a class. Accordingly, it can't accommodate changes made to member variables that could generate a ripple—for example, adding 40 days to a date, which would change "tm_mon," and possibly "tm_year" as well. It has the following sub-parts:

struct tm {
      int tm_sec;
      int tm_min;
      int tm_hour;
      int tm_mday;
      int tm_mon;
      int tm_year;
      int tm_wday;
      int tm_yday;
      int tm_isdst;};

The sub-part tm_hour starts at 0 and ends at 23, while tm_mday returns the day of the month, beginning at 1. The value for tm_mon varies from 0 through 11. The object's year is tm_year + 1900. The sub-part tm_wday defines 0 as Sunday, and ascends to 6 for Saturday. The sub-part tm_yday starts at 0 and ends at 365, depending upon leap-year status. If Daylight Savings Time is not in effect, tm_isdst is false.

If the name of a weekday or month is required, construct an array of strings and reference this with tm_wday or tm_mon for their respective names (see the example later in the chapter and in Chapter 12, *Pseudo-Date Functions*).

Although struct tm cannot be directly dumped as a string, the function (asctime()) exists for this purpose. The output format of asctime() is constant ('Thu Jan 01 00:00:00 1998'), but it is useful when logging and debugging. An interesting and undocumented feature of asctime() is its ability to return a full month name if 12 is added to tm_mon, or a full week name if 7 is added to tm_wday. For example, if you put "13" in place of "01," it will return "January."

The advantages of using struct tm are clear, since it accounts for month- and year-length variations. For example, with struct tm it is easy to add years (dateA.tm_year += 1). Adding months is almost as simple, but it requires a couple of lines of code to make sure that tm_mon remains between 0 and 11 (discussed further in the chapter). After changes have been made to tm_year and/or tm_mon, you must correct it for the weekday, if the weekday is required. Do so by converting the struct tm to a time_t format and then back again (see the examples under localtime() and mktime(), later in the chapter.)

Example

```
#include <time.h>
#include <stdio.h>
#include <dos.h>

char * weekdayname[] = {"Sunday", "Monday", "Tuesday",
"Wednesday",
                        "Thursday", "Friday", "Saturday"};
char * monthname[] = {"January", "February", "March", "April",
"May",
                      "June", "July", "August", "September",
                      "October", "November", "December"};

void main(void)
{
    struct tm dateA;

    dateA = *localtime(0);
    printf("Old = %s\n", weekdayname[dateA.tm_wday]);
    printf("Old = %s\n", monthname[dateA.tm_mon]);
    dateA.tm_mon +=20;
    while(dateA.tm_mon<0){ dateA.tm_year--; dateA.tm_mon+=12;}
    while(dateA.tm_mon>11){ dateA.tm_year++; dateA.tm_mon-=12;}
    // the two preceding lines should follow any month
alteration
    printf("New = %s\n", monthname[dateA.tm_mon]);
    // the new dateA ->tm_wday is incorrect, as it has last
been
    // calculated with the last localtime() call
    // see the next section for a fix
}
```

localtime() and mktime() functions

The function localtime() converts a time_t variable to a struct tm. The function mktime() converts a struct tm to a time_t.

Usage

```
dateA = localtime(&t);
t = mktime(&dateA);
```

Returns

The complimentary variable type.

localtime() arguments

The single argument is mandatory.

PART	TYPE	DESCRIPTION
t	time_t	the seconds since January 1, 1970 to be converted into a struct tm

mktime() arguments

The single argument is mandatory.

PART	TYPE	DESCRIPTION
dateA	struct tm	the struct tm to be converted into seconds since January 1, 1970

If localtime() is fed a zero, the result will obviously be January 1, 1970. On the other hand, if mktime() receives a NULL, the result will be a time_t of –1.

The localtime() function has one notable characteristic: it assigns its struct tm to one spot in memory and returns a pointer. This seems simple enough, as one could use struct tm pointers to identify the address, but there is a problem—localtime() always writes over the same location in memory! Work around this by using simple (non-pointer) struct tm variables and de-referencing localtime(), thereby using a copy of the struct instead of an address. By merely placing an asterisk (*) in front of localtime() you won't have a problem.

Example

Get the current time from the system as a type time_t, convert it to a struct tm, change the contents, correct it, and redisplay as struct tm and type time_t.

```
#include <time.h>
#include <stdio.h>
#include <dos.h>

void main(void) {
    time_t t;
    struct tm dateA;

    t = time(NULL);
    printf("Number of seconds since January 1, 1970 %ld\n",t);
    t += 500 * (60*60*24);    // add 500 days
    dateA = *localtime(&t);   // convert to struct tm
    printf("dateA: %s\n", asctime(&dateA));

    dateA.tm_mon += 20;       // add 20 months
    while(dateA.tm_mon<0){ dateA.tm_year--; dateA.tm_mon+=12;}
    while(dateA.tm_mon>11){ dateA.tm_year++; dateA.tm_mon-=12;}
    // the preceding two lines account for month range

    t = mktime(&dateA);       // convert to time_t then
    dateA = *localtime(&t);   // back to update weekday
```

C Date Functions

```
        printf("Finished date: %s\n", asctime(&dateA));

        t = mktime(&dateA);
        printf("Number of seconds after alterations %ld\n",t);
}
```

difftime() function

The difftime() function finds the amount of time between two type time_t variables.

t3 = difftime(t2, t1);

Returns

The difference between t2 and t1 as a double.

Arguments

This argument is mandatory.

PART	TYPE	DESCRIPTION
t1	time_t	secondary time
t2	time_t	reference time

If t2 is greater than t1, the result will be a negative number.

Unfortunately, difftime() can only return the number of seconds between the two dates. In actuality, it is much easier to simply subtract the two times.

With integer division, you can measure the elapsed time in units of minutes, hours, days, or weeks. However, you need to convert both dates into struct tm format and perform some arithmetic to measure in subjective time units, such as calendar weeks, months, or years.

Example
```
#include <time.h>
#include <stdio.h>
#include <dos.h>

void main(void) {
    time_t t1;
    time_t t2;
    time_t t3;
    t1 = time(NULL);
    t2 = time(NULL) + 37497600;   // (37497600 = 14 months)
    t3 = difftime(t2, t1);
    printf('%ld\n', t3);
}
```

PART V

Code Scanners

CHAPTER 18

Code Scanner Design and Theory

Using a code-scanner to automate your conversion process makes sense. It will save time and will help find *hidden date data*.

WARNING

It's unsafe to rely entirely on automated scanning. Test converted code thoroughly so that no date instances escape to cause problems later.

The basic business logic is:

- Gather all source code into a central file system
- Assemble a file of search strings
- Scan source files for all occurrences of these search strings
- Report on, and store, findings
- Manually check every reported occurrence and related code

My flowchart for a simple code scanner illustrates the theory behind code-scanning applications. It is followed by some pseudo-code, which forms the core of a generic scanner. This generic framework can easily be converted to any programming-code framework. I introduced the scanner in pseudo-code so that the concept can be implemented on your platform of choice.

There are major shortcomings to this pseudo-code that you need to be aware of. For example, multiple occurrences of search strings on the same line are not accommodated—this design still reports every line that meets the search criteria but shortens the output report, so don't assume there are no other important occurrences on the same line. If you don't have suitable programmers and design staff to adapt the code to your special requirements, you would be better served by purchasing a system with verifiable references and support.

Following this chapter you will find a scanner prototype written in Visual Basic 5. I chose this language and platform for developing a scanner because VB is conducive to Rapid Application Development (RAD), as well as to prototyping. Windows-based PCs are very common, so all you'll have to do to use this program is download all of the source files in text format to your PC, then scan. If this isn't possible, the VB code is fundamentally BASIC (and simple), and can be re-developed quite easily on another platform.

To download the Visual Basic scanner, navigate your browser to:

http://www.oreilly.com/catalog/y2knut

Code Scanner Design

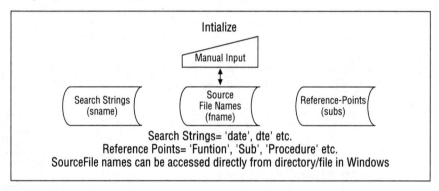

Figure 18-1: Scanner flowchart

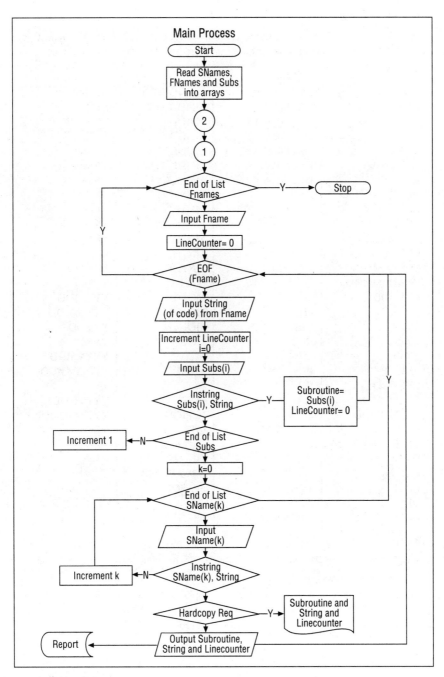

Figure 18-1: Scanner flowchart (continued)

Search Strings

This list should include all possible combinations ("99," "00," etc.), not just "dte" and "date." The following table contains many possible search criteria.

Table 18-1: Search Criteria

AGE	DDMMCCYY	MMDDCCYY	STAMP
ANN	DDMMCYY	MMDDCYY	STMP
ANNIV	DDMMMCYY	MMDDY	TMSTMP
ANNIVERSARY	DDMMMYYY	MMDDYY	YYY
ANNV	DDMMMYYYY	MMDDYYY	YEAR
APR	DDMMYY	MMDDYYYY	YEARS
AUG	DDMMYYY	MMMCCYY	YMD
BDAY	DEC	MMMCYY	YR
BIRTHDAY	DMY	MMMYY	YRDAY
CCCC	DOB	MMMYYY	YRMODA
CCMMDDYY	DT	MMMYYYY	YRS
CCYY	DTE	MNTH	YY
CCYYMMDD	DURATION	MNTHS	YYDDD
CCYYMMMDD	FEB	MO	YYMM
CENTURY	FINISH	MODY	YYMMDD
CLOSING	FISCAL	MONTH	YYMMMDD
CYD	GREGORIAN	MONTHS	YYYDD
CYM	INTERVAL	MOS	YYYDDD
CYMD	JAN	MTH	YYYMMDD
CYY	JUN	MTHS	YYYMMMDD
CYYDDD	JUL	NOV	YYYY
CYYMMDD	JULIAN	OCT	YYYYDDD
CYYMMMDD	LEAP	PERIOD	YYYYMMMDD
DAT	LEAPYEAR	QTR	99
DATE	LPYR	QUARTER	9999
DATES	MAR	QUOTIENT	
DAY	MAY	REMAINDER	
DAYS	MDY	SEASON	
DD	MM	SEP	
DDD	MMDD	SPAN	

Notes

1. Some words are abbreviated in this table, so the full word should also be listed.

2. Be on the lookout for underscores used to separate key strings.

3. Case variations should be tested where applicable. (The VB Prototype accommodates "case" through the use of "UCase.")

4. Customize this list for your environment and programming language.

Scanning for variations on "99" will produce horrendously long output, so you will need to apply Boolean logic and combination strings to the process.

Input Files

The two input files (search strings and subroutine names) and the source-code files should be prepared manually. All should be in standard text-file format.

Pseudo-code Code Scanner

```
Main
Load all search strings into array SNames()
Load all reference points into array Subs()
Load all file names into array FNames()
J=0
For all files
 Filename = FName(j)
    j=j+1
    LineCounter = 0
    While not(EOF) Filename
AA:
        SString = Input line from Filename
        LineCounter = LineCounter +1
for all of array Subs()
    //if currentline = sub/func name, move along
if SString is InString(Subs(I)) then
                                SubroutineName = Subs(I)
                                LineCounter = 0
                                Goto  AA
end if
                                next
                                for all of array SName()
//expand recursive search functionality to
        //accommodate multiple occurrences of search
        //criteria on the same line (if required)
        //at this point
        //
        //Store findings for future use
                if SString is InString(SName(k)), then
                        Print SubroutineName
                        Print LineCounter
                        Print SString
                end if
            next
        end while
        Close FName
    Next
    Close all files
End.
```

CHAPTER 19

Visual Basic Code Scanner Prototype

The simple source-code scanner prototype presented here is written in Visual Basic (VB), a popular Rapid Application Development (RAD) language for PCs. Most of the processing code is in the code module (.BAS file), and can easily be re-written in another language.

The screens and code, including event handlers for the forms, are supplied in this chapter. However, I have excluded the form-definition code. This code is generated automatically when you create the forms.

Although I have tested this application, there's no guarantee that it can find all occurrences of date-related text—it only reports the first occurrence of a date instance in any line, so these lines should always be double-checked for additional dates. Nor can I promise that it is entirely bug free. The scanning process is safe in that it does not write to the input files: all findings are written to output files in a different directory. It uses the first six characters of the input file name and a two-digit counter as a naming convention.

I recommend testing your own version of this application thoroughly before full-scale use.

System Function Calls and Events

The row of text boxes labeled "Total" displays the cumulative total of the boxes listed on the row labeled "Current." The file buttons below open a text editor, then display the contents of the files. This lets the operator edit the input files and customize search criteria.

The operator should group all files to be scanned in one directory for selection. The code limits individual file size to 5 MB.

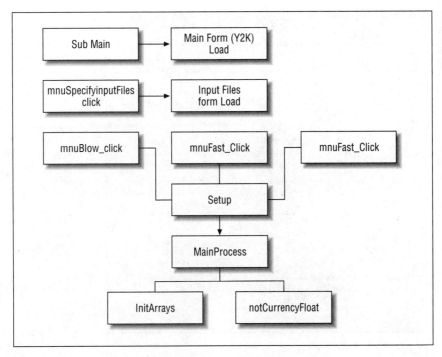

Figure 19-1: VB code scanner

Output Files

Output files should be placed in the "Outfiles" directory, and are named using a combination of the first six characters of the input file and the files-processed counter.

```
Main Form
Declarations
Option Explicit

Private Sub cmdStop_Click()
    EmergencyStop = True
End Sub

Private Sub Form_Load()
    Load frmLookup
    mnuprocess.Enabled = False
    mnuPrintOutput.Enabled = False
End Sub

Private Sub mnuFast_Click()
    Setup (0)
End Sub

Private Sub mnuInputFiles_Click()
    frmLookup.Visible = True
End Sub
```

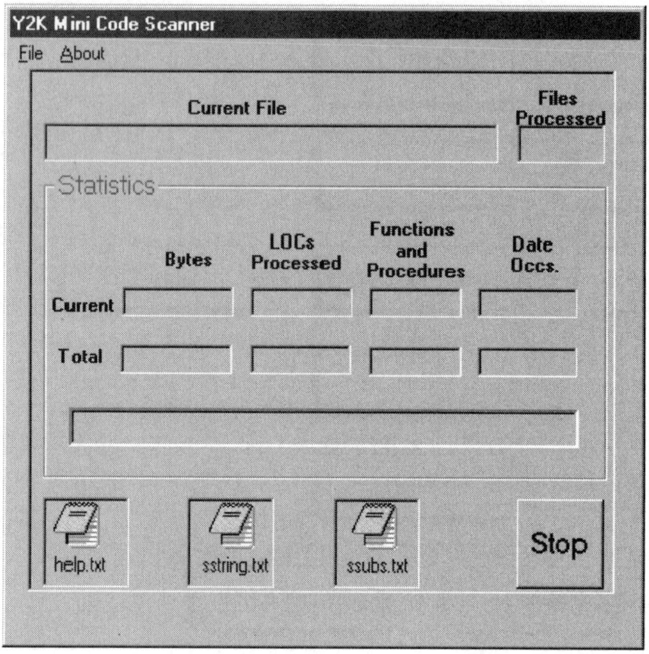

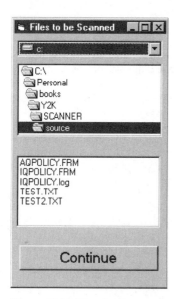

Figure 19-2: Main screen

Figure 19-3: File selection screen

```
Private Sub mnuAbout_Click()
    frmAbout.Show 1
End Sub

Private Sub mnuExit_Click()
    End
End Sub

Private Sub mnuprocess_Click()
    mnuInputFiles.Enabled = False
End Sub

Private Sub mnuSlow_Click()
    Setup (1)
End Sub
```

Code module functions

```
Option Explicit

Global CurrentFileName$, InputFile1$, OutputFile1$,
OutputFileNum1%, InputFileNum1%
Global tt1(5000) As String, tt2(5000) As String
Global LCount1%, Lcount2%
Global Linecounter%
Global EmergencyStop%
Global SStrings(500) As String
Global SSubs(500) As String
Global Findings(5000) As String
Global subsIndex%
Global stringsIndex%
Global i%, Ins$
Global mm2&
Global AppPath

Sub InitArrays()
    Dim x, qq
    On Error GoTo ErrInitArrays
    'initialize 3 arrays
  'search-strings, subroutine names
  'and output
    For x = 0 To 500
        SStrings(x) = ""
        SSubs(x) = ""
    Next
    For x = 0 To 5000
        Findings(x) = ""
    Next
    stringsIndex = 0
    InputFileNum1 = FreeFile
  'read searchstrings into array
    Open AppPath & "\SString.txt" For Input As InputFileNum1
    While Not EOF(InputFileNum1)
        Line Input #InputFileNum1, Ins
```

```
            Ins = Trim(Ins)
            if Len(Ins) > 0 then
                SStrings(stringsIndex) = Ins
                stringsIndex = stringsIndex + 1
            end if
      Wend
      Close InputFileNum1
      subsIndex = 0
      InputFileNum1 = FreeFile
   'read subroutine heading into array
      Open AppPath & "\SSubs.txt" For Input As InputFileNum1
      While Not EOF(InputFileNum1)
            Line Input #InputFileNum1, Ins
            Ins = Trim(Ins)
            if Len(Ins) > 0 then
                SSubs(subsIndex) = Ins
                subsIndex = subsIndex + 1
            end if
      Wend
      Close InputFileNum1
      Exit Sub
ErrInitArrays:
   MsgBox "Error accessing Search Strings " & Err
   Exit Sub
End Sub




Sub Main()
      frmY2K1.Show
End Sub




Function notCurrencyFloat(locc%, sstring$)
      Dim II$, xx%, qq$, kk$, flag%, OFlag%
      Dim locc2%
      If Not (IsNumeric(sstring)) Then
          notCurrencyFloat = True
          Exit Function
      End If
      locc2 = locc
      II = Ins
   'expand functionality to accommodate
   'variations on 18,19,19xx etc. here
      Do
          OFlag = True
          flag = False
          qq = ""
          xx = 0
          kk = Mid$(II, locc2 + xx, 1)
      'build numeric string inc. decimals
          While kk = "." Or kk = "," Or IsNumeric(kk)
              xx = xx + 1
```

```
                qq = qq & kk
                kk = Mid$(II, locc2 + xx, 1)
        Wend
        'occurrence contains a decimal point
        If InStr(qq, ".") > 0 Or InStr(qq, ",") > 0 Then
                flag = True
                OFlag = False
        End If
        If flag Then
                'look at remainder of string
                II = Mid$(II, locc2 + xx, Len(II) - locc2 + xx)
                locc2 = InStr(1, II, sstring, 1)
                If locc2 > 0 Then
                        flag = True      'another instance
                Else
                        flag = False
                End If
        End If
    Loop While flag
    notCurrencyFloat = OFlag
End Function


Sub MainProcess(way)
    Dim LC%, FC%, k%, x%, subroutine$,
    Dim FS&, locc%, tt$, CharCase%, dd%, ee%
    Dim ShortOut$
    Dim occtot%, MM&, mm3%
    On Error GoTo errMainProcess
    InitArrays
    InputFileNum1 = FreeFile
    LC = 0
    FC = 0
    x = 0
    Open InputFile1 For Input As InputFileNum1
    MM = FileLen(InputFile1)
    frmY2K1.txtBytes.Text = Format(MM, "#,###,###")
    DoEvents
    frmY2K1.txtBytes.Refresh
    mm3 = 0
    frmY2K1.ProgressBar1.Value = 0
    Dim tmp%
    tmp = 0
    'scan whole file
    While Not EOF(InputFileNum1)
        'increment progress bar
        If way Then
            tmp = tmp + 1
            if tmp < frmY2K1.ProgressBar1.Max then
                frmY2K1.ProgressBar1.Value = tmp
            End If
            DoEvents
        End If
        If EmergencyStop Then GoTo bb:
```

```
'skip over blank lines
        Do
            Line Input #InputFileNum1, Ins
            Ins = Trim(Ins)
        Loop Until (Len(Ins) > 0 Or EOF(InputFileNum1)) And
Left(Ins, 1) <> "~"
        LC = LC + 1
        If way Then
            frmY2K1.txtCurrentLOCs.Text = LC
            frmY2K1.txtCurrentLOCs.Refresh
            frmY2K1.txtToTalLocs.Text = frmY2K1.txtToTalLocs.Text + 1
            frmY2K1.txtToTalLocs.Refresh
        End If
        Ins = Trim(Ins)
        Linecounter = Linecounter + 1
        'check if input string is a subroutine name
        For i = 0 To subsIndex - 1
            If InStr(1, SSubs(i), Ins, 1) Then
                subroutine = SSubs(i)
                Linecounter = 0
                FC = FC + 1
                If way Then
                    frmY2K1.txtCurrentFuncs.Text = FC
                    frmY2K1.txtCurrentFuncs.Refresh
                    frmY2K1.txtTotalFuncs.Text= frmY2K1.
txtTotalFuncs.Text + 1
                    frmY2K1.txtTotalFuncs.Refresh
                End If
                GoTo AA
            End If
        Next
        If EmergencyStop Then GoTo bb:
        'check input string for date occurrences
        For k = 0 To stringsIndex - 1
            If EmergencyStop Then GoTo bb:
            Ins = UCase(Ins)
            SStrings(k) = UCase(SStrings(k))
            locc = InStr(1, Ins, SStrings(k), 1)
            If locc > 0 Then
                'skip processing if only currency or float
                If notCurrencyFloat(locc, SStrings(k)) Then
                    'save string containing occurrence, shorten to
        ' first 50 chars if too long
                    Findings(x) = Trim(subroutine) & "--" &
Trim(Ins)
                    dd = Len(Findings(x))
                    ee = Len(SStrings(k))
                    If dd > 50 Then
                        Findings(x) = Left$(Findings(x), 48) & " "
& Left$(SStrings(k), 9) & Space(10 - ee) & " #" & Linecounter
                    Else
                        Findings(x) = Findings(x) & Space(50 - dd)
& " " & Left$(SStrings(k), 9) & Space(10 - ee) & " #" & Linecounter
                    End If
```

```
                        x = x + 1
                        'update screen
                        If way Then
                            frmY2K1.txtCurrentOCCs.Text = x
                            frmY2K1.txtCurrentOCCs.Refresh
                            frmY2K1.txtToTOCCS.Text= frmY2K1.
txtToTOCCS.Text + 1

                            frmY2K1.txtToTOCCS.Refresh
                        End If
                    End If
                Exit For
                End If
        Next
        If EmergencyStop Then GoTo bb:
AA:
    Wend
        frmY2K1.txtCurrentOCCs.Text = x
        frmY2K1.txtCurrentOCCs.Refresh
        frmY2K1.txtToTOCCS.Refresh
        frmY2K1.txtToTalFiles.Text = frmY2K1.txtToTalFiles.Text + 1
        frmY2K1.txtToTalFiles.Refresh
bb:
Close InputFileNum1
        'dump findings array to file
        OutputFileNum1 = FreeFile

        If Len(CurrentFileName) > 6 Then
            OutputFile1 = Left(CurrentFileName,
(Len(CurrentFileName) - 2)) & frmY2K1.txtToTalFiles.Text & ".txt"
            Else
                OutputFile1 = CurrentFileName & frmY2K1.
txtToTalFiles.Text & ".txt"
            End If
            Dim tDir$, Myname$, MyPath, FoundFlag
''new next ???
            MyPath = AppPath & "\"
            Myname = Dir(MyPath, vbDirectory)    ' Retrieve the
first entry.
            FoundFlag = False
            Do While Myname <> "" And Not (FoundFlag) ' Start the
loop.
                ' Ignore the current directory and the encompassing
directory.
                If Myname <> "." And Myname <> ".." Then
                    ' Use bitwise comparison to make sure MyName is
a directory.
                    If (GetAttr(MyPath & Myname) And vbDirectory) =
vbDirectory Then
                        If Myname = "outfiles" Then
                            FoundFlag = True
                        End If
                    End If
                End If
            Myname = Dir    ' Get next entry.
```

```
        Loop
        If FoundFlag Then
                Open AppPath & "\outfiles\" & OutputFile1 For
Output As OutputFileNum1
                Else
                    MkDir AppPath & "\outfiles"
                    Open AppPath & "\outfiles\" & OutputFile1 For
Output As OutputFileNum1
                End If
        Write #OutputFileNum1, OutputFile1
        Write #OutputFileNum1, ""
        Write #OutputFileNum1, ""
        For i = 0 To x - 1
            Write #OutputFileNum1, Findings(i)
            k = Len(Findings(i))
        Next
        Close OutputFileNum1
        Exit Sub
errMainProcess:
    MsgBox "Error in MainProccess " & Err & " was generated by " _
            & Err.Source & Chr(13) & Err.Description
End Sub


Sub Setup(way%)
    '"way" indicates display method for scan process
    '0 = fast, don't update screen every line
    '1 = slow, update screen every line
        Dim tDir$, Myname$, MyPath, FoundFlag      ''new/next
MyPath = AppPath & "\"
        Myname = Dir(MyPath, vbDirectory)    ' Retrieve the
first entry.
        FoundFlag = False
        Do While Myname <> "" And Not (FoundFlag) ' Start the
loop.
            ' Ignore the current directory and the encompassing
directory.
            If Myname <> "." And Myname <> ".." Then
                ' Use bitwise comparison to make sure MyName is
a directory.
                If (GetAttr(MyPath & Myname) And vbDirectory) =
vbDirectory Then
                    If Myname = "outfiles" Then
                        FoundFlag = True
                    End If
                End If
            End If
            Myname = Dir     ' Get next entry.
        Loop
        If FoundFlag Then
            Open AppPath & "\outfiles\" & OutputFile1 For
Output As OutputFileNum1
            Else
                MkDir AppPath & "\outfiles"
```

```
                Open AppPath & "\outfiles\" & OutputFile1 For
Output As OutputFileNum1
            End If
        Write #OutputFileNum1, OutputFile1
        Write #OutputFileNum1, ""
        Write #OutputFileNum1, ""
        For i = 0 To x - 1
            Write #OutputFileNum1, Findings(i)
            k = Len(Findings(i))
        Next
        Close OutputFileNum1
        Exit Sub
errMainProcess:
    MsgBox "Error in MainProccess " & Err & " was generated by " _
            & Err.Source & Chr(13) & Err.Description
End Sub


Sub Setup (way%)
    '"way" indicates display method for scan process
    '0 = fast, don't update screen every line
    '1 = slow, update screen every line
    Dim Myname$, Mypath$, x%, y&, TotalBytes&
    AppPath = "C:\Scanner"
    frmY2K1.mnuInputFiles.Enabled = False
    'init counters
    frmY2K1.txtToTalLocs.Text = 0
    frmY2K1.txtToTalFiles.Text = 0
    frmY2K1.txtToTOCCS.Text = 0
    frmY2K1.txtTotalFuncs.Text = 0
    EmergencyStop = False
    TotalBytes = 0
    'for all files in the list
    For x = 0 To frmLookup.File1.ListCount - 1
        'for all files selected for scanning
        If frmLookup.File1.Selected(x) = True Then
            'get filesize
            y = FileLen(frmLookup.Dir1&"\" & frmLookup.File1.
List(x))
            TotalBytes = TotalBytes + y
        'if file too big, exit
            If y > 5000000 Then
                MsgBox "Individual File Size Limit of 5Mb. exceeded
(" & frmLookup.File1.List(x) & ") - Processing " & InputFile1 & "
Aborted"
                Close
                Exit Sub
            End If
        End If
    Next
    If TotalBytes = 0 Then
        MsgBox "No Files or Empty Files Selected"
        frmY2K1.mnuInputFiles.Enabled = True
        Exit Sub
```

```
        End If
    'format display
        frmY2K1.txtToTbytes = Format(TotalBytes, "#,###,###")
    'either setup progress bar limits or delay message
        If way Then
            mm2 = 0
            TotalBytes = TotalBytes / 28                    'LOCs > 100
            While TotalBytes > 100
                TotalBytes = TotalBytes / 10
                mm2 = mm2 + 1
            Wend
        Else
            Dim tmp%, hrs%, mins%
            tmp = TotalBytes / 3000
            hrs = tmp \ 3600
            mins = tmp \ 60
            If mins = 0 Then mins = 1
            If hrs > 1 Then
                MsgBox "This process could take up to " & hrs & " hour/
s"
            Else
                MsgBox "This process could take " & mins & " minute/s"
            End If
        End If
    'scan all files
        For x = 0 To frmLookup.File1.ListCount - 1
            frmY2K1.MousePointer = 11
            If EmergencyStop Then Exit For
            If frmLookup.File1.Selected(x) = True Then
                InputFile1 = frmLookup.Dir1&"\" & frmLookup.File1.
List(x)
                CurrentFileName = frmLookup.File1.List(x)
                frmY2K1.txtCurrentLOCs.Text = 0
                frmY2K1.txtCurrentOCCs.Text = 0
                frmY2K1.txtCurrentFuncs.Text = 0
                frmY2K1.Label8(4) = InputFile1
                MainProcess (way)
            End If
        Next
Beep:   Beep
        If EmergencyStop Then
            MsgBox "Process Aborted", 64
        Else
            MsgBox "Done", 64
        End If
        frmY2K1.mnuInputFiles.Enabled = False
        frmY2K1.MousePointer = 0
        frmY2K1.mnuInputFiles.Enabled = True
End Sub
```

APPENDIX A

Year-2000 Resources

This appendix lists Year-2000 resources available on the World Wide Web. The listings have been grouped into several major categories that provide relevant Year-2000 information or services.

The categories have been separated into the following Year-2000 topics, ranging from the most general (so there are a large number of vendor sites) to the most specific (where there are fewer user group sites):

Vendors
Tools
Testing
Legal Issues
Services
Embedded Systems
User Groups

Within each category you will find an alphabetical listing of subjects and their corresponding URLs. This is by no means a definitive list, but each category contains many useful web sites. The sites that are listed are meant to provide useful information, and can be used as a starting point when searching the World Wide Web for Year-2000 information.

Year-2000 Vendors

If you have a specific Year-2000 related product or company in mind, this list is a good place to get their URL.

Acer Year 2000 Information
http://www.acer.com/aac/support/year2000/index.htm

Adobe
http://www.adobe.com/supportservice/custsupport/NOTES/227e.htm

Alpha Databases
http://support.alphasoftware.com/alpha5/y2k.html

American Software
http://www.amsoftware.com

Apple
http://product.info.apple.com/pr/letters/1997/961210.pr.ltrs.macos2000.html

Bind View
http://www.bindview.com/special/year2000.html

Bridge IMS
http://www.BridgeIMS.com

Bridging Data Technology
http://www.bridging.com

CACI
http://year2000.caci.com

CDG 2000, Inc.
http://www.cadvision.com/cdg/

Centurian Solution
http://www.centuria.net/default.htm

Cisco Systems
http://www.cisco.com/warp/public/752/2000/

Claris Products
http://www.claris.com/news/docs/year2000-c.html

Cognos - Power2000
http://www.cognos.com/power2000/index.html

Coopers & Lybrand
http://www.za.coopers.com/ey2k/ey2k.htm

Corel
http://www.corel.com/2000.htm

Data Commander
http://www.datacommander.com.

DATA21 Enterprise Software Solutions
http://www.data21.com

Dell Y2K Q&A
http://www.dell.com/year2000/faq/faq.htm

Dell Year-2000 System Tools
http://www.dell.com/year2000/tools/tools.htm

DGEN2000
http://www.dgen2000.com

Dortech Electronics Limited
http://www.dortech.demon.co.uk/

EasiRun
http://www.easirun.com

Edge Information Group
  http://www.edge-information.com

Gateway Support Center
  http://www.gateway.com/home/support/cs_techdocs/y2k/default.html

Global Software, Inc.
  http://www.global-software.com

HCL James Martin, Inc. TSRM
  http://www.hcl-jmi.com

HP LaserJet Printers
  http://www.hp.com/cposupport/printers/support_doc/bpl02816.html

HP OfficeJet Printer/Fax/Copier/Scanners
  http://www.hp.com/cposupport/multifunction/support_doc/bpu50193.html

IBM
  http://www.software.ibm.com/year2000/method10.html

IBM —Year 2000
  http://www.ibm.com/year2000

IBM DOS
  http://www.software.ibm.com/os/dos/2000/

IBM PC Hardware Timer Setting
  http://www.s390.ibm.com/stories/pc.html

IBM Year-2000 Technical Support
  http://www.software.ibm.com/year2000

IBM: 'Meeting the Year-2000 Challenge'
  http://www.software.ibm.com/year2000/y2kasweb.html

i-Cube: IT consulting
  http://www.i-cube.com

Information Management Resources, Inc.
  http://www.imri-ca.com

Intel
  http://support.intel.com/support/year2000/

ITAA
  http://www.itaa.org/year2000.htm

JBA
  http://2000.jbaworld.com/index.asp

JGW Systems
  http://www.jgw.com

Lexmark
  http://www.lexmark.com/printers/year2000.html

Lotus
  *http://www.lotus.com/world/uk.nsf/8eedc7b0ca2d78278525630f004e7aba/
  00002126*

Resources

MacKinney Systems
http://www.mackinney.com/yr2000.htm

McAfee
http://www.mcafee.com/prod/2000.asp

Micro Focus
http://www.microfocus.com/year2000

Microsoft
http://support.microsoft.com/support/kb/articles/Q155/6/69.asp

http://mspress.microsoft.com/prod/books/sampchap/1032.htm

Microsoft Year 2000
http://www.microsoft.com/ithome/topics/year2k/default.htm

Microsoft Year-2000 Compliance
http://www.microsoft.com/ithome/topics/year2k/y2kcomply/y2kcomply.htm

Microsoft Year-2000 Resource Center
http://www.microsoft.com/ithome/topics/year2k/product/product.htm

Millennia III
http://www.millennia3.com

MillenniumPlus Consulting
http://www.millenniumplus.com

MITRE/ESC
http://www.mitre.org/research/y2k

Nova Technology, Inc.
http://www.novatechnology.com

Novell Patches
http://www.novell.com/p2000/patches.html

Novell Project Compliance
http://www.novell.com/p2000/index.html

Oracle - RDB Beyond the Year 2000
http://www.oracle.com/products/servers/rdb/html/y2000.html

Oracle Products & Year-2000 Compliance
http://www.oracle.com/support/html/2000.htm

pi Technologies
http://www.pitechnologies.com/

Platinum TranCentury Date Simulator Year 2000
http://www.platinum.com/products/year2k/b_time.htm

Precision Computing, Inc.
http://www.precomp.com

Pretoria Software Solutions (PTY) Ltd.
http://www.pss.co.za/year2000.html

Prince Software, Inc.
http://www.PRINCEsoftware.com

Princeton Softech
http://www.princetonsoftech.com

QNX
http://www.qnx.com/literature/y2k.html

Quarterdeck
http://www.qdeck.com/qdeck/products/qd2000.html

Real Time 2000
http://www.RTEL.Co.UK

Renew 2000
http://www.renew2000.com

RiskTrak
http://www.risktrak.com/

Rockwell Software
http://www.software.rockwell.com/year2000/index.htm

Sterling Software VISION
http://www.sterling.com/products/vision.html

Sun Year-2000 Program Compliant Product List
http://www.sun.com/y2000/cpl.html

Sun's Year-2000 Information Site
http://www.sun.com/y2000

Symantec
http://www.symantec.com/y2k/y2k.html

Texas Instruments
http://www.ti.com/corp/docs/year2000/index.htm

Thinking Tools
http://www.thinkingtools.com

Transcend 2000
http://www.transcend2000.com

Turn of the Century Solution
http://www.tocs.com

UltiMIS
http://www.ultimis.com

UNISYS 2200 Series
http://www.marketplace.unisys.com/year2000/faq/2200faq.htm

Viasoft, Inc.
http://www.viasoft.com

VisualSoft
http://www.visualsoft-india.com/vshift1/ie/4/0.html

WRQ Software
http://support.wrq.com/techdocs/2000.htm

Y2K Vendor List
http://www.year2000.com/y2k-vendors.html

Year-2000 Tools

This list contains web sites where you can find information about the many Year-2000 conversion tools that are available.

19T0
> *http://www.19t0.com*

2000 Technologies corporation
> *http://www.2000technologies.com*

2000 Tools Are you Ready?
> *http://www.2000tools.com*

21st Century COBOL Conversions, Inc.
> *http://www.year2000.com/vendors/21cent/21cent.html*

ACR's Year-2000 Resource Guide
> *http://www.acrhq.com/yr2000.htm*

Acucobol
> *http://www.acucobol.com/Services/year2000.html*

Advanced Software Products Group, Inc.
> *http://www.aspg.com/Products/products.htm*

Ardes 2k
> *http://www.ardes2k.com/website/visitors/visitors.htm*

AstraTek
> *http://www.Astratek.com/*

Avatar Solutions, Inc.
> *http://www.avatars.com/y2ksol.html*

Banyan
> *http://www.banyan.com/products/y2k/year2000.html*

BMR Software
> *http://www.bmrsoftware.com/*

Bozeman Legg Inc.
> *http://www.bozemanlegg.com/year2000.html*

Breakpoint 2000
> *http://www.b2d.com/bpdwnld.htm*

Calders DR-DOS Solutions
> *http://www.caldera.com/dos/*

Catch/21
> *http://www.catch21.com/Catch21.htm*

Cipher Systems, Ltd.
> *http://www.ciphersys.com*

Class Solutions Ltd.
> *http://www.class-solutions.com/vds2000.htm*

Computer Information Analysis, Inc.
> *http://www.cia-cas2000.com*

Computer Performance Engineering
http://www.y2kok.com/vhunt.htm

CSW Source Analyzer
http://www.lls.se/csw

Digital Year-2000 Ready
http://ww1.digital.com/year2000/

Electric Utilities and Year 2000
http://www.euy2k.com

EYE_T Technology Ltd.
http://www.eye-t.com

EZD8
http://www.ezd8.com

FieldEx 2000 AD
http://www.fieldex.com.ph

FIX-IT 2000
http://www.fixit2000.com

GAS Software
http://www.gas.co.za/

GE Medical Systems
http://www.ge.com/medical/year2000/index.htm

IBM
http://www.pc.ibm.com/year2000/year2000b.html

IBM VisualAge 2000
http://www.software.ibm.com/ad/va2000/y2k

IBS Conversions, Inc.
http://WWW.IBS2000.COM

Intersolv Factory2000
http://www.intersolv.com/factory2000/frameset_factory2000.html

Isogon
http://www.isogon.com

Lexibridge
http://www.lexibridge.com

LogicWare Corp.
http://www.LogicWare-inc.com

McCabe Visual 2000 Environment
http://www.mccabe.com/yr2000/Index.html

Metro Information Systems Corporation
http://www.metroinfo.com/c2000/pressrel/19970417.html

Micro Focus' Challenge 2000
http://www.mfltd.co.uk

Microsoft Year-2000 Tools Guide
http://www.microsoft.com/ithome/topics/year2k/tools/OFFICE-TOOLS/v_excel.htm

MILLENIX
http://www.millennix.com

Mitre Tools and Services
http://www.mitre.org/research/y2k/docs/VENDORS.html

MS Millennium
http://www.msmillennium.com

Mycroft Systems Ltd.
http://www.mycroft.co.nz

New Art Technologies
http://www.newarttech.com/naexcel.htm

PC Check
http://www.pccheck.com/cdg2000.htm

PC Profile
http://www.pcprofile.com

PC-Aid 2000
www.pcaid2000.com

Peritus
http://www.peritus.com/prodserv.html

Piercom Ltd.
http://www.piercom.ie

Pinnacle Decision Systems, Inc.
http://www.pinndec.com/year2k.html

Plant Y2Kone
http://www.planty2kone.com/fr_main.html

Power Software Year 2000
http://www.power-soft.co.uk

Preparations and Plans for the Year-2000 Date Change
http://www.state.ma.us/dls/year2k.htm

Progeni
http://www.progeni.com

Prove It 2000
http://www.proveit2000.com

PSR Metrics System
http://www.psrinc.com/metsys.htm

Quantech CorrecTime© - Time for your PC
http://www.quantech.co.uk/quantech/index.htm

Ravel Software, Inc.
http://www.unravel.com

Real World Training Systems
http://www.real2000.com

Reasoning Systems - The Year-2000 Problem
http://www.reasoning.com/y2k.html

ReGenisys Corporation
http://www.regenisys.com

Rhône-Valley Systems
http://www.rhone-valley.ch

Rigel Desktop Solutions
http://www.rigel.co.nz

RX2000 Solutions Institute
http://www.rx2000.org

SBT
http://www.sbt.com

SCA Millennium Resource
http://www.sca-net.co.uk/millennium

Shelby Software
http://www.shelby-software.com

SIMCOM
http://www.simcomcity.com/

Software Management Network
http://www.softwaremanagement.com

Software Migrations Limited
http://www.smltd.com/

Solutions 2000
http://www.solutions2000.com/index.html

Source Retrieval
http://www.sourceretrieval.com/welcome.html

Survive 2000 PC Checking Tool
http://www.survive-2000.com

Technologic Software
http://www.technologic.com

The Guide Associates
http://www.2000won.com

Transition Software Corp
http://www.transition-software.com

ViaSoft's Enterprise 2000
http://www.viasoft.com/sltns/e2000/index.htm

Visionet Systems
http://www.visionets.com

Whitfield Software Services
http://www.wssnet.com

WRQ Express 2000 Suite
http://www.wrq.com/express2000/

Xpress Software
http://www.xpsoft.com

Y2K PC Software, Inc.
http://www.y2kpc.com/products.htm

Y2KSOLVR
http://www.y2ksolvr.com

Y2Ktool
http://www.y2ktool.com/

Year-2000 Testing

If you're looking for information on the testing and development of Year-2000 conversion projects, this list will help.

Apple
http://www.apple.com/macos/info/2000.html

Metro Information Systems Corporation Year-2000 Test Center
http://www.metroinfo.com/y2k/center/pressrel/19970310.html

Microsoft Year-2000 Test Criteria
http://www.microsoft.com/ithome/topics/year2k/product/criteria.htm

NRF Survival 2000 EDI Project
http://www.nrf.com/hot/yr2000/mission.htm

Open Mainframe Solutions LLC - Mainframe testing on your site 24x7
http://www.openmainframe.com

Princeton Softech Ager 2000
http://www.princetonsoftech.com/products/ps-ager2000.htm

Softbridge
http://www.sbridge.com

SQE
http://www.sqe.com

Synergy 2000, Inc.
http://www.Synergy2000.com

Tallecom Software
http://www.talc.com.au

TargetFour Year-2000 Home Page
http://www.target4.com/year2000.htm

Testing for the Year 2000 - a Tutorial
http://www.itworks.be/y2ktestingtutorial.html

Testing Tips: Lessons Learned
http://www.sentrytech.com/sqttest.htm

The A Consulting Team Inc.
http://WWW.TACT.com

Year-2000 Solutions
http://www.sector7.com/sector7_year2000/year2000.htm

Year-2000 Legal Issues

Below you'll find some web sites covering Year-2000 legal issues.

2000 LEGAL.COM
http://www.2000legal.com

2000Compliance.com
http://www.2000compliance.com

2001: A Legal Odyssey
http://www.year2000.com/archive/legal.html

AMS Group International, Corp.
http://www.amsgrp.com

Comlinks.com Legal Papers
http://www.comlinks.com/mmenu.htm

IT2000
http://www.it2000.com/legal/index.html

Legal Guidelines for Millennium Date Change Issues
http://www.tarlo-lyons.co.uk/newinfo.html

The Millennium Time Bomb (Legal Brief - English Law)
http://www.ffwlaw.com/1096bomb.htm

The Writing's on the Wall
http://www.y2k.com/doliab.htm

The Year-2000 Challenge: Implications for Directors & Managers
http://www.year2000.co.nz/y2krws01.htm

The Year-2000 Legal Coalition
http://www.actr.com/actr/y2k

UK Weblaw
http://www.weblaw.co.uk/index.htm

Westergaard Year-2000 Litigation
http://www.y2ktimebomb.com/Litigation

Y2K - Year-2000 Compliance/Warranties
http://www.gahtan.com/year2000/

Y2KEXPERTS.com
http://www.y2kexperts.com

Year-2000 Law Center
http://www.year2000.com/lawcenter/

Year-2000 Liability Resource to Legal Information
http://www.2000law.com/index.htm

Year-2000 Services

The list below contains web sites that cover a myriad of general Year-2000 services and issues.

Alydaar
http://www.alydaar.com

ANSTEC Year-2000 Services
http://www.anstec.com/YR2000.HTM

AnswerThink's Millennium | solutionsSM
http://www.answerthink.com/millennium/

APAA Year-2000 Issues
http://www.apaa.org/yr2000.htm

Ascent Logic Corporation
http://www.alc.com/Y2kfaq.html

Audit Serve Inc.
http://www.auditserve.com

Blackhawk
http://www.blackhawkis.com

Blueshift
http://www.blueshift.com/shift2000

Bretton Woods, Inc.
http://www.bretton-woods.com/

Bridgeway Systems
http://www.bridgeway2k.com

Bytewise
http://www.bytewise.com

Centennial 2000
http://www.centennial.co.uk

Century Technology Services
http://www.ctsi2000.com

Computer Task Group
http://ctg2.com/about/year2k.htm

Core Software
http://www.core-soft.com

Cutter Consortium
http://www.cutter.com/consortium/

Cybermetrix
http://www.cybermetrix.co.uk

Data Dimensions
http://www.data-dimensions.com

Data Ease Services
http://www.dataease.co.uk/services/milleniu.htm

Digital Year-2000 Program
http://www.digital.com/info/LI01U0/

Elsys - Year 2000
http://www.elsys.com/y2k.htm

FSB: Year-2000 Challenge
http://www.fsb.co.za/2000.htm

InterTech
http://it.org/cobol.html

Keane, Inc.
http://www.keane.com

KPMG - The Year 2000
http://www.kpmg.co.za

MatlenSilver Information Technology Services
http://www.matlensilver.com

Millennium Date Corporation Ltd.
http://www.milleniumdate.co.uk

Millennium PC Services
http://www.mpcs2000.com

Millennium Plus Year-2000 Page
http://millenniumplus.com/Y2KPage.htm

Millennium Technology Consulting Group
http://mtcg.com/year2000.htm

MST The Year-2000 Resource Book
http://www.mstnet.com/year2000/yr2000.htm

NCC's Year-2000 Solutions
http://www.ncc.co.uk/y2k.html

NewTech
http://Newtech-Solutions.com

PKS Information Services, Inc.
http://www.pksis.com

Questicon Incorporated
http://questicon.com

Rescue 2000 Problem
http://rescue2000.com

Softdata Consulting
http://www.softdata.com

TechForce/COSMOS Information Center
http://www.cosmos2000.com/y2kcntr.html

Terasys, Incorporated Year-2000 Projects
http://www.terasys.com/premierframes.html

The National Bulletin Board for Year 2000
http://it2000.com

TQM Consulting, Inc.
http://www.tqminc.com

VM and the Year 2000
http://www.vm.ibm.com/year2000/

Y2Khelp.net
http://www.y2khelp.net/

Year-2000 Services Conversion Centre Limited
http://www.conversion-centre.co.uk/index_yr2k.htm

Year-2000 & Embedded Systems

This list covers issues on embedded systems and the Year-2000 process.

2000 Dangers for Engineers
http://www.iee.org.uk/2000risk

3Com Year-2000 Product Compliance
http://www.3com.com/products/yr2000.html

Automation 2000 Home Page
http://www.auto2000.ndirect.co.uk/y2kindex.htm

Automotive Industry Action Group Year-2000 Information
http://www.aiag.org/project/year2000/year2000.html

Biomedical Engineering Database
http://www.y2k.gov.au/biomed

Center for Devices & Radiological Health
http://www.fda.gov/cdrh/yr2000.html

Embedded Systems and Y2K
http://www.iee.org.uk/2000risk/guide/year2k76.htm#E11E88

Embedded.com
http://www.embedded.com/

EPRI's Year-2000 Issues for Embedded Systems
http://www.epriweb.com/year2000/

Otis Elevators ... and the Year 2000
http://www.nao.otis.com/year2000.html

Penn Computing Year 2000
http://www.upenn.edu/computing/year2000/

Project Damocles
http://www.year2000.com/y2kdamocles.html

Real-Time Operating Systems
http://www.realtime-info.be/encyc/market/rtos/rtos.htm

Rockwell Automation and the Year 2000
http://www.ragts.com/webstuff/y2k.nsf

Softaid's Embedded Web
http://www.softaid.net/embedded.html

The Bruker Year-2000 Home Page
http://www.bruker.com/y2000

The Pocket Gateway to Year 2000
http://www.cix.co.uk/~parkside/y2kweb.htm

Utilities and Year 2000
http://www.euy2k.com/index.htm

Year 2000 and Bently Nevada Products
http://www.bently.com/support/2000list.htm

Year 2000 and Dover Elevators
http://www.doverelevators.com/whatsnew/y2k.html

Year-2000 Embedded Systems Issues
http://www.state.id.us/y2k/embed.htm

Year-2000 Embedded Systems Vendors, Associations, and Manufacturers
http://ourworld.compuserve.com/homepages/roleigh_martin/y2k_com.htm

Year-2000 Program Process Control Devices and Embedded Microprocessors
http://www.wa.gov/dis/2000/survey/process/process.htm

Year-2000 Readiness GE Fanuc PLC & IO Products
http://www.ge.com/gemis/gefanuc/PDFs/year2000.pdf

Year-2000 Test Results
http://www.modicon.com

Year-2000 & User Groups

Look here for some of the Year-2000 user groups.

Atlanta Year-2000 Users Group
http://www.bytewise.com/atlyear2000/

Group West Year 2000
http://www.groupwest.ca/techexp/2000.htm

ICS Year 2000/Euro Special Interest Group
http://www.iol.ie/sysmod/y2ksig05.htm

Irish Computer Society Year 2000 & Euro SIG
http://www.iol.ie/~pobeirne/y2ksig.htm

Johns Hopkins Medicine Center for Information Services Year 2000
http://jhmcis.med.jhu.edu/y2000/y2menu.htm

Nutmeg Centurians
http://www.effectivebydesign.com/nutmeg/

Ohio 2000
http://www.ccai.net/ohio2000

San Francisco Bay Area Year-2000 User Group
http://www.sf2000.com

San Francisco Computer Consultants, Inc.
http://www.sfconsult.com

The Disaster Center Year-2000 Page
http://www.disastercenter.com/year2000.htm

The Information Management Forum
http://www.infomgmtforum.com

The Year-2000 Information Center
http://www.year2000.com/cgi-bin/y2k/NFyear2000.cgi

Tick, Tick, Tick
http://www.tickticktick.com

Y2K User Groups
http://www.year2000.com/y2kusergroups.html

Year-2000 Homepage
http://www.year2000.com

Index

Symbols and Numbers

- (minus) symbol, 147
$ (currency) symbol, 147
* (asterisk) symbol, 148
+ (plus) symbol, 147
, (comma) symbol, 146
. (period) symbol, 146
... (ellipsis) symbol, 110
/ (slash) symbol, 146, 191
[ ] brackets, 110
{ } curly braces, 110
0 (zero) symbol, 146
9's complement, 65
B (blank) symbol, 146
Z symbol, 148

A

ACCEPT verb, 123
Access, date conversion rules, 78
ADD verb, 127
ADVANCING clause, 149
AFTER phrase, 134, 183
analyzing Year-2000 problem, 45, 48
ANSI standards, 55, 109
applications
  front-end, 68–70, 81
  off-the-shelf, 75
arithmetic in COBOL, 126, 182
arrays (see tables, COBOL)

AS/400, tools for conversion, 20
ASSIGN clause
  file alias, 142
  with direct access files, 160–162
  with MERGE verb, 159
  with SORT verb, 153
asterisk (*) symbol, 148
AT END clause, 158
automation tools, Year-2000, 74, 273, 278

B

BEFORE phrase, 183
beginning a Year-2000 project, 44, 46
benefits of complying, additional, 18
bibliography, COBOL programming, 211
BINARY items, 119
blank (B) symbol, 146
brackets [ ], 110
budget (see cost of compliance)
buffer, record, 143

C

C language
  functions (see date functions, C
    language)
  time_t type, 266
  tm structure, 267
calendar, Julian, 61

About the Author

Norman Shakespeare is a private consultant with twenty years' experience in electronics, PC and mini hardware, networking, programming, and training. Before writing this book he spent two years consulting at a large financial institution on asset-finance, insurance, and telephonic banking. A significant part of this job was programming in Visual Basic and Access. He enjoys this hands-on side of computing and is in the process of developing a code-scanning tool specifically for Year-2000 use.

Prior to the financial position he was the academic head of the Computer Training Institute where his leadership and technical input to the popular computer science courses resulted in his admission as a Member of the prestigious City and Guilds of London Institute (MCGI). He was responsible for writing much of the courseware at the Institute, experience that set him up for full-time technical authoring. He has a long list of advanced computing and technical diplomas and qualifications, the acquisition of which appears to be one of his hobbies.

Originally from Zimbabwe, he has lived in South Africa and Canada and traveled through Europe, Asia, and America (where he gleaned much of his knowledge for another of his hobbies, fiction writing).

Colophon

The animal featured on the cover of Year 2000 in a Nutshell is a rooster. Roosters, also known as cocks, are male chickens having reached maturity at the age of one year. Today there are over 200 recognized breeds of chickens including the Rhode Island Red, White Leghorn, and Cornish. Over centuries of breeding some varieties have produced striking traits, such as a Japanese breed called the Yokohama, whose tail can grow up to 18 feet long. Though they quickly spread through the ancient world, chickens probably originated in Asia and may have been fully domesticated as early as 2000 BC—as seen in a painting of a rooster found in the tomb of the pharaoh Tutankhamen and frequent references to the breed in 4th and 5th century BC Greek literature. The cock was admired in the ancient world as today not only for his early morning crow symbolizing daybreak, but also for his pride and courage. Cockfighting, which readily displays these characteristics, may have been the original reason for domestication even before the bird was valued for its meat and eggs.

Paula Carroll was the production editor for this book. TIPS Technical Publishing handled production services. The illustrations were created by Robert Romano with Macromedia Freehand 7.0. Edie Freedman designed the cover, using an original drawing by Susan Hart. The cover layout was produced by Kathleen Wilson with QuarkXPress 3.32 using the ITC Garamond font. The inside layout was designed by Edie Freedman and modified by Nancy Priest and implemented in FrameMaker by Mike Sierra. The text and heading fonts are ITC Garamond Light and Garamond Book. This colophon was written by Angela Tyletta Daley.

Whenever possible, our books use RepKover™ or Otabind™ lay-flat binding. If the page count exceeds the limit for lay-flat binding, perfect binding is used.

More Titles from O'Reilly

Unix Programming

Programming Python

By Mark Lutz
1st Edition October 1996
906 pages, ISBN 1-56592-197-6

Programming Python describes how
to use Python, an increasingly popular
object-oriented scripting language.
This book, full of running examples, is
the most comprehensive user material
available on Python. It's endorsed by
Python creator Guido van Rossum and complements reference
materials that accompany the software. Includes CD-ROM
with Python software for all major UNIX platforms, as well
as Windows, NT, and the Mac.

POSIX Programmer's Guide

By Donald Lewine
1st Edition April 1991
640 pages, ISBN 0-937175-73-0

Most UNIX systems today are POSIX
compliant because the federal
government requires it for its
purchases. Given the manufacturer's
documentation, however, it can be
difficult to distinguish system-specific
features from those features defined
by POSIX. The *POSIX Programmer's Guide*, intended as an explanation of the POSIX standard and as a reference for the POSIX.1
programming library, helps you write more portable programs.

UNIX Systems Programming for SVR4

By David A. Curry
1st Edition July 1996
620 pages, ISBN 1-56592-163-1

Presents a comprehensive look at the
nitty gritty details on how UNIX interacts
with applications. If you're writing an
application from scratch, or if you're
porting an application to any System
V.4 platform, you need this book. It
thoroughly explains all UNIX system calls and library routines
related to systems programming, working with I/O, files and
directories, processing multiple input streams, file and record
locking, and memory-mapped files.

Power Programming with RPC

By John Bloomer
1st Edition February 1992
522 pages, ISBN 0-937175-77-3

RPC (Remote Procedure Calling) is
the ability to distribute the execution of
functions on remote computers. Written
from a programmer's perspective, this
book shows what you can do with RPCs,
like Sun RPC, the de facto standard
on UNIX systems. It covers related
programming topics for Sun and other UNIX systems and
teaches through examples.

POSIX.4

By Bill O. Gallmeister
1st Edition January 1995
568 pages, ISBN 1-56592-074-0

A general introduction to real-time
programming and real-time issues,
this book covers the POSIX.4 standard
and how to use it to solve "real-world"
problems. If you're at all interested in
real-time applications—which include
just about everything from telemetry
to transaction processing—this book is for you. An essential
reference.

Pthreads Programming

By Bradford Nichols, Dick Buttlar &
Jacqueline Proulx Farrell
1st Edition September 1996
284 pages, ISBN 1-56592-115-1

POSIX threads, or pthreads, allow
multiple tasks to run concurrently
within the same program. This book
discusses when to use threads and
how to make them efficient. It features
realistic examples, a look behind the scenes at the implementation and performance issues, and special topics such as
DCE and real-time extensions.

O'REILLY™

TO ORDER: **800-998-9938** • **order@oreilly.com** • **http://www.oreilly.com/**
OUR PRODUCTS ARE AVAILABLE AT A BOOKSTORE OR SOFTWARE STORE NEAR YOU.
FOR INFORMATION: **800-998-9938** • **707-829-0515** • **info@oreilly.com**

C and C++

C++: The Core Language

By Gregory Satir & Doug Brown
1st Edition October 1995
228 pages, ISBN 1-56592-116-X

C++: The Core Language is a primer for C programmers transitioning to C++, an object-oriented enhancement of the C programming language fast becoming the language of choice for serious software development. Designed to get readers up to speed quickly, this book tells you just what you need to learn first.

This book covers a subset of the features of C++. The subset consists of features without which it's just not C++, and a handful of others that make it a reasonably useful language. You can actually use this subset (using any compiler) to get familiar with the basics of the language.

C++: The Core Language includes sidebars that give overviews of all the advanced features not covered, so that readers know they exist and how they fit in. It covers features common to all C++ compilers, including those on UNIX, Windows NT, Windows, DOS, and Macs.

Practical C++ Programming

By Steve Oualline
1st Edition September 1995
584 pages, ISBN 1-56592-139-9

Practical C++ Programming is a complete introduction to the C++ language for the beginning programmer, and also for C programmers transitioning to C++. Unlike most other C++ books, this book empha-
sizes a practical, real-world approach, including how to debug, how to make your code understandable to others, and how to understand other people's code. Topics covered include good programming style, C++ syntax (what to use and what not to use), C++ class design, debugging and optimization, and common programming mistakes. At the end of each chapter are a number of exercises you can use to make sure you've grasped the concepts. Solutions to most are provided.

Practical C++ Programming describes standard C++ features that are supported by all UNIX C++ compilers (including gcc) and DOS/Windows and NT compilers (including Microsoft Visual C++).

Practical C Programming, 3rd Edition

By Steve Oualline
3rd Edition August 1997
454 pages, ISBN 1-56592-306-5

There are lots of introductory C books, but this new edition of Practical C Programming is the one that has the no-nonsense, practical approach that has made Nutshell Handbooks® so popular. C programming is more than just getting the syntax right. Style and debugging also play a tremendous part in creating programs that run well and are easy to maintain.

Practical C Programming teaches you not only the mechanics of programming, but also how to create programs that are easy to read, debug, and maintain. This third edition introduces popular Integrated Development Environments on Windows systems, as well as UNIX programming utilities, and features a large statistics-generating program to pull together the concepts and features in the language.

Checking C Programs with lint

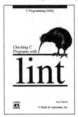

By Ian F. Darwin
1st Edition October 1988
84 pages, ISBN 0-937175-30-7

The lint program checker has proven time and again to be one of the best tools for finding portability problems and certain types of coding errors in C programs. lint verifies a program or program segments against standard libraries, checks the code for common
portability errors, and tests the programming against some tried and true guidelines. linting your code is a necessary (though not sufficient) step in writing clean, portable, effective programs. This book introduces you to lint, guides you through running it on your programs, and helps you interpret lint's output.

O'REILLY™

TO ORDER: **800-998-9938** • **order@oreilly.com** • **http://www.oreilly.com/**

OUR PRODUCTS ARE AVAILABLE AT A BOOKSTORE OR SOFTWARE STORE NEAR YOU.

FOR INFORMATION: **800-998-9938** • **707-829-0515** • **info@oreilly.com**

Database

Oracle PL/SQL Programming, 2nd Edition

By Steven Feuerstein with Bill Pribyl
2nd Edition September 1997
1028 pages, Includes diskette
ISBN 1-56592-335-9

The first edition of *Oracle PL/SQL Programming* quickly became an indispensable reference for both novice and experienced PL/SQL developers. Packed with examples and recommendations, it helped everyone using PL/SQL make the most of this powerful language.

Oracle8 presents PL/SQL programmers with new challenges by increasing both the possibilities and complexities of the language. This new edition updates the original book for Oracle8, adding chapters on the new PL/SQL object features (object types, collections, object views, and external procedures). It also contains a much-requested chapter on tuning PL/SQL, as well as expanded discussions of debugging and tracing PL/SQL execution. A companion diskette contains the Companion Utilities Guide for Oracle PL/SQL Programming, an online tool that includes more than 100 files of source code and documentation prepared by the authors.

Even if you've already read the first edition of *Oracle PL/SQL Programming*, you'll find an enormous amount of new and revised information in this second edition and on its companion diskette. If you're new to PL/SQL, you'll soon find yourself on the road to mastery.

Oracle8 Design Tips

By Dave Ensor & Ian Stevenson
1st Edition September 1997
130 pages, ISBN 1-56592-361-8

The newest version of the Oracle DBMS, Oracle8, offers some dramatically different features from previous versions, including better scalability, reliability, and security; an object-relational model; additional datatypes; and more. To get peak performance out of an Oracle8 system, databases and code need to be designed with these new features in mind. This small book tells Oracle designers and developers just what they need to know to use the Oracle8 features to best advantage.

Mastering Oracle Power Objects

By Rick Greenwald & Robert Hoskin
1st Edition March 1997
508 pages, Includes diskette
ISBN 1-56592-239-5

Oracle's new Power Objects is a cross-platform development tool that greatly simplifies the development of client/server database applications. With Power Objects, you can develop applications for Windows, Windows 95, Windows NT, and the Macintosh in a remarkably short amount of time; for example, you can build a master-detail application that can add, update, and select records via a user interface—all in 30 seconds, with no coding!

This is the first book that covers Power Objects Version 2. It's an in-depth work, aimed at developers, that provides detailed information on getting the most from the product. It looks thoroughly at the most advanced features of Power Objects, covering specific application issues such as lists, reports (using both the native report writer and the Crystal Reports product), built-in methods, moving data, implementing drag-and-drop, etc. It also focuses on the use of object-oriented principles, global functions and messaging, OCXs, debugging, and cross-platform issues. The book also includes chapters on using PL/SQL with Power Objects and integrating the World Wide Web with the product. It provides a wealth of developer tips and techniques, as well as understandable explanations of the internal workings of Power Objects. The accompanying disk contains practical and complete examples that will help you build working applications, right now.

Oracle Design

By Dave Ensor & Ian Stevenson
1st Edition March 1997
546 pages, 1-56592-268-9

This book looks thoroughly at the field of Oracle relational database design, an often neglected area of Oracle, but one that has an enormous impact on the ultimate power and performance of a system. Focuses on both database and code design, including such special design areas as data models, enormalization, the use of keys and indexes, temporal data, special architectures (client/server, distributed database, parallel processing), and data warehouses.

O'REILLY™

TO ORDER: **800-998-9938** • **order@oreilly.com** • **http://www.oreilly.com/**

OUR PRODUCTS ARE AVAILABLE AT A BOOKSTORE OR SOFTWARE STORE NEAR YOU.

FOR INFORMATION: **800-998-9938** • **707-829-0515** • **info@oreilly.com**

Database

Advanced Oracle PL/SQL *Programming with Packages*

By Steven Feuerstein,
1st Edition Oct.1996, 690 pages,
plus diskette, ISBN 1-56592-238-7

Steven Feuerstein's first book, *Oracle PL/SQL Programming*, has become the classic reference to PL/SQL, Oracle's procedural extension to its SQL language. His new book looks thoroughly at one especially advanced and powerful part of the PL/SQL language—the package. The use of packages can dramatically improve your programming productivity and code quality, while preparing you for object-oriented development in Oracle technology. In this book, Feuerstein explains how to construct packages—and how to build them the right way. His "best practices" for building packages will transform the way you write packages and help you get the most out of the powerful, but often poorly understood, PL/SQL language.

Much more than a book, *Advanced Oracle PL/SQL Programming with Packages* comes with a PC disk containing a full-use software companion. Developed by Feuerstein, RevealNet's PL/Vision Lite is the first of its kind for PL/SQL developers: a library of thirty-plus PL/SQL packages. The packages solve a myriad of common programming problems and vastly accelerate the development of modular and maintainable applications.

Oracle Built-In Packages

By Steven Feuerstein
1st Edition March 1998
600 pages), Includes diskette
ISBN 1-56592-375-8

Oracle's built-in packages extend the power of the PL/SQL language in significant ways. Oracle makes built-ins available to all developers, but few developers know how to use them effectively. This book is a complete reference to all of the built-ins, including the new packages available with Oracle8. It provides extensive examples and comes with a diskette containing an online tool developed by RevealNet, Inc., that provides point-and-click access to the many files of source code and online documentation developed by the authors.

Oracle Performance Tuning, 2nd Edition

By Mark Gurry & Peter Corrigan
2nd Edition November 1996
964 pages, Includes diskette
ISBN 1-56592-237-9

The first edition of *Oracle Performance Tuning* has become a classic for programmers, managers, database administrators, system administrators, and anyone who cares about improving the performance of an Oracle system. This second edition is a complete revision, with 400 pages of new material on new Oracle features that will be helpful whether you are running Oracle6, Oracle7, or Oracle8. It updates all the original information, incorporating new advice about disk striping and mirroring, RAID, client-server, distributed databases, MPPS, SMPs, and other architectures. It also includes new chapters on parallel server, parallel query, backup and recovery, the Oracle Performance Pack, and more.

The book comes with a PC disk containing all of the SQL and shell scripts described in the book, as well as additional tuning scripts that can help monitor and improve performance at your site.

Oracle Scripts

By Brian Lomasky & David C. Kreines
1st Edition May 1998
200 pages, Includes CD-ROM
ISBN 1-56592-438-X

Database administrators everywhere are faced with the ongoing job of monitoring Oracle databases for continuous reliability, performance, and security. This book provides the first central source of previously created, tested, and documented scripts for performing these monitoring tasks. The accompanying Windows CD-ROM contains all of the scripts discussed in the book.

O'REILLY™

TO ORDER: **800-998-9938** • **order@oreilly.com** • **http://www.oreilly.com/**

OUR PRODUCTS ARE AVAILABLE AT A BOOKSTORE OR SOFTWARE STORE NEAR YOU.

FOR INFORMATION: **800-998-9938** • **707-829-0515** • **info@oreilly.com**

How to stay in touch with O'Reilly

1. Visit Our Award-Winning Site

http://www.oreilly.com/

★ "Top 100 Sites on the Web" —*PC Magazine*
★ "Top 5% Web sites" —*Point Communications*
★ "3-Star site" —*The McKinley Group*

Our web site contains a library of comprehensive product information (including book excerpts and tables of contents), downloadable software, background articles, interviews with technology leaders, links to relevant sites, book cover art, and more. File us in your Bookmarks or Hotlist!

2. Join Our Email Mailing Lists

New Product Releases

To receive automatic email with brief descriptions of all new O'Reilly products as they are released, send email to:
listproc@online.oreilly.com
Put the following information in the first line of your message (*not* in the Subject field):
subscribe oreilly-news

O'Reilly Events

If you'd also like us to send information about trade show events, special promotions, and other O'Reilly events, send email to:
listproc@online.oreilly.com
Put the following information in the first line of your message (*not* in the Subject field):
subscribe oreilly-events

3. Get Examples from Our Books via FTP

There are two ways to access an archive of example files from our books:

Regular FTP
- ftp to:
  ftp.oreilly.com
  (login: anonymous
  password: your email address)
- Point your web browser to:
  ftp://ftp.oreilly.com/

FTPMAIL
- Send an email message to:
  ftpmail@online.oreilly.com
  (Write "help" in the message body)

4. Contact Us via Email

order@oreilly.com
To place a book or software order online. Good for North American and international customers.

subscriptions@oreilly.com
To place an order for any of our newsletters or periodicals.

books@oreilly.com
General questions about any of our books.

software@oreilly.com
For general questions and product information about our software. Check out O'Reilly Software Online at **http://software.oreilly.com/** for software and technical support information. Registered O'Reilly software users send your questions to:
website-support@oreilly.com

cs@oreilly.com
For answers to problems regarding your order or our products.

booktech@oreilly.com
For book content technical questions or corrections.

proposals@oreilly.com
To submit new book or software proposals to our editors and product managers.

international@oreilly.com
For information about our international distributors or translation queries. For a list of our distributors outside of North America check out:
http://www.oreilly.com/www/order/country.html

O'Reilly & Associates, Inc.
101 Morris Street, Sebastopol, CA 95472 USA
TEL   707-829-0515 or 800-998-9938
       (6am to 5pm PST)
FAX   707-829-0104

O'REILLY™

TO ORDER: **800-998-9938** • **order@oreilly.com** • **http://www.oreilly.com/**
OUR PRODUCTS ARE AVAILABLE AT A BOOKSTORE OR SOFTWARE STORE NEAR YOU.
FOR INFORMATION: **800-998-9938** • **707-829-0515** • **info@oreilly.com**

International Distributors

UK, EUROPE, MIDDLE EAST AND NORTHERN AFRICA (except France, Germany, Switzerland, & Austria)

INQUIRIES
International Thomson Publishing Europe
Berkshire House
168-173 High Holborn
London WC1V 7AA, UK
Telephone: 44-171-497-1422
Fax: 44-171-497-1426
Email: itpint@itps.co.uk

ORDERS
International Thomson Publishing Services, Ltd.
Cheriton House, North Way
Andover, Hampshire SP10 5BE,
United Kingdom
Telephone: 44-264-342-832 (UK)
Telephone: 44-264-342-806 (outside UK)
Fax: 44-264-364418 (UK)
Fax: 44-264-342761 (outside UK)
UK & Eire orders: itpuk@itps.co.uk
International orders: itpint@itps.co.uk

FRANCE

Editions Eyrolles
61 bd Saint-Germain
75240 Paris Cedex 05
France
Fax: 33-01-44-41-11-44

FRENCH LANGUAGE BOOKS
All countries except Canada
Telephone: 33-01-44-41-46-16
Email: geodif@eyrolles.com

ENGLISH LANGUAGE BOOKS
Telephone: 33-01-44-41-11-87
Email: distribution@eyrolles.com

GERMANY, SWITZERLAND, AND AUSTRIA

INQUIRIES
O'Reilly Verlag
Balthasarstr. 81
D-50670 Köln
Germany
Telephone: 49-221-97-31-60-0
Fax: 49-221-97-31-60-8
Email: anfragen@oreilly.de

ORDERS
International Thomson Publishing
Königswinterer Straße 418
53227 Bonn, Germany
Telephone: 49-228-97024 0
Fax: 49-228-441342
Email: order@oreilly.de

JAPAN

O'Reilly Japan, Inc.
Kiyoshige Building 2F
12-Banchi, Sanei-cho
Shinjuku-ku
Tokyo 160 Japan
Tel: 81-3-3356-5227
Fax: 81-3-3356-5261
Email: kenji@oreilly.com

INDIA

Computer Bookshop (India) PVT. Ltd.
190 Dr. D.N. Road, Fort
Bombay 400 001 India
Tel: 91-22-207-0989
Fax: 91-22-262-3551
Email: cbsbom@giasbm01.vsnl.net.in

HONG KONG

City Discount Subscription Service Ltd.
Unit D, 3rd Floor, Yan's Tower
27 Wong Chuk Hang Road
Aberdeen, Hong Kong
Telephone: 852-2580-3539
Fax: 852-2580-6463
Email: citydis@ppn.com.hk

KOREA

Hanbit Publishing, Inc.
Sonyoung Bldg. 202
Yeksam-dong 736-36
Kangnam-ku
Seoul, Korea
Telephone: 822-554-9610
Fax: 822-556-0363
Email: hant93@chollian.dacom.co.kr

TAIWAN

ImageArt Publishing, Inc.
4/fl. No. 65 Shinyi Road Sec. 4
Taipei, Taiwan, R.O.C.
Telephone: 886-2708-5770
Fax: 886-2705-6690
Email: marie@ms1.hinet.net

SINGAPORE, MALAYSIA, AND THAILAND

Longman Singapore
25 First Lok Yan Road
Singapore 2262
Telephone: 65-268-2666
Fax: 65-268-7023
Email: daniel@longman.com.sg

PHILIPPINES

Mutual Books, Inc.
429-D Shaw Boulevard
Mandaluyong City, Metro
Manila, Philippines
Telephone: 632-725-7538
Fax: 632-721-3056
Email: mbikikog@mnl.sequel.net

CHINA

Ron's DataCom Co., Ltd.
79 Dongwu Avenue
Dongxihu District
Wuhan 430040
China
Telephone: 86-27-83892568
Fax: 86-27-83222108
Email: hongfeng@public.wh.hb.cn

AUSTRALIA

WoodsLane Pty. Ltd.
7/5 Vuko Place, Warriewood NSW 2102
P.O. Box 935,
Mona Vale NSW 2103
Australia
Telephone: 61-2-9970-5111
Fax: 61-2-9970-5002
Email: info@woodslane.com.au

ALL OTHER ASIA COUNTRIES

O'Reilly & Associates, Inc.
101 Morris Street
Sebastopol, CA 95472 USA
Telephone: 707-829-0515
Fax: 707-829-0104
Email: order@oreilly.com

THE AMERICAS

McGraw-Hill Interamericana Editores, S.A. de C.V.
Cedro No. 512
Col. Atlampa 06450
Mexico, D.F.
Telephone: 52-5-541-3155
Fax: 52-5-541-4913
Email: mcgraw-hill@infosel.net.mx

SOUTHERN AFRICA

International Thomson Publishing Southern Africa
Building 18, Constantia Park
138 Sixteenth Road
P.O. Box 2459
Halfway House, 1685 South Africa
Tel: 27-11-805-4819
Fax: 27-11-805-3648

O'REILLY™

TO ORDER: **800-998-9938** • order@oreilly.com • http://www.oreilly.com/

OUR PRODUCTS ARE AVAILABLE AT A BOOKSTORE OR SOFTWARE STORE NEAR YOU.

FOR INFORMATION: **800-998-9938** • 707-829-0515 • info@oreilly.com

O'Reilly & Associates, Inc.
101 Morris Street
Sebastopol, CA 95472-9902
1-800-998-9938

Visit us online at:
**http://www.ora.com/
orders@ora.com**

O'REILLY™

O'REILLY WOULD LIKE TO HEAR FROM YOU

Which book did this card come from?

_____

Where did you buy this book?
- ❏ Bookstore
- ❏ Direct from O'Reilly
- ❏ Bundled with hardware/software
- ❏ Computer Store
- ❏ Class/seminar
- ❏ Other _____

What operating system do you use?
- ❏ UNIX
- ❏ Windows NT
- ❏ Macintosh
- ❏ PC(Windows/DOS)
- ❏ Other _____

What is your job description?
- ❏ System Administrator
- ❏ Network Administrator
- ❏ Web Developer
- ❏ Programmer
- ❏ Educator/Teacher
- ❏ Other _____

❏ Please send me O'Reilly's catalog, containing
a complete listing of O'Reilly books and
software.

Name _____ Company/Organization _____

Address _____

City _____ State _____ Zip/Postal Code _____ Country _____

Telephone _____ Internet or other email address (specify network) _____

Nineteenth century wood engraving
of a bear from the O'Reilly &
Associates Nutshell Handbook®
Using & Managing UUCP.

PLACE
STAMP
HERE

NO POSTAGE
NECESSARY IF
MAILED IN THE
UNITED STATES

BUSINESS REPLY MAIL

FIRST CLASS MAIL   PERMIT NO. 80   SEBASTOPOL, CA

Postage will be paid by addressee

O'Reilly & Associates, Inc.
101 Morris Street
Sebastopol, CA 95472-9902